PORTRAITS OF THE SEVENTIES

PORTRAITS OF THE SEVENTIES

BY

GEORGE W. E. RUSSELL

WITH 52 ILLUSTRATIONS

Essay Index Reprint Series

 BOOKS FOR LIBRARIES PRESS
FREEPORT, NEW YORK

First Published 1916
Reprinted 1970

STANDARD BOOK NUMBER:
8369-1717-0

LIBRARY OF CONGRESS CATALOG CARD NUMBER:
73-117834

PRINTED IN THE UNITED STATES OF AMERICA

TO

CHARLES ROBERT

EARL SPENCER

IN HONOUR OF A LONG FRIENDSHIP

AND OF

SOME OLD FRIENDS

NOTE

NOT long ago an enterprising publisher approached me with suggestions about what he was good enough to call "the book we are all waiting for." When I asked him to be a little more explicit, he replied on this wise: "I suppose, Mr. Russell, that, in the course of your career, you must have had a great many interesting things told you in confidence." "Well, perhaps some." "So I imagined. Now I think that those things would make a very readable book." "I quite agree—very readable indeed; but I am afraid that there is an obstacle in the way." "Obstacle? I don't see it. Of course the book would be anonymous; and the anonymity would stimulate the sale." When I mildly suggested that even tho prospect of a sale could not justify one in revealing things told "in confidence," the publisher looked as much upset as Matthew Arnold's friend Nick when he heard the word "delicacy"; and I felt that it would be unkind to labour the point. " ' Collect your-self, my friend,' said I, laying my hand on his shoulder ; ' you are unmanned ' "[1] ; and he retired in disorder.

These inconvenient obligations of confidence pressed themselves on my mind when Mr. Fisher Unwin asked me to write a book about people eminent in the Seventies and Eighties, as a sequel to Mr. Justin McCarthy's *Portraits of the Sixties.* I felt, and now feel, that in this kind of writing one goes perilously near the edge of what is confidential ; but, on full con-sideration of the case, I decided to make the attempt. My endeavour has been to describe only what must have been seen and heard by many besides myself, whether in public or in social life ; and, whenever a point was doubtful, I have cultivated reticence at the expense of piquancy.

I have had the advantage of being able to refresh my memory by reference to a diary which I have kept ever since I was twelve years old.

That this collection of portraits is palpably incomplete is due to the fact that I have, in previous books, described a good many eminent

[1] *Friendships' Garland,* p. 71.

people of my time—such as Lord Shaftesbury, Lord Houghton, Lord Coleridge, Lord Goschen, Sir Alexander Cockburn, Sir William Harcourt, Sir Frederick Leighton, Bishop King, Bishop Westcott, Dr. Pusey, Charles Kingsley, and R. H. Hutton. I have been unwilling to borrow from myself except when it was absolutely necessary; and then, like Lord Morley, I have justified my action by "the old Greek principle that a man may once say a thing as he would have it said, δις δὲ ὀυκ 'ενδέχεται—he cannot say it twice."

G. W. E. R.

CONTENTS

ILLUSTRATIONS

PORTRAITS OF THE SEVENTIES

CHAPTER I

JUSTIN McCARTHY [1]

A PORTRAIT of Mr. McCarthy rightly occupies the first place in a book which tries to continue his *Portraits of the Sixties*. The McCarthy of the Sixties was a journalist and a novelist. The McCarthy of the Seventies and the Eighties was also a politician and an historian. For reasons which will presently appear, he and I did not always agree in politics. All the more pleasing on that account was his unfailing amiability in private life. The tone and spirit of our social intercourse are happily illustrated by the following quotation from his *Reminiscences* :—

" My next and last anecdote on the subject of visitors to the House of Commons I tell partly, of course, for the instruction or amuse-

---

[1] 1830–1912.

ment of the public; but partly also for the
especial benefit of my friend Mr. George W. E.
Russell.   An American friend and his wife came
to see me in London some years ago.   It
was arranged that my daughter and I should
accompany them to the House of Commons, and
that we should have a little dinner there.   In
the course of conversation on our way to the
House and through the House, I discovered
that my American friends had some odd notions
with regard to the manners of the British
aristocracy; it seemed to be a fixed article of
faith in their minds that every one in England
who had a direct connexion with a family in the
peerage was wont to bear himself with haughty
demeanour towards his humbler fellow-subjects,
and was especially inclined to vaunt his superi-
ority over any native of the great American
Republic, where merit is marked by no hereditary title.   We endeavoured to controvert this
opinion without making too much of it, and we
hoped that even in the intercourse of a short
visit our friends might acquire other views as
to the ways of the British aristocrat.   We had
a pleasant little dinner, and one or two Members
of the House of Commons made part of our
company; Mr. George Russell was one of these

JUSTIN McCARTHY.

To face p. 16.

guests. Everything went on delightfully until
we were about to break up after dinner, and
then our American friends told me that they
had a letter of introduction to a Member of
the House who then held a position in Her
Majesty's administration. I said I had not
seen him in the House that night; but Mr.
Russell came to the rescue and explained that
the man we were speaking of was at that time
working in a private room which he had within
the precincts of the House.

"I did not happen to know where the room
was, and George Russell benignly said, 'It's
the easiest place to find; go into the Central
Hall and you will see the entrance to it just
behind my uncle's statue.' Every one who
has been in the Central Hall knows the statue
to the late Earl Russell, the Lord John of historic memory. Mr. Russell shortly after left
us, having to go back into the House; and we
went to conduct our visitors to the friend whom
they desired to see. But on the way they both
broke out, as if with one thought and one voice,
'There! did we not tell you? Were we not
right? "Behind my uncle's statue." Yes, to
be sure, "Behind my uncle's statue!" Just to
show us untitled Americans what poor things

we are—we who have no noblemen-uncles, with
statues to consecrate their nobility.'

"Mr. Russell has never, I am sure, heard this
story before; but if he should happen to read
it in these pages, I hope it may prove a lesson
to him to abate his fierce aristocratic pride, and
to be sure that on no future occasion does he
ever, from no matter what good-natured purpose,
endeavour to help us, the lowly born, upon our
humble way by any allusion to 'my uncle's
statue.'"

Justin McCarthy was born at Cork in 1830,
and we, who knew him in his placid and gentle-
man-like maturity, always delighted in the
recollection that he had begun life as a rebel.
At eighteen, he was one of "the men of '48,"
and was only precluded by his tender years
from attaining immortality in Thackeray's ballad
of the "Battle of Limerick":—

> O the lovely tay was spilt
> On that day of Ireland's guilt;
> Says Jack Mitchil, "I am kilt! Boys, where's the back door?
> 'Tis a national disgrace:
> Let me go and veil me face;
> And he boulted with quick pace from the Shannon shore.

Foiled in his early desire to head or help a
revolution, Justin McCarthy became a journalist;

first at Cork, then at Liverpool, and finally
in London. He edited the *Morning Star*,
when it was John Bright's organ and the oracle
of Radicalism; and from the *Star* he passed
to the service of the *Daily News*. Here, under
the austere direction of F. H. Hill, and in the
congenial companionship of Andrew Lang, Peter
Clayden, and Mr. Herbert Paul, he plied for
long years a busy and graceful pen. "The Ditto
Press" was in those days an uninvented phrase,
but the truth which it expresses was always
with us; and the *Daily News* said Ditto to the
leaders of the Liberal party with touching
regularity. But in 1879 Justin McCarthy
entered Parliament for the County of Longford,
and, before two years were over, he found
himself, under Parnell's leadership, constrained
to fight the Liberal party with all his might.
"Ditto" in the *Daily News* was difficult to
combine with denunciation in the House,
obstruction in the Lobby, and hostility in
the constituencies; but McCarthy's tact and
amiability enabled him to play his rather complicated part without, as far as I know, losing
a single friend.

Gladstone's conversion to Home Rule, announced by the "Hawarden Kite" in December

1885, solved these difficulties. Thenceforward his hostility—not a very deadly passion—was reserved for his former chief, John Bright, and the other Liberals who still upheld the Union; and he was again able to co-operate whole-heartedly with Gladstone, Harcourt, John Morley, and other devotees of the new policy. So all was plain sailing until the fateful month of November, 1890, when the high hopes of Home Rulers, ancient and modern, were quenched in the foul air of the Divorce Court. Then came the decisive hour of McCarthy's life, and he acquitted himself nobly in it. He must choose between Parnell's leadership and what he believed to be best for the cause of Irish Nationalism. It was a choice which might have tried the moral fibre of a stronger-seeming nature; but McCarthy never wavered. He put the Cause above the Man, and thereby involved himself in a furious and fratricidal strife, from which his soul must have revolted.

In the angry scene which concluded the long-drawn-out drama of " Committee Room No. 15," [Parnell turned on Justin McCarthy with the taunt, " You have been wanting to step into my shoes all the time." To assert that Parnell never said anything more untrue

than this would perhaps be bold. He certainly
never said anything more unjust. His subsequent
saying that his successor in the Irish leadership was "a nice old gentleman for a quiet tea-
party," though borrowed from O'Connell, was
less unjust. Some men seek for greatness ;
others have greatness thrust upon them. Justin
McCarthy was of these last, if ever man was.
Not long before, Parnell, speaking in a very
different spirit, had dubbed him the "*beau ideal*
of an Irish member." If Parnell meant what he
said, he must indeed have felt that the time had
come to beat the swords of a fighting party
into plough-shares. "Quiet in manners, polished
in speech, retiring and urbane in temperament,
Justin McCarthy was the fly in amber of the
Irish Parliamentary party." The only thing
his colleagues ever lamented in him was "his
distressing want of native ferocity." They did
not, indeed, doubt his fortitude. He had been a
familiar figure in the Reporters' Gallery almost
before Parnell was born, and a Nationalist
member while yet Parnell was only a sporting
squire. He had proved his faithfulness to the
Irish cause through many a year of storm and
stress ; and one of his colleagues was kind
enough to breathe the pious wish that McCarthy

might be hanged for high treason, "to show how calmly a quiet man could die for Ireland." To be sure, he was scarcely a milder or more harmless-seeming revolutionary than Mr. J. F. X. O'Brien, M.P. for South Mayo, who had actually been sentenced to be hanged, drawn, and quartered for that very offence.

With, and through, the strife of Parnellite and anti-Parnellite, McCarthy seemed to develope a new nature. Small in stature, delicate in constitution, pacific in temperament, he suddenly proved himself equal to exertions and endurances of which one would have judged him physically incapable. His natural fluency became eloquence; and to moral courage he added a complete indifference to bodily peril. In the House of Commons he became ten times more effective and more considerable than he had ever been before. His prudence in counsel, his anxiety to avoid needless offence, and his dignified demeanour, were exactly the qualities which a parliamentary leader requires; and it was observed that "his qualities and even his defects marked him out as the easiest man for his colleagues to rally round in the place of their deposed dictator." All friends of Ireland deplored the day when shattered health and impaired eyesight compelled him to retire.

Of McCarthy's novels there is no need to speak in detail. A critic said of them, very happily, that they were like their writer, agreeable after-dinner companions. *Dear Lady Disdain*, was the most popular, and *Miss Misanthrope* ran it close. *Waterdale Neighbours* is notable for its excellent description of a Tory Democrat, written long before Lord Randolph Churchill had been heard of.

In 1878 McCarthy, suddenly developing a new line of talent, published his *History of Our Own Times*. No history since J. R. Green's —few since Macaulay's—ever attained so wide and so sudden a popularity. It is painted with a broad brush, and the drawing bestows little attention on details. But its facts, so far as they go, are accurate; it gives a clear, though perhaps a superficial, view of all the leading persons and events of the time which it covers; and it is written in graceful, flowing, and easy English. Its most distinguishing feature is about the last which one would expect in a book written by an active and lifelong politician—an absolute impartiality. I remember the astonishment, touched with indignation, of an old Whig when he came to the passage describing the bellicose attitude of Napoleon III

in 1858, and of the military advisers who urged
him on. " Certainly this Mr. McCarthy is the
most impartial gentleman I ever came across.
He says, 'Let us be just to the French Colonels.'
No, really, I must draw the line at those dangerous
ruffians."

To be just to every one, even to French
Colonels, was inherent in McCarthy's nature;
and, if he was sometimes too generous or too
gentle, those are not very heinous faults.

CHAPTER II

LORD BEACONSFIELD [1]

THE Whigs, among whom I was reared, never could be induced to take Lord Beaconsfield seriously. To them he was just "Dizzy," a purely comic figure, whose antics were always incalculable and generally amusing. They felt none of that violent animosity to him which prevailed among the Tories until his genius had brought Toryism into subjection. They merely regarded him as a droll adventurer, who was always trying to play solemn parts and say impressive things. They were ready enough to allow that he was a good hand at parliamentary banter; but the notion that he could be a serious statesman never crossed their minds. As the representative of the "Country Party" and leader of the "Landed Interest," he seemed particularly comic, but

[1] 1804–81.

supremely so when he figured as the champion of the Church, declaring himself "on the side of the angels," and dating letters to his clerical constituents on "Maundy Thursday." In their graver moods the Whigs condemned him as an unprincipled adventurer, who had bamboozled the Conservative party, and wormed his way into a place which properly belonged to men of higher character; but, whether grave or gay, they despised him, ignored his genius, and never dreamed that he could be formidable.

This habit of mind was natural enough in men whom the adventurer had spent his life in caricaturing, and any one of whom might have sate for the portrait, in *Endymion*, of "a haughty Whig peer, proud of his order, prouder of his party, freezing with arrogant reserve and condescending politeness." Furthermore, it is to be remembered that, though Disraeli had dethroned Peel and made himself leader of the Conservative party in the House of Commons, yet he had always been hampered by the hindrances and perplexities which beset a thoroughly false position; and that, as long as Palmerston lived, he had striven in vain for an opportunity in which his real powers could be displayed.

LORD BEACONSFIELD.

To face p. 26.

Reared in this tradition, I had certainly no prepossession in favour of the enigmatical Member for Buckinghamshire, who in July 1866 succeeded Gladstone as Chancellor of the Exchequer and Leader of the House of Commons. Indeed, any prejudices which a boy of thirteen might have entertained would probably have lain in the opposite direction; for the event which brought Disraeli into power was the defeat of my uncle's last Reform Bill; and I can remember the indignant surprise of the Whigs when Lord Derby, accepting office on my uncle's resignation, announced that he reserved to himself entire liberty to deal with the question of Parliamentary Reform whenever suitable occasion should arise. Parliament met for the new Session in February 1867, and the Derby-Disraeli Reform Bill was introduced in March.

I now approach one of the happy accidents of my life. I was shortly going to Harrow; but I happened to be in London when the Bill was in Committee. My father, being then Sergeant-at-Arms, could admit me to a seat under the gallery whenever he chose, and so it came about that I heard some of the most memorable debates of that great controversy. Gladstone and Bright and Lowe and Lord

Cranborne (who next year became Lord Salisbury), and Sir John Coleridge (afterwards Lord Chief Justice), and Ayrton and Kinglake and Horsman and Henley—it is a notable list of speakers, and might be greatly prolonged. But one figure appeared to me to tower head and shoulders above the rest, and that was the leader of the Conservative party, the ridiculed and preposterous "Dizzy." His mastery of the House, on both sides, seemed absolute. Compared to him, Gladstone played a secondary and an ambiguous part. At every turn in the debate Disraeli manifested two qualities in which, as Gladstone once told me, he surpassed all his predecessors—his political audacity [1] and his readiness in throwing a colleague overboard. I was not surprised, but only confirmed in my boyish impression, when in later years I read in Lord Houghton's Life an entry relating to this period: "Gladstone seems quite awed by the diabolical cleverness of Dizzy"; and this record by Bishop Wilberforce: "Disraeli . . . has been able to teach the House of Commons

[1] Mrs. Disraeli, famous for her conversational oddities, once said to a friend of mine: "Dizzy has the most wonderful moral courage, but no physical courage. When he has his shower-bath, I always have to pull the string."

almost to ignore Gladstone, and at present lords it over him, and, I am told, says that he will hold him down for twenty years."

Those debates interested me acutely, both because they first taught me the democratic as against the Whig idea of Government; and because they displayed, in the contrast between Disraeli and those who surrounded him, the difference between genius and talent.

The Reform Bill passed into law on the 15th of August, 1867. On the 25th of February, 1868, Lord Derby having resigned, Disraeli became Prime Minister. Even now the Whigs could not take him seriously. "Old Diz. Prime Minister!" This seemed the best joke of all. "The last government was the Derby; this is the Hoax," was a pleasantry which passed from mouth to mouth. "I give him six months," was the word at Brooks's; but fate gave him nine.

The General Election of November 1868 returned a majority of a hundred for Gladstone and Irish Disestablishment. Disraeli, though of course leader of the Opposition, took very little share in the debates on the Irish Church which occupied the Session of 1869, and his speech on the Second Reading of the disestablishing Bill was likened at the time to "a Columbine's skirt, all flimsiness and spangles." At the moment his energies were engaged in a quite unsuspected quarter, as was discovered at the beginning of May 1870, when he astonished the world by publishing *Lothair* (for which, by the way, he got £10,000). On the eve of publication Lord Houghton wrote: "There is an immense and most malevolent curiosity about Disraeli's novel. His wisest friends think that it must be a mistake, and his enemies hope that it will be his ruin. He told Longman he believed he was the first ex-Premier who had ventured on a work of fiction. If he had said this to me, I should have suggested M. Guizot's *Meditations Religieuses*."

This is not the proper place for an analysis of what Froude held to be Disraeli's greatest achievement in literature, but I can recall the fact that once again it shook the Whigs with laughter. Certainly the descriptions of aristocratic life, embellished with portraits which every one could recognize, were droll enough. Even after the lapse of forty-five years I can hear the mock-heroic tone of my father's voice as he read out the description of a country house [1] where there were "salt-cellars a foot high" and state beds "borne by silver poles." But all this flummery is contained in the first volume: whoever has the patience to wade through it, or the courage to skip it, will find in the second and third volumes a vividly interesting chapter of modern history. The Garibaldian rising of September 1867, with its disastrous conclusion at Mentana, has never been described with such intimate knowledge. Mentana was historical, and, though the author might embellish the story with some fantastic touches of his own, even the Whigs could not say that he had invented it. But throughout the narrative Disraeli harps upon one theme— "The only strong things in Europe are the Catholic Church and the Secret Societies." The Whigs knew something about "the Catholic Church," and partly hated it, partly despised it. But the idea of Secret Societies, undermining the political soil of Europe, and ready, at any favourable moment, to break out in armed insurrection, seemed to them too absurd to be even intended for reality. "Here's old Diz. 'cramming' us again! All this bogey-stuff about Secret Societies! What will the old boy

[1] Drawn from Knole.

try to make us believe next?" But, before ten years were over, the Whigs, or such of them as survived, discerned to their amazement that Disraeli had been telling them the literal truth about a real and most formidable force in international politics. It was not for nothing that he, who noticed everything and never forgot anything, had been the most important member of the Cabinet when Fenianism was at its height; and what he had learned in office he revealed in *Lothair*, even to the personal appearance and social habits of some of the chief conspirators. When the Fenian General, Gustave Paul Cluseret, who had played so sinister a part in the Commune, wrote his experiences in *Macmillan's Magazine*, we saw that, in describing "Captain Bruges" and his operations in London and in Ireland, Disraeli had been narrating historical facts which had fallen under his official observation.

When *Lothair* was once launched on its highly successful voyage ("The pecuniary results," Dizzy said to my father, "have been eminently gratifying") the author was free to return to his political duties as leader of the Opposition, and critic of the Gladstonian administration. His opponents gave him abundant opportunity for the exercise of his unequalled powers of sarcasm and ridicule. At this point a story may be interjected—

In early life Disraeli had been fond of riding, and in his Letters to his Sister there is a preposterous account of a run with Sir Henry Smythe's hounds, near Southend, in 1834. "Although not in pink, I was the best-mounted man in the field, riding an Arabian mare, which I nearly killed; a run of thirty miles, and I stopped at nothing."

A later and much better authenticated performance is thus recorded by an eye-witness In October 1873 Disraeli, who had not crossed a horse for thirty years, was staying with Lord Bradford at Weston, in Shropshire. To the astonishment of his fellow-guests, his host persuaded him to go out cub-hunting. My informant met him at Chillington, five miles from Weston. "He was wearing low shoes and white cotton socks, and trousers which rucked up nearly to his knees." To Mr. Giffard, the owner of Chillington, he said, in his slow, impressive way, "I like your place; it is so stately." He did not get back to Weston till after luncheon, and, when he got off his horse in the stable-yard, he was so exhausted that he reeled, and almost fell against the wall. "It was a plucky performance for an old man who never rode."

By the end of 1873, Gladstone's government, which, when formed in 1868, seemed a Ministry of all the Talents, had become, in Disraeli's admirable phrase, "a range of exhausted volcanoes." Weary of rebuffs, Gladstone suddenly dissolved Parliament, and was astonished by the completeness of his overthrow. In February 1874 Disraeli became Prime Minister for the second time, and for the first time found himself not only in office but in power. Before this he had held office on sufferance: he was now entrusted by the country with absolute authority. His enemies had been made his footstool. Crown, Parliament, and populace were united in his support.

A schoolboy has few opportunities of seeing great men, and an undergraduate not many more. From my early boyhood, as I said before, I had followed Disraeli's career with interest. I took my degree at Oxford in 1876, and thenceforward, going a good deal into society both in London and in the country, and having as many friends among Tories as among Liberals, I had frequent opportunities of seeing Lord

Beaconsfield (as he became in 1876) at close
quarters. He was indeed a striking, and even
a startling, figure. He was a good deal bowed,
and walked with a rather shuffling gait. His
face was of a death-like pallor, and what remained of his once luxuriant hair was dyed
to an inky blackness, the curl over his forehead being fixed in its place with gum. His
eyelids drooped, and there was about him a
general air of incipient paralysis, which was
only dispelled by the brightness of his eyes
and his singularly clear and deliberate enuncia-
tion. He was always rather elaborately dressed;
in winter he wore an Astrakhan-lined great-coat,*
and in summer, when he was wandering about
the woods and lanes of Hughenden, he displayed
a velvet jacket, a "fancy" waistcoat, and a
Tyrolean hat. He still stayed a good deal in
country houses, such as Hatfield and Bretby and
Welbeck, and even once at Woburn, but his health
was failing and he was no longer good company.
The processes of his toilet were too elaborate to
allow of his appearing before luncheon-time, and
then he was easily tired. He took scarcely any
part in conversation, but sate for long stretches
in moody silence, only broken now and then by

* See the cartoon in *Vanity Fair*, Dec. 10, 1879.

some sententious or epigrammatic remark. The late Lord Bath declared he was the dullest guest who ever visited Longleat, but the fact that both host and guest cordially disliked each other may have accounted for this impression. The late Sir William Fraser, who was one of the most abandoned bores in London, and a devoted adherent of Lord Beaconsfield, left this artless record :—

" During his last Premiership I dined with him in Downing Street : on entering, he replied to my commonplace hope that he was no worse for the bitter weather, with a feeble groan. I ventured to add that I found him surrounded by his illustrious predecessors ; he groaned again. ' Sir Robert Walpole over the chimney-piece ! ' He feebly bleated the word ' Walpole.' At first I thought he must be dying ; then, harmless as were my words, I thought they might have shocked him. I waited for a minute or two : and was followed by the Duke of Buckingham and Chandos, his intimate personal friend from boyhood : a nobleman of by no means formal manners ; his words bore close resemblance to my own : to my relief Disraeli replied in the same ghastly manner. I felt that he could not survive the night. Within a quarter of an hour, all being seated at dinner, I observed him talking to the Austrian Ambassador, Count Apponyi, with extreme vivacity: during the whole of dinner their conversation was kept up: I saw no sign of flagging.

"This is difficult to account for. One theory has been that Disraeli took carefully measured doses of opium; and, these being calculated to act at a given time, that the effect of the subtle drug was as I have described. I never saw such phenomena in any other person: in fact I remember diverting the late Lord B——, who was a great admirer of Disraeli, by telling him that I believed D—— was in reality a corpse, which occasionally came to life; and that, if he had ever been a human being, it must have been at a far distant period of the world's existence."

Sir William's bland irrecognition of his own conversational infirmity has always struck me as a warning.

When Lord Beaconsfield roused himself to speak, he always spoke carefully, and his phrases were bandied about from mouth to mouth. "Have I read the 'Greville Memoirs'? No, and I have no intention of reading them. Charles Greville was the most conceited person

with whom I have ever been brought in contact,
though I have read Cicero and known Bulwer-
Lytton." Once the late Lord Alington drove
him over to visit the great Lord Shaftesbury at
St. Giles's, and when he was leaving the house
he said, "Farewell, my dear Lord. I have to-
day seen one of the most impressive sights—a
great English nobleman, living in patriarchal
state in his own hereditary halls." A fervent
admirer once said, "Lord Beaconsfield, I am
going to ask a great favour. Will you let
me bring my boy to see you, and will you
give him one word of counsel which may stand
him in stead all his life?" The old gentleman groaned, but consented; and, when young
hopeful was presented, he said, "My dear
young friend, your good papa has asked me
to give you a word of counsel; here it is:
Never ask who wrote the 'Letters of Junius,'
or on which side of Whitehall Charles I was
beheaded; for if you do you will be considered
—a bore, and that is something too terrible for
you, at your tender age, to understand." To
a friend of my own, a brilliant and ambitious
Jew, he said, "You and I belong to a race
which can do everything but fail." A well-
known and delightful lady tried to make him

read the *The New Republic*, and write a favourable word about it for the author's encouragement. He replied, "I am not as strong as I was, and I cannot undertake to read your young friend's romances; but give me a sheet of paper." So then and there he sate down and wrote : "Dear Mrs. S——, I am sorry that I cannot dine with you next week, but I shall be at Hughenden. Would that my solitude could be peopled with the bright creations of Mr. Mallock's fancy!" I have always thought that "bright creations," as an epitome of a book which one had not read, was a stroke of genius.

The following story, not less characteristic, I had direct from Lord Randolph Churchill.

When Lord Randolph was beginning to take politics seriously, he thought it would be a good move to ask Lord Beaconsfield to dinner. When the ladies left the dining-room, he placed himself where Lady Randolph had been sitting, by the great man' side. "Will you have some more claret, Lord Beaconsfield?" "No thank you, my dear friend. It is admirable wine—true Falernian—but the gout holds me in its horrid clutch." When the guests had gone, and the host and hostess were talking over the events of the evening, Lord Randolph said, "I think the old gentleman enjoyed himself, and I know he liked his claret." "Claret? He didn't touch it! He drank brandy and water all dinner-time."

Of Disraeli's phrases in debate there is no need to speak, for they are historic and proverbial, and most of them belong to a period anterior to that which we are now considering. But one is embedded in my memory of 1878. The beloved and admired Princess Alice, Grand Duchess of Hesse, died of diphtheria, which she had contracted through kissing her sick boy. One would have thought that an incident so natural and touching could not, by any ingenuity, have been vulgarized, but Lord Beaconsfield was equal to the occasion. In moving a Vote of Condolence to the Queen, he indulged in some terrible phrases about "The Kiss of Death," and said it was an incident worthy to be portrayed in "painting, sculpture, or gems." *Gems!* what an inconceivable bathos! But, as a critic at the time remarked, the author of it belonged to the race which gave us jewellery and mosaic.

On the 8th of June, 1878, Lord Beaconsfield set out for the Congress of Berlin. He arrived on the day before the Congress opened, and slept at the British Embassy. My cousin, Lord Odo Russell, afterwards Lord Ampthill, was then our Ambassador; and in the evening Lord Beaconsfield's Private Secretaries came to him with anxious faces. " We are in a great scrape," they said; " the Chief has determined to open the proceedings to-morrow in French; and his pronunciation is so grotesque that we shall be the laughing-stock of Europe. He pronounces the French word for Grocer as if it rhymed with Overseer. Of course we dare not tell him so. Can you help us ? " Lord Odo replied, " It is a delicate mission, but I like delicate missions, and will see what I can do." So he repaired to the state-bedroom, where the Premier-Plenipotentiary of Great Britain was being dismantled for the night. "My dear Lord, a dreadful rumour has reached us. We are told that you are going to open the proceedings to-morrow in French. Of course no one is more competent to do so than you; but, after all, speaking French is a commonplace accomplishment; but you will be the only man in Congress who could make an oration in English. The Plenipotentiaries of all the other countries have come to Berlin expecting the greatest intellectual treat of their lives

—a speech by the greatest living master of the English language. Now, will you disappoint them?" Lord Beaconsfield fixed his monocle, gazed earnestly at his host, and said that he would consider the point. Next day he opened the proceedings in English. The question has always been whether he perceived the hint, or swallowed the flattery.

Lord Beaconsfield now stood on the top of golden hours. On the 16th of July he had returned in triumph from Berlin, bringing back what he called "Peace with Honour." He had acquired an ascendency over the Queen such as no other Minister ever approached, and the methods by which he acquired it were vividly described in the *Quarterly Review* for April 1901. The House of Lords, in spite of old prejudices against adventurers and upstarts, was at his feet. In the House of Commons he commanded a majority which some professed Liberals were not ashamed to swell; and he was the idol of the mob. His lease of supreme power lasted for six years, and in March 1880 he advised the Queen to "recur to the sense of her people." It was remarked at the time that the nonsense of her people might have served his purpose better; but sense prevailed, and he was beaten

even more decisively than Gladstone in 1874.
When all was over some one casually mentioned the name of Mr. W. B. Skene, who had
been chief organizer of the Conservative party.
"What!" exclaimed the dethroned chief, in his
deepest tones, "has that unhappy man not fled
the country?"

I was returned, as a vehement opponent of
Lord Beaconsfield's policy, for Aylesbury, then
one of those widely extended "Agricultural
Boroughs" which were as large as modern
divisions of counties. The limit of my borough,
in one direction, touched Hughenden, and there
I discovered that the great man was by no means
so popular as his toadies had declared. The
causes of his unpopularity were amusing, and
characteristic both of him and of his neighbours. "As long as he sate for the county,"
said one, "he used to deal with the local tradesmen, but as soon as he became Lord Beaconsfield, he went to the Co-operative Stores."
"Yes," said another, "and, when he goes back to
London from Hughenden, he always takes the
cold meat with him."

Whatever were the causes of his downfall
nothing ⸢in his political life became him so
well as his way of leaving it. Having met and

harangued his disheartened followers in the Picture Gallery of Bridgewater House, he returned to Hughenden, which he genuinely loved—to his roses and his peacocks and his trout-stream; to his " German Forest " and his " Golden Gate," for by such picturesque appellations he was wont to dignify the appurtenancies of a very moderate villa. He loved bright colours; and his drawing-room paper of green with gold fleur-de-lys, and the crimson satin furniture with which he embellished his new house in London, were more than æsthetic flesh and blood could bear without a cry of pain.

During the year of life that remained to him after he had left office, he was a good deal alone. He always read during dinner, allowing ten minutes to elapse between the courses, and keeping some favourite book in readiness. " When the servants are not in the room," he said, "I have 'some bright spirit to my minister.'" At the beginning of 1881, he took possession of 19, Curzon Street, which he had bought with the proceeds of *Endymion*, and resumed his attendance in the House of Lords; and even went a little into society. On the 18th of March, 1881, he dined with Lord and Lady Airlie, in the house which had once been

Macaulay's on Campden Hill. He paid Matthew Arnold, who was one of the guests, some effusive compliments, saying that he was "the only living Englishman who had become a classic in his own lifetime." An account of the conversation may be found in the second volume of Arnold's Letters; but one of Lord Beaconsfield's speeches uttered on that occasion, though not recorded, is too good to be lost. "You have heard me called a flatterer." Arnold could not deny it. "Yes, and it is true. Every one likes flattery; and, when you come to Royalty, you should lay it on with a trowel."

Lord Beaconsfield had always been fond of exercising hospitality, but he only gave one dinner in Curzon Street. His guests were the Duke and Duchess of Sutherland, Lord and Lady Granville, Lord and Lady Spencer, Lady Chesterfield, Lady Dudley, Lady Lonsdale, Lord and Lady Barrington, Lord and Lady Cadogan, Lord Bradford, Sir Frederick Leighton, Mr. Henry Manners, and Mr. Alfred de Rothschild. Those whose social memories cover thirty years will realize that it was a well-chosen party. Perhaps it was in view of this occasion that he said to a friend of mine, "I want an earl to complete my table. I believe there are a hundred of them; but I'll be hanged if I can remember the name of one "—a characteristic gibe at the aristocracy which he had subjugated.

Very soon after this dinner, his last illness began. It was bronchial asthma, gouty in origin, and aggravated by the bitter winds of March. He struggled on bravely, and the story of those painful weeks, narrated by one of the doctors who attended him, may be read in the *Nineteenth Century* for 1889. One night I was at a political party at Lord Granville's house, and I heard Lord Wolverton, who had been Liberal Whip, say to a great lady on the Liberal side, "Old Dizzy is very ill," to which she replied, with a wink of triumphant intelligence, "Oh yes! I know—dying." The illness was protracted, and that mordant critic, Bernal-Osborne, was reported to have said, "Overdoing it—as he always overdid everything."

Lord Beaconsfield died on the 19th of April, 1881; and the proposal to bury him in West-minster Abbey elicited the curious story about Mrs. Brydges-Willyams, which has been told in full in the third volume of his *Life*. She had been his benefactress, and he had promised her that they should be buried side by side; but it was impossible to admit her remains to the Abbey, so he rests beside his wife and his friend in the churchyard of Hughenden.

W. E. GLADSTONE.

To face p. 47.

CHAPTER III

WILLIAM EWART GLADSTONE[1]

I WAS reared in the Gladstonian tradition. Unlike most Whigs, my father both admired and trusted the brilliant recruit from Toryism who sate for the University of Oxford and, till he joined Lord Palmerston's government, still described himself as "A Liberal Conservative." My uncle, Lord Russell, though he often dissented from Gladstone's policy and expressed his dissent unhesitatingly, yet loved and admired the man; and in the Eastern Question of 1876–79, the whole of my family, then united for the last time, supported Gladstone in his triumphant opposition to Lord Beaconsfield.

For my own part, my interest in Gladstone was first aroused by his attack on the Irish Church in 1868. I was then a boy at Harrow, but already what foolish people call "a

---

[1] 1809–98.

ritualist"; and I was delighted to see the spiritual nature of a church, as distinct from its legal and secular position, maintained in practice by a statesman of first-class import- ance. When the great administration of 1868– 74 began, I followed its reforming course with high hopes, and shared the general dis- appointment at the failure and discredit in which it ended. But the Eastern Question of 1876 revived all one's boyish fervour, and I went into the General Election of 1880 as men go into a crusade—

> Bliss was it in that dawn to be alive,
> But to be young was very heaven.

It was during the Eastern Question that I became personally acquainted with Gladstone, for my occasional glimpses of him at my father's house when I was a boy could scarcely be called acquaintance. In July 1878, just after Lord Beaconsfield's triumphant return from Berlin, I was asked to dinner at short notice by an apologetic hostess, who said, "It would really be a charity if you would come, for the Gladstones are coming, and every one refuses to meet him." A year later *Vanity Fair* inscribed under an excellent portrait of him, "The most

popular man in England"; and at Easter 1880
he attained the summit of his greatness.

Thus from 1878 to 1898 I saw Gladstone
pretty constantly, and received from him unbounded kindness. A phrenologist once said of
him that "he was at heart a solitary man,"
and I believe that the guess, for it could have
been nothing more, was sound; but, for all that,
he often spoke to me with the most impressive
freedom on topics which ordinary men keep to
themselves, and this although he was forty-three
years my senior.

Let me say at once that I did not always
agree with my leader. His exclusive absorption
in the Irish Question from 1885 onwards
seemed to me disastrous; and his apparent
condonation of crime and outrage was painfully
akin to the process which has been described
as "praising with faint damns." But a life
prolonged to the verge of ninety is bound to
show signs of impairment somewhere. Gladstone's natural force was unabated, and his
intellect as clear as when he was thirty; but
he had never had much sense of proportion
and perspective, and where the advocacy of
Ireland was concerned he seemed to have
forgotten all that is meant by fitness.

I will now try to describe him as I knew him and shall always remember him—the greatest man, taking him all round, with whom I have ever been brought in contact.

The late Lord Granville, a Gladstonian of the deepest dye, once said, "Don't talk to me of Gladstone's wonderful mind—we know all about that—what I envy is his wonderful body." Lord Morley expressed the same feeling when he spoke of "the incomparable physical gifts which seemed to encase a soul of fire in a frame of pliant steel." To us who knew Gladstone only in the second half of his life, it is odd to think that he was once considered delicate; chiefly, I imagine, because of his ivory-pale complexion; and to remember that he spoke of himself as being far less robust than the contemporaries whom he followed to the grave. The truth, I suppose, is that he inherited that mysterious and invaluable endowment which is called "a good constitution," and that, through habitual temperance in the widest sense, a reasonable rule of life, and the incessant care of a wife who was "no inconsiderable physician," he became stronger and stronger with succeeding years. In a word, his health was perfect; and the slightest impairment of it, such as a cold

or an indigestion, always seemed to affect him
with a quaint surprise.

Every one who ever met him at close quarters
will recollect that the index-finger of his left
hand was only a stump which he protected by
a black finger-stall. This injury was the result
of an accident in 1845; his gun burst as he
was loading it and the finger was shattered.
When the surgeon saw it, he pronounced that
amputation was necessary. Gladstone laid his
hand on the table, and the finger was sawn off.
This, be it remembered, was before the days of
chloroform, and was surely a triumph of passive
endurance. His active endurance was not less
conspicuous. It was shown in his favourite
exercise of tree-felling; and in his inexhaustible
powers of walking—" a measured mile in twelve
minutes "; a twenty-five mile stretch on the
hills of Balmoral; the ascent of Snowdon after
he had turned eighty. At eighty-five he told
me that, though his eyesight and his hearing
had failed, the stethoscope could detect nothing
amiss. " The trunk is sound." His healthiness
was evinced in his hearty appetite for simple
food—clear soup and fish plainly cooked, roast
beef, rice pudding, bread - and - cheese. Nor
should his love of wine, especially port, be

forgotten. Archbishop Temple told me that, when he went up to Oxford in the Forties, he was assured that men drank less than had once been the custom because Gladstone had been conspicuously abstemious in the Thirties; and yet in old age Gladstone told me that he would not trust himself to write a paper or compose a speech with a bottle of port in the room. "I should drink it out to the last drop," he said, so conscious was he of the helpful stimulus. When he was thirty-seven, and therefore, I suppose, in the perfection of his powers, he divided the twenty-four hours of the day into ten for sleep, food, and recreation, and fourteen for work. The food and the recreation probably did not take very long, but his needs for sleep were great, and he slept as soundly as a tired child.

It is worth remembering that, though Gladstone had one of the strongest and most serviceable intellects of his generation, he had not been a precocious infant. His development came comparatively late, but it was rapid, and by the time he was twenty-one it was complete. His powers of "grind" were from first to last the astonishment of all who saw him at work, and he used to say that, the more distasteful the subject was, the harder he felt impelled to work at it. Superficiality was to him as impossible as idleness. Whatever the thing was on which he was engaged, if it was only a novel which he meant to review, he eviscerated it. There was no fragment of it that he had not discovered and dragged out. His humility was absolutely unaffected, and I am convinced that he meant exactly what he said when he once told me that he had no mental gift which every one did not share, except perhaps the power of being absorbed in what he was doing. In that power he was indeed unequalled. When he was busy, one could go into the room and go out of it, take down a book from the shelf, even poke the fire, and he would not look up from his work. If it was necessary to attract his attention, he raised his eyes with the dazed expression of a man suddenly aroused from sleep.

It has been commonly said that he had no sense of humour. "Gladstone's jokes are no laughing matter" was the great Lord Derby's just tribute. I should rather say that he had a sense of humour, but that it was scanty, incalculable, and inexplicable. He would take what was meant for a joke with the most alarming seriousness, and plunge into a strenuous argument about some obvious and intended absurdity. On the other hand, he would laugh consumedly at babyish riddles—"the sort of thing" as one of his colleagues said, "that my boys gave up when they left a private school"; and odder still was his love of having a story retold to him, even when he knew every turn in it from start to finish. Thus he once said to me, "Tell me that droll story about 'Providence'." "I don't think I know it." "Yes, you do. It was about an old farmer who had lost everything, and whose clergyman tried to comfort him by saying that it was the doing of Providence;" and so on, till I recalled a pastoral experience of the late Dr. Jessop in East Anglia, which Gladstone evidently remembered in every detail.

Most hopeless of all was an attempt to tickle his fancy with a story which depended for its point on some trait of cynicism, baseness, or sharp practice. Robert Browning told me of his own experience in this particular. One year, at the Banquet of the Royal Academy, Lord Beaconsfield said to Browning, "What a terrible display! How entirely destitute is our English School of all spirituality, all ideality, in painting!" But, when he rose to speak after dinner, he said that the feature which most

forcibly struck him in the surrounding show
was the high tone of spirituality and ideality
which marked it. Browning reported this
characteristic incident to Gladstone, who replied,
with kindling eye, "Do you call that story
amusing, Browning? I call it devilish."

But, if tales of trickery or humbug shocked
him, even more vehemently was he affected by
anything which savoured of cruelty or oppression;
and it was fine to see his brows contract and
his onyx-eyes flash, when

> Some tale of injury called forth
> The indignant spirit of the North.

In general conversation he did not, in my
opinion, excel. In fact, he did not converse.
He was always intensely interested in something,
and, whatever that something was, he would
harangue upon it with inexhaustible eloquence,
but without much reference to the question
whether it interested his hearers. When he
dined with Queen Victoria, he would break in
upon the reverent undertones, in which courtiers
delight, with dissertations on the Athanasian
Creed, or the relation of Zeus to the minor
deities; whereas the astuter Beaconsfield would
bracket the Queen and himself in the subtile

phrase "We authors," or lead the conversation to water-colour drawing, and the cousinships of German princes. At my own table, I have heard Gladstone lecture to a parcel of eager Radicals, who never entered a church, on the proper place for the organ, and the best rendering of *Dies Irae*. He treated with equal eloquence the improvement of dentistry, the price of wine, and the convenience of lifts. Lord Morley's chapter on his Table-Talk is a faithful and formidable reproduction.

Conversely, his absolute sincerity forbade him to simulate an interest in subjects which did not appeal to him. Certainly this trait left him a wide field over which he could roam at will, for theology, finance, history, poetry, music, and philosophy as long as it was not metaphysical, were topics with which he was thoroughly familiar. One only had to start him on a sub-division of one of these, and he would talk till bedtime. Happily he did not, as a rule, talk about politics; though, at a hot moment in the Irish Question, I heard him abuse Pitt and the Union (which he likened to the Massacre of St. Bartholomew) until he was constrained to exclaim, "I have lost my temper." But there was one large and conspicuous gap in his intellectual range. He had not the slightest interest in physical science, in any one of its aspects or applications. Pathetic was the failure when the late Professor James Stuart sought to interest him in the mechanical marvels of the Cambridge University Workshop. Once under strong pressure he promised to go to Greenwich on a night when a peculiarly interesting eclipse of the moon was promised, and his joy when a thick fog came on and forbade the attempt resembled that of a schoolboy who has got an unexpected half-holiday. When a friend who was interested in the public health informed him, as a most important fact, that a leper had been discovered in Dublin, he only replied, "Do you happen to know if he is a Nationalist?"

Another habit of his that militated against conversation, as that phrase is commonly understood, was his love of arguing. Disputation was to him what fencing is to some men—at once an exercise and a delight; and this without the slightest regard to the importance of the question in dispute, which indeed as often as not had no importance whatever. Whether there is more to eat in a poached egg or a boiled, and whether one man can be expected to harness a pair of horses, are questions on which I have known him nearly as earnest as when he was arguing that Homer foresaw the doctrine of the Trinity, or that Dante was educated at Oxford.

If all this is true, and only very hardy idolaters will deny it, the reader may ask what the charm was that drew one irresistibly to his company. One of its elements of course was the conviction, which deepened with one's deepening knowledge, that he was on the whole, and in the combination of physical, moral, and intellectual gifts, the finest piece of God's handiwork that one had ever seen. With rare self-knowledge, he once described himself as having a "vulnerable temper and impetuous moods"; and these traits, mastered by a strong self-control, did not detract from, but rather enhanced, the interest of his society. There are some people who appear to the best advantage on the distant heights, elevated by intellectual eminence above the range of scrutiny, or shrouded from too close observation by the misty glamour of great station and great affairs. Others are seen at their best in the middle distance of official intercourse, and in the friendly but not intimate relations of pro-

fessional and public life. But the noblest natures
are those that are seen to the best advantage
in the close communion of the home, and there
Gladstone was pre-eminently attractive. His
courtesy was invariable and universal; and
alike to men and women, to old and young,
he paid the compliment of assuming that they
were on his own intellectual level, and furnished
with at least as much knowledge as would enable
them to follow and to understand him. He
was equally free from official pomposity and
from intellectual arrogance. It was commonly
said of him that he was a good judge of MAN
and a bad judge of men. I do not dispute the
proposition as a general truth; and yet I feel
disposed to place on record certain judgments
on particular men which may tend to modify it.
In August 1895, when Gladstone had left his
parliamentary life behind him, I was staying
with him at Hawarden, and one day our talk
turned on the men who had been his colleagues
in his last administration, their qualities and
their prospects. It was obvious to mention
Lord Rosebery, who had succeeded him in the
Premiership. "Rosebery is a most incalculable
politician. All politicians are incalculable, and
tend to become increasingly so as the pressure

of the constituencies increases. But Rosebery, who has no constituents, is the most incalculable of all."

"Harcourt?" "If you think Harcourt is likely to lead a strenuous Opposition, you greatly misconceive him. Besides, Harcourt is not a young man" (as if that was poor Harcourt's fault!).

"John Morley?" "Morley has done admirable work for Ireland, but he has lost his seat, and he need not be in a hurry to return. There will be nothing for him to do in this Parliament."

"Lord Spencer?" "The best of men, but he made no resistance to the Naval Estimates which the Sea Lords forced on him. Mad and drunk, I call them."

"My friend George Trevelyan?" "Oh, the House of Lords is the right place for Trevelyan."

"Asquith?" "Asquith makes a very good speech on a legal point—very much so."

So we ran through the late Cabinet, and, when I had finished my catechism, Gladstone said, "But you have left out the most important man of all, and he is an Under-Secretary— Edward Grey. There's the man with the real parliamentary gift." This was a shrewd judgment, which the events of twenty years have abundantly confirmed.

One might long continue this analysis of the different qualities which constituted the charm of Gladstone's presence; and which led one, even from afar, to follow his banner and call oneself by his name. The list is by no means exhausted; but I place last what, as regards my own case, perhaps I ought to have placed first in the enumeration. It has been my happiness to know great saints in various communions; but they have been either ministers of religion by profession or recluses from the world by choice. Here was a man who did his human work and fought his human battles with the most scrupulous diligence and the most masterful resolution; and yet all the while was dwelling (to use his own phrase) "in the inner court of the sanctuary, whereof the walls are not built with hands."

If ever we should be tempted to despond about the possibilities of human nature, we may bethink ourselves of him and take courage. If our faith should ever be shaken by

> Blank misgivings of a creature
> Moving about in worlds not realized,

the memory of his strong confidence may re-assure us. If ever we should be told by the flippancy of scepticism that "religion is a disease," then we who knew him can point to one who, down to the very verge of ninety years, displayed a fulness of vigorous and manly life beyond all that we had ever known.

The last and the truest word was uttered by Bishop Westcott, in a letter acknowledging a memorial sketch which I wrote when Gladstone died : "I think he will be remembered for what he was rather than for what he did."

CHAPTER IV

THE DUKE OF ARGYLL[1]

GEORGE DOUGLAS CAMPBELL, eighth Duke of Argyll and chief of the Clan Campbell, was one of the most conspicuous personages of the Victorian age; but, though he lived through the Eighties, he culminated in the Seventies. His character, his mental gifts, and his early training, all marked him out from the common run of British nobility; indeed, he stands in my memory as unique. His pedigree, even when tried by the exacting tests of historical research, was one of the most illustrious in Europe; his forefathers had played great parts in the history of two kingdoms; and his widespread territory covered some of the most famous tracts of Scottish soil. But it was not in these respects that he was unique. The peerage contains plenty of men with long descents, historic

[1] 1823–1900.

ancestries, and great estates, but they have commonly been fashioned in the same mould, domestic and educational, and have been stamped by it into conventional forms. Not so the Duke of Argyll. He was born the younger son of a younger son; and when, by the deaths of his uncle and his elder brother, he became Marquess of Lorne and heir to the Dukedom of Argyll, his life was deemed too precious to be exposed to the perils of school and college. When other boys of his position were firding their level at Eton and Christ Church, or Harrow and Trinity, Lord Lorne posted about Europe in a travelling-carriage with a tutor and a courier; conversed and corresponded with learned men who were his father's friends; and trained himself to face the great problems of thought and nature by silent meditation in the fastnesses of his Highland home. His mental development was twofold. He became, through his early habits of personal investigation, one of the most expert naturalists of his time; and he learned, as few naturalists learn, to look through phenomena to the power behind them, and to investigate the laws of spiritual and intellectual being. All this was remarkably unlike the normal training of a

DUKE OF ARGYLL.

To face p. 64.

young nobleman in the Forties of the last century, and other circumstances increased the unlikeness. The disputes which produced the disruption of the Church of Scotland in 1843 forced even secularly-minded and indifferent people to consider the force of spiritual conviction in the affairs of this life, and Lord Lorne, whose temperament was eagerly religious, dashed into the controversy. In 1842 he published "A Letter to the Peers, from a Peer's Son, on the duty and necessity of immediate legislatory interposition in behalf of the Church of Scotland"; and this didactic instinct clung to him all through life. Forty years later Lord Houghton, replying to him in the House of Lords, said: "The noble Duke began advising us when he was nineteen, and has been advising us ever since."

Lord Lorne became Duke of Argyll in 1847, and thenceforward he added political activity to his theological and philosophical and scientific preoccupations. He had married, in 1844, a daughter of the Duke of Sutherland, and so entered that "sacred circle of the Great-Grandmotherhood," which, disguised under the title of the Whig party, played so great a part in Victorian politics.

When the ill-starred Coalition of 1853 was
formed, the Duke of Argyll, not quite thirty,
was admitted to the Cabinet; and, after Lord
Aberdeen's downfall, he remained in it as a
colleague of Lord Palmerston. By 1858 Palmerston's government had lost its popularity,
and Matthew Arnold, dining with Lord Granville
at the opening of the Session, "found all the
Ministerial people saying, 'What a stormy
time we shall have!'. There is no doubt that
between India and the 'French Colonels'
Bill,' the government are in a critical situation. It is said that Lord Derby is both
willing and eager to come in. The Duke of
Argyll said, with a sublime virtue, that we were
not to shrink from doing what was right because other people did and said what was
wrong."

That saying of the Duke was eminently
characteristic. Throughout a long life he persisted in "doing what was right," without
reference to party or convention or authority
or popularity. He was from first to last a
man of his own mind, and a striking instance
of political independence. Gladstone used to
say that the ever-increasing pressure of the
constituencies on their members, inevitable under

a widely-extended franchise, made it more and more difficult for a Member of Parliament to exercise independent judgment. The Duke of Argyll was never tried by that test; but I suspect that at any period of his life he would have flung away his seat sooner than give a vote which did not wholly commend itself to his conscience and judgment.

The Duke left office with the other Whigs in 1858, and returned to it with them in 1859. It was in the two years immediately ensuing that he made his noblest and most signal manifestation of political independence. The slave-owners' rebellion in the United States broke out in 1861; and the upper classes of England, almost to a man, rallied to the Southern side. The Duke of Argyll pronounced unhesitatingly for the North :—

> In him Demosthenes was heard again ;
> Liberty taught him her Athenian strain ;
> She clothed him with authority and awe ;
> Spoke from his lips, and in his looks gave law.

At this point it is natural to say a word about the Duke's most striking gift. His accomplishments, as I said before, were many and various. It was not by the mere accident of

birth that he became President of the British
Association in 1855, and Fellow of the Royal
Society in 1857. *The Reign of Law*, published
in 1866, marked him out as one of the most
original thinkers of his time, and ran to nineteen editions. His treatise on the Eastern
Question (1879) is still authoritative. *The
Unseen Foundations of Society*, published in
1893, showed his mental powers in unabated
force, and in *The Philosophy of Belief* (1896)
he returned to the theological interests of his
early youth. Still I can conceive that theologians
may have dissented from his presbyterianism;
that metaphysicians may have said that his
philosophy was more dogmatic than demon-
strative; even that naturalists may have dissented from his observations on the flight of
birds. But I cannot conceive that any one,
competent to judge, would have denied that
he was an orator. Gladstone was accustomed
to say that the Duke of Argyll was one of the
three men of the time who had the greatest
faculty of public speech. The trio, oddly enough,
did not include Bright; and, naturally, did not
include Gladstone himself. I should add both,
and I should put the Duke at the head of the
gifted five. Bright's eloquence, at once simple and

sonorous, reads more effectively than that of any other man. Gladstone was, in my experience, unrivalled in the art of mixing argument with rhetoric, and in unravelling a complicated theme. But the Duke of Argyll spoke like a man inspired. I have heard that Lord Beaconsfield, newly arrived in the House of Lords and hearing the Duke for the first time, exclaimed, "And this has been going on all these years, and I have never found it out!" When the Duke had wound up one of his most impetuous harangues by saying, "Your Lordships must not suppose that I am influenced in what I have said by feeling," Lord Beaconsfield said, in his reply, "If, my Lords, the speech of the noble Duke, admirable as it was, is a specimen of his style when not under the influence of feeling, I look forward with considerable apprehension to what I may have to encounter when he shall be under that influence." It is true that the Duke's reputation as a writer, a naturalist, and an amateur theologian, distracted public attention from his oratorical power; and I have been told that he himself did not realize it. Yet orator indeed he was, in the highest implication of the term. He always spoke under the in-

fluence of fiery conviction, and the live coal
from the altar seemed to touch his lips.   He
was absolute master of every mood of oratory—
pathos, satire, contemptuous humour, ethical
passion, noble wrath; and his unstudied
eloquence flowed like a river through the successive moods, taking a colour from each and
gaining force as it rolled towards its close.

There were two great controversies in which
the Duke's eloquence rose to its highest flights
—the Eastern Question of 1875–79, and the
Irish Question of 1886–95.   But before I come
to these it may be expedient to say that
he joined Gladstone's government of 1868
as Secretary of State for India, and that of
1880 as Lord Privy Seal.   He resigned in 1881,
disapproving of the Irish Land Bill, and never
again held office.   His greatest triumphs always
were in Opposition.   Throughout the Eastern
Question his consuming zeal and fiery eloquence made him the fervent champion of the
Christian cause in the House of Lords, and
the most formidable opponent of the Turk
and his allies.   The House of Lords is a
singularly democratic assemblage, and the fact
that it has no Speaker and no Rules of Order
gives its members a fine latitude of angry

speech. Of this latitude the Duke availed himself to the uttermost; and Lord Salisbury was wont thus to epitomize one of the Duke's attacks on him: "The noble Marquess opposite has told the House a lie, and knows it."

When the Home Rule controversy arose, the Duke revolted against all panic-stricken concessions to a treasonable and murderous conspiracy. To speak against Home Rule in the House of Lords was indeed to preach to the converted; so the Duke, though an old man and in broken health, betook himself to the platform, and poured the liquid fire of his scorn and indignation into the Parnellite host. After the General Election of 1886 had shown conclusively that the country was not going to be rushed into Home Rule, the half-hearted Home Rulers on one side, and the more moderate Unionists on the other, began to make delicate approaches to each other. There was a kind of half-expressed desire to substitute some sort of practicable autonomy for the blank separation proposed by the defeated Bill, and so to replace Gladstone in power. The Duke saw the manœuvre, and quoted, with happy sarcasm, from his favourite Wordsworth :—

Ye blessed creatures! I have heard the call
Ye to each other make.

On the 6th of September 1893 I heard the Duke speaking on the Second Reading of the second Home Rule Bill. He was then seventy years old and his health was failing; the speech attempted little in the way of argument, and was desultory beyond belief. But suddenly there came a passage which lifted the whole debate into a nobler air. The orator described himself standing on the western shores of Scotland, and gazing across towards the hills of Antrim. " We can see the colour of their fields, and in the sunset we can see the glancing of the light upon the windows of the cabins of the people. This is the country, I thought the other day when I looked upon the scene—this is the country which the greatest English statesman tells us must be governed as we govern the Antipodes." And he emphasized the last word with a downward sweep of his right hand which in a commonplace speaker would have been frankly comic, but in this great master of oratory was a master-stroke of dramatic art.

It remains to say a word about the Duke's personal appearance and demeanour. He was very short, but made the most of his few inches by a vigorous and rather challenging carriage. His hair was as vividly red as that of his famous namesake Rob Roy, and was brushed straight back and up from a truly intellectual brow. His manner suggested a combination of the Highland Chief with the University Professor. When his eldest son married Princess Louise, *Punch* exactly hit the Duke's sense of his own importance by the words which it put into the mouths of two imaginary clansmen : " MacCullum Mohr's son's goin' to get marrit to the Queen's young dochter." " Eck! The Queen mun be the Proud Woman." The Duke had inherited the tradition of the time when his forefathers exercised " heritable jurisdiction," and the dwellers on their lands were in good earnest subject to their rule. The world had changed a good deal in a hundred years, but the eighth Duke of Argyll had scarcely accommodated himself to the change ; and the development of political independence in a district which his name had so long dominated seemed to him a very disquieting phenomenon.

A quality not easily distinguished from arrogance showed itself in the Duke's social bearing.

He never seemed to realize that his associates were in any sense his equals. As a
professor, he harangued and expounded and
laid down the law. As a chieftain, he summoned one guest to his side and then in
turn dismissed him to make way for another.
He spoke as the Elder of the Kirk when he
rebuked episcopacy; as the President of the
Geological Society when he reproved Evolution;
and as the hoary Whig when he preached the
sanctity of property to the socialistic and inex-
perienced Gladstone, who was fourteen years
his senior.

But always and in all things, at all times
and in all circumstances, he was the self-
sufficing and self-governing man,

> Who never sold the truth to serve the hour,
> Nor paltered with Eternal God for power.

CHAPTER V

ROBERT LOWE [1]

CERTAINLY one of the most conspicuous figures of the Seventies was Robert Lowe (created in 1880 Lord Sherbrooke); but even in the Seventies the main achievement of his life was past. This achievement was the defeat of the Russell-Gladstone Reform Bill of 1866. Emerging from a kind of half-obscurity in which he had long dwelt, Lowe attacked that extremely mild measure of reform with a passion, an energy, and an insistence which elevated him for a moment to the highest point of parliamentary importance. His speeches delivered during the Sessions of 1866 and 1867 constitute the most forcible and most eloquent indictment of Democracy which is to be found in English literature. Aided by the Tories, and some jaundiced Whigs such as A. W. Kinglake the

[1] 1811–92.

historian of the Crimea, and Edward Horsman the "Superior Person" of Disraeli's sarcasm, he defeated the Bill in Committee. The scene of his triumph was thus described by an eye-witness :—

"His hair, brighter than silver, shone and glistened in the brilliant light. His complexion had deepened into something like bishop's purple. There he stood, that usually cold, un-demonstrative, intellectual, white-headed, red-faced, venerable arch-conspirator ; shouting himself hoarse, like the ring-leader of a school-boys' barring-out."

The descriptive touches in this paragraph need some amplification. Lowe was one of the strangest-looking people one ever beheld. He was an Albino, with snow-white hair, a crimson complexion, and eyes so short-sighted as to be almost blind. Fearing the total loss of sight, he left Oxford after a brilliant career, and went out to Sydney, where he hoped to make a competence at the Bar before blindness should disqualify him. He made the competence and escaped the blindness. Returning to England in 1850, he became a leader-writer in the *Times*, and in 1852 was returned to Parliament for Kidderminster, sitting as a Palmerstonian Whig.

ROBERT LOWE.

To face p. 76.

He subsequently sate for Calne, and from 1868 to 1880 for the University of London. When Gladstone became Prime Minister for the second time, he offered Lowe a peerage, and induced the Queen to make the peerage a Viscountcy. The Queen demurred, on the ground that Lowe had not particularly distinguished himself in the various offices he had held; but Gladstone replied that the position which he had made for himself in the debates on Reform in 1866 was such as to justify the higher dignity. Considering that Lowe's achievement in 1866 had been the destruction of Gladstone's pet measure, I have always thought this a very remarkable instance of magnanimity. The nature of Lowe's relations with the reformers may be inferred from his reply to a member of the Reform League, who had asked his opinion of the demonstrations in favour of Reform which followed the rejection of the Bill in 1866:—

"The Reform League, having fastened upon me assertions which I have not made, has loaded me with the most virulent abuse, and has striven to make me an object of the hatred, perhaps a mark for the vengeance, of my fellow-countrymen.

"With such a body and its leaders, of whom

you appear to be one, I have no courtesies to interchange. When I think proper to give an opinion on the recent popular demonstrations, it is not to the Reform League that I shall offer it "

Lowe's career in office was singularly ill-starred. He became a placeman almost as soon as he entered Parliament, and in 1864 he was Vice-President of the Committee of Council on Education. Lord Robert Cecil, afterwards Lord Salisbury, carried in the House of Commons a Resolution censuring him for having mutilated the reports of his Inspectors. It is only fair to say that a Parliamentary Committee afterwards exonerated him, and rescinded the Resolution; but of course it had the immediate effect of driving him out of office. The *Owl* described him in a couplet which he was fond of quoting—

> "To vote, contents his natural desire;
> He draws no stipend, but he eats no mire."

He was a private Member when the Reform Bill of 1866 was introduced, and he used his freedom with remarkable effect. But, having turned out the Liberal government as a penalty for their timid concession to democracy, he was appalled to find that the Tories, who succeeded them, presented a really democratic Reform Bill in 1867, and, with the aid of Liberals, established Household Suffrage. Seeing that power had passed finally out of the hands of the middle classes into those of the artisans, Lowe exclaimed, with insight and with acrimony; "Now we must educate our masters"; and the saying was repeated by Lord Haldane in 1915.

About this time Lowe was very bad company. "What was a conflict last year," he said, "is a race now"—and a race to perdition. Bishop Wilberforce wrote, after meeting him in a country house, "It was enough to make the flesh creep to hear his prognostications for the future of England." However, nothing dreadful happened. The newly-enfranchised electors sent Disraeli (who, with Lord Derby, had given them Household Suffrage) to the right-about, and returned Gladstone with a majority of a hundred, pledged to the disestablishment of the Irish Church. Lowe, who abhorred all religious establishments, had attacked the Irish Church with exceeding vehemence; so Gladstone, forming his administration at the end of 1868, made him Chancellor of the Exchequer. There never was a more unfortunate appointment. Beginning with the doctrine that

the function of the Chancellor of the Exchequer
is to distribute a certain amount of human
misery and that he who distributes it most
equally is the best Chancellor, Lowe went to
work distributing it right and left; and he
accompanied the distribution with an amount of
personal disagreeableness which doubled the
resentment of his victims. His opposition to
Reform had made him intensely unpopular with
Liberals, and now the entire Tory party joined
the chorus of depreciation. Disraeli said, not
untruly, that Lowe possessed a natural faculty
of inspiring aversion, and that he could not
appear on the hustings of a popular election
without risk to his life—to remedy which misfortune, Disraeli pleasantly said that he had
invented a non-popular seat for him, by giving
the University of London a Member of Parliament. Day by day storms of angry criticism
assailed the Chancellor of the Exchequer, and
in reply he found himself to be, in Gladstone's
expressive phrase, " as helpless as a beetle on
its back." His culminating folly was a feature
of the Budget of 1871, when, to every one's
amazement, he levied a tax on matches—for
no conceivable reason unless it was to indulge
a pedantic play on words. He proposed that

each match-box should bear a Latin motto:
Ex luce lucellum. Some people, misled by
sounds, thought that this must mean "Out of
light, a little light," and they said what a
clever man Mr. Lowe must be, and what a fine
thing a classical education was. When they
found that it meant "Out of light, a little gain,"
and that the little gain was scarcely more than
half a million, they justly said that such a sum
was certainly not worth the trouble and incon-
venience which the tax must cause, and rose in
insurrection against it. A regiment of match-
girls, whose wretched bread Lowe imperilled,
marched in procession to the House of Commons;
every one felt sorry for them; every one disliked
Lowe, and the tax was dropped. Rather happily,
Lowe turned the joke against himself in a couplet
which was widely quoted:—

> *Ex luce lucellem* we very well know,
> But, if Lucy won't sell 'em, what then, Mr. Lowe?

Lowe disappeared from office with the rest
of the Liberal Government after the General
Election of 1874, and never returned to it. No
Minister was ever less regretted. He renewed
his anti-democratic activities as a bitter opponent of the Agricultural Labourers' Suffrage;
and, when the government of 1880 was formed,

the state of his health prevented his inclusion
in the Cabinet. He then disappeared into the
House of Lords.

So far, I have described Lowe only as he
appeared in public life. In private life he was
a very different and a much more attractive
person. By common consent he was one of the
cleverest men of his time, but in public life his
cleverness only accentuated his offensiveness: in
private life it manifested itself in more agreeable
forms. He was perfectly good-tempered and good-
natured; quite free from formality or pomposity;
easy, natural, and accessible. His range of knowledge was extremely wide, and even perplexingly
various. It seemed impossible to tap a subject
with which he was unfamiliar, and I suspect that
his enormous memory was sometimes reinforced
by inventive skill. In the distant days when the
plague of Acrostics devastated society, smart
women, whose education had been neglected,
always turned to " dear Mr. Lowe " for quotations, references, and allusions. They seldom
turned in vain; and, if they had chanced to
stumble on something that the oracle did not
know, the oracle would have been quite equal to
the occasion. In public, Lowe could only speak
after the most elaborate preparation, but in

private his rapidity of thought and phrase was
as remarkable as his erudition. A foolish decrier
of classical learning once said to him, " I have
the greatest contempt for Greek and Latin," and
Lowe replied: "Not, I should think, the contempt which familiarity breeds." Once a lady
asked him, in my hearing, to go with her to the
Opera. She had got a box, and wanted to take
some one with her. No, he was engaged. "Oh!
I see the Bishop of Gibraltar. I'll try him."
"That's no good—Gibraltar can never be taken."
In the rapid give-and-take of ordinary society
Lowe was as light and gay as a clever undergraduate; but, when it came to the serious work
of after-dinner conversation, in houses where '34
port was still procurable, he was as instructive
as Dr. Johnson, and a great deal more amiable.

CHAPTER VI

LORD HARTINGTON

IN this case I use the name which was current
in the Seventies and Eighties, though later
it was merged in a higher designation. Spencer
Compton Cavendish, born in 1833, was Lord
Cavendish till 1858, Marquess of Hartington from
1858 to 1891, and eighth Duke of Devonshire
from 1891 till his death in 1908.

C'est dommage quand les rois sont mal élevés.

Hartington was born to a very great position
—one of the greatest in England as to rank and
property—and his education was the worst that
could have been devised for his character and
condition. For the heir-apparent to a great title
and corresponding wealth to be educated among
his father's dependents is the most spoiling of
experiments. The son of a Southern planter,
reared among the slaves who would soon be his

own chattels, could not be more unfortunately placed than an English boy, of vigorous mind and imperious will, brought up among grooms and gamekeepers, and fed from his cradle on the thick flattery which is the appointed diet of an eldest son. The seventh Duke of Devonshire, though he had been educated at Eton, disliked Public Schools, and his three sons were brought up at home. Intellectually, the boys probably gained by this arrangement, for no better equipped teacher could have been procured than the Duke, who had been Second Wrangler, Smith's Prizeman, and Eighth Classic; but in other ways the experiment was risky. The younger sons, Lord Frederick and Lord Edward Cavendish, emerged from it unspoilt, partly through an inherent simplicity and fineness of disposition, and partly through the fact that neither of them was the heir-apparent. The tradition of English life, in families which hold titles and land, hedges the eldest son with a divinity which no one is hardy enough to dispute ; and Hartington's was a nature which took this divinity very much as a matter of course. Eton would have been his salvation, for there he would have had to find his level among a thousand schoolfellows, to whom his prospects in life would have been matter of complete indifference.   Mr. Herbert Paul, himself an Etonian, has justly observed that " Eton is thoroughly democratic, and a little rough handling is not a bad thing when bestowed upon

Some tenth transmitter of a foolish face."

Some other epithet than " foolish" must be used to describe the faces of the Cavendishes ; but the " rough handling," whether physical or mental, would have been an admirable training for the future Duke of Devonshire.   Unfortunately, he did not get it, but got instead the incessant, solicitous, and interested homage which is bestowed by neighbours and dependents on the boy who will some day be master of 200,000 acres and a proportionate income.   This method of education left its mark on Hartington for all time.   He was absolutely selfish; and he did not, as others of the same temperament have often done, attempt to conceal the selfishness under an air of courtesy or consideration.   He had no manners.   He observed no social usages.   If he was engaged to dine at eight, he came at nine. If you asked him a question, he either stared in stony silence or else drawled a monosyllable which sounded like " Whor ? " and meant " What ? ". When the Cabinet decided to drop an Education

Bill at which Sir John Gorst, as Vice-President
of the Committee of Council, had been toiling,
the Duke of Devonshire, then Gorst's official chief,
strolled into his room, and, after standing some
time in silence with his back to the fire, said
"Well, Gorst, your d——d Bill's dead." Here
are the less desirable fruits of a domestic
education.

Yet he was not pompous. Pomposity is the
vice of the snob, and, in spite of his rough
exterior, he was at heart a gentleman. His view
of society was illustrated by what I once heard
him say when, after the Socialist riots of 1887,
people spoke with horror of the probability of a
mob in Hyde Park. "Mob? Whenever I go
into the Park I see a mob—only some of the
mobs are better dressed than others." His
uncivil behaviour was due, not to any vulgar
notion of a social eminence which justified
incivility, but to the circumstances of his
upbringing. He had been motherless from his
seventh year. His father was a man of retiring habits, a student and a man of business,
shy even of his own sons; and the circle in
which the heir to Chatsworth moved was such
as always surrounds the "home-keeping youth"
who is heir to great possessions. He was un-

civil, because he had not been taught, at the age when nature is receptive, that other people had claims and feelings and susceptibilities, and that consideration for these should be the distinctive mark of high breeding.

Let me turn for a moment to personal description. Hartington was tall, and strongly, though loosely, built. When he overcame a natural tendency to slouch, and held himself upright, he was what is called "a fine figure of a man." On an occasion of ceremony or state he moved and carried himself with dignity; and, although his ordinary dress was rough and untidy, he appeared to advantage in the scarlet and ermine of the peerage, or the black-and-gold robes of the Chancellor of the University of Cambridge. His features were massive, and strongly marked; his light brown beard concealed a wide mouth and a very determined chin. His way of looking, or rather staring, at a stranger who addressed him, was eulogized by an admiring foreigner as a "You-be-d——d-ness of demeanour." To the end, he looked younger than his years, and I remember a mild sensation among descriptive paragraph-writers when he first used glasses in the House of Commons.

As to his tastes, habits, and occupations, they

LORD HARTINGTON.

(Duke of Devonshire.)

To face p. 88.

were pretty much what might be expected in a
man of his antecedents, who did not marry till
he was fifty-nine. He might be truly said, in
Whyte-Melville's words, to "have played the
game all round." As a young man, he had
been fond of hunting and shooting, and very
fond of fishing; but in his mature age I should
say that amusements which involved money
pleased him best. Lord Redesdale has described
the rhadamanthine gravity with which he used
to play whist; and some more adventurous
games seemed even to excite him. On race-
courses and at Monte Carlo his habitual phlegm
disappeared, and I have seldom heard him
speak with greater animation than when he
was protesting against the restrictions imposed
in this country on public gambling—" I own
two towns which would be splendid places for
gaming-tables. Not Barrow—Barrow is too
businesslike. But Buxton and Eastbourne—both
full of idle people and invalids. Gaming-tables
are just what they want."

His physical nature was strong, enduring,
rough, perhaps rather coarse. He had a large
appetite, and thoroughly enjoyed a good dinner;
but could tackle an office-luncheon of roast beef
and cabbage with exemplary appetite. He had,

in a remarkable degree, what novelists call
"Temperament"; and, when he was just leaving Cambridge, that temperament, quite uncon-
trolled by social considerations, nearly landed
him in a most undesirable marriage. His father
called some friends of the family into council,
and propounded the question—Was there any
counter-attraction strong enough to break the
spell? and the unanimous reply was "Politics."
So, almost against his will and wholly against
his natural inclination, Hartington became at
twenty-four M.P. for North Lancashire, and
thenceforward sate in the House of Commons
till he ascended to the Lords. When he was
thirty he accepted minor office under Lord Palmerston, and in 1866 he entered Lord Russell's
Cabinet as Secretary of State for War.

Those were the days when a young man of
family who voted straight might reckon on
political advancement; but no one ever questioned Hartington's competence for office. His
intellect was sound, strong, and capable. At
Cambridge he was found to have inherited a
good deal of his father's mathematical ability;
and, with very little reading, he obtained a
Second Class in the Mathematical Tripos.
Though he held some of the most exacting of

the posts in the government, he was never found wanting. His mind was, as he himself said, slow, but it was sure; and an excellent feature of his character was, whatever office he undertook, he prided himself upon doing the work thoroughly. He was indeed as good an instance of the great nobleman in politics as could easily be adduced. No one on earth was less of a courtier, but Queen Victoria liked to have him near her, just because he resembled the Ministers of her early reign—a sportsman, a man of the world, a country gentleman, a little of a gambler; not a professional politician like Mr. Chamberlain, nor a metaphysician like Mr. Balfour, nor a man of science like Lord Salisbury, nor a scholastic theologian like Mr. Gladstone.

Hartington's political career was marked by some curious vicissitudes. He has been nick-named, I think rightly, "The Last of the Whigs." In 1859 he moved the vote of want of confidence which displaced Lord Derby's government and made Palmerston dictator for the rest of his life. Under Palmerston, and later under Russell, he was thoroughly at home. But Gladstone's leadership often strained his allegiance. Through the great reforming days of 1868–74, and again from 1880 to 1885, he held office in Gladstone's administrations; and yet his attitude towards the Liberal ideal always had in it something that reminded one of Sancho Panza—"following by an attraction he cannot resist that poor, mad, scorned, suffering, sublime enthusiast, the Modern Spirit; following it, indeed, with constant grumbling, expostulation, and opposition, with airs of protection, of compassionate sympathy, with an incessant by-play of nods, shrugs, and winks addressed to the spectators; following it, in short, with all the incurable recalcitrancy of a lower nature; but still following it."

Probably the most disgreeable period of Hartington's political life was the year 1879. Gladstone, having led his party into the wilderness of opposition, having abandoned them there, and having left Hartington to shepherd them as well as he could, now began to show unmistakable signs of an intention to resume the Premiership whenever he could oust Lord Beaconsfield. Hartington, who had been formally elected leader of the Liberal party in the House of Commons, and, according to all political usage, was entitled to expect that supreme reward for himself, was naturally incensed. If he had obeyed his own inclination, he would have withdrawn from an ostensible leadership, which had now become a mockery; but he was advised that any such action on his part would split the party, and he doggedly held on till the dissolution of March 1880. People praised his loyalty to Gladstone, but he said to me in later days—"I thought that Gladstone had not behaved well to me, and I did not feel the least 'loyalty' to him. That is quite the wrong word." That he subordinated all merely personal considerations to the one great object of defeating Lord Beaconsfield, is illustrated by the following letter, which he addressed to me, though he knew well that I was a Gladstonian and a Radical:—

"I write a line to express my sincere wishes for your success in your contest at Aylesbury. The names of Russell and Cavendish have been so long associated together in the history of the country that I cannot help feeling something more than a common interest in your success."

When Lord Beaconsfield's overthrow was complete, the Queen did her utmost to secure Hartington for her Prime Minister. "She set her back against the table, and fought her hardest"; but without avail. Hartington realized both that Gladstone would decline to serve

under him, and that to form a Liberal administrative with Gladstone outside it would be a
hopeless task. As Hartington's action at this
crisis subsequently became the subject of some
malicious and ignorant gossip, it may be well to
publish the following memorandum which he
wrote for me in 1892 :—

" The advice which Lord Hartington gave to
the Queen in 1880, from first to last, was that
H.M. should send for Mr. Gladstone and consult
him as to the formation of a Government, and
that if he should be willing to undertake the
task, she should call upon him to form an
Administration.

" Lord H. had up to that time had no com-
munication with Mr. G. on the subject, and
did not know what his views as to returning to
office might be. With the Queen's permission,
Lord H. on his return from Windsor informed
Mr. Gladstone and Lord Granville, but no other
person, of what had passed between H.M. and
himself, and neither Lord H. nor any other
person is at liberty now to make those communications public. From the time when Lord H.
was first sent for to Windsor, to the time when
Mr. G. was sent for by the Queen, Lord
H. neither saw nor came in contact with

any of his friends or former colleagues except
Lord Granville and Mr. Gladstone."

So Gladstone became Prime Minister, and
Hartington joined his Cabinet, where he re·
mained uneasily till 1885; and, as Secretary of
State for War, he had a principal part in the
tragical folly of sending Gordon to Khartoum.
Then occurred the great conversion which shattered the Liberal party for twenty years, and
gave Hartington the opportunity of his lifetime.
Never before had he shown a tenth part of the
intellectual energy which he threw into the fight
against Home Rule; and, roused at last from
his habitual lethargy, spoke both in the House
and in the country with a power which no one
believed him to possess.   Once on a time he
had been observed to yawn in the middle of
one of his own speeches, and, when a friend
commented on this irregular proceeding, he replied, "Well, but it was d——d dull, wasn't it?"
Henceforth there was no yawning in his speeches,
but every word struck home with a massive
force which crushed verbiage and flummery into
powder.

The General Election of 1886 dismissed Home
Rule and the Liberal government with it.
The great part which Hartington had played

in the struggle was recognized by Lord Salisbury, who generously offered to serve under him
in a Coalition government. Hartington again
declined the Premiership; and did so yet once
more, when, at Christmas 1886, Lord Randolph Churchill's resignation shook the Cabinet.
I believe that no other man has ever three
times refused to be Prime Minister of England.

Throughout the remaining years of the controversy about Home Rule, Hartington, first as
a private Member of Parliament, and then as a
peer, fought the battle of the Union with unabated vigour, and in the House of Lords helped
to throw out Gladstone's second Home Rule Bill
by the remarkable majority of 419 to 41.

When Lord Rosebery's brief and dismal administration came to its ignominious end in
1895, Hartington, who had now become Duke of
Devonshire, joined Lord Salisbury's government,
and remained in it when Mr. Balfour succeeded
his uncle. When the controversy about Tariff
Reform arose, and Mr. Balfour shilly-shallied
and split straws, the Duke declared firmly,
though not precipitately, for Free Trade. He
had the majority of his colleagues against him,
and he quitted the Cabinet. His resignation
brought his official career to a close, and also,

more than any other individual act, it saved
Free Trade.

What was the dominant characteristic of
Hartington's nature? I say Honesty. Slow-
ness, selfishness, obstinacy, pride, and several
other attributes may be imputed to him; but,
alike in his public and in his private life,
they were dominated by his honesty. A professional politician on my own side once said
to me, with a significant snuffle: "Hartington
can't be bought." By special grace I was enabled to forbear the too obvious reply; but the
politician was right. Not the strongest induce-
ments that political life has to offer ever prevailed to move Hartington, by a hair's breadth,
from the course which commended itself to his
judgment. He said what he meant, and meant
what he said. He had plain thoughts and expressed them in plain words. I well recall the
effect produced in the House of Commons when
Hartington, who never made any ethical profes-
sions, defended the evacuation of Kandahar:
"We go away now because we do not want Kandahar, and because we have no right to be
there." That was Hartington all over. No
sympathy with glittering policies, no false shame
about imaginary loss of "prestige," but simply

reason and justice. We did not want Kandahar; therefore it was foolish to stay. We had
no right to be there; therefore we ought to go.

The same straightforwardness which he practised he expected from others, and, where there
was any departure from it, he did not spare the
offender. In this connexion a small but characteristic incident recurs to my memory. A man
who had cheated at cards and had been turned
out of his clubs became engaged to a girl
young enough to be his daughter, whom he met
abroad. The girl's parents had vaguely heard
a rumour of the man's misconduct, but did not
know the facts, and were naturally anxious to
ascertain them. At my suggestion they wrote
to Hartington, and, in a case where most men
would have hesitated about the right course and
shrunk from consequences, Hartington wrote a
plain statement, in black and white, of what he
had observed, and of the consequences which had
followed from it.

SIR WILFRID LAWSON.

To face p. 99.

CHAPTER VII

SIR WILFRID LAWSON[1]

IF I had never entered Parliament, I suppose I should never have known Sir Wilfrid Lawson; and in that case I should have lost a great honour and a great pleasure. He was a pure and single-minded patriot, and one of the most delightful companions in the world.

A life of absolute and calculated sacrifice for the redemption of degraded humanity is, in sober truth, a Christ-like life, and it must surely spring from that "naturally Christian soul" in which the fathers of the faith believed. It is a rare glory to have spent one's "length of days" in persistent and unconquerable effort for the service of those who are least able to help themselves, and to have accepted no reward except the loving gratitude of hearts inspired and emboldened by a high example.

[1] 1889–1906.

It is a pity that Sir Walter Scott never encountered the name of "William de Wybergh,
of Wybergthwaite," for surely he would have
immortalized it in *Ivanhoe* or *The Talisman*.
The pedigree of Wybergh bristles with romantic
appellations, and the demesne of Clifton in
Westmorland has been possessed by the Wy-
berghs "in an unbroken male descent since the
thirty-eighth year of Edward III."

Wilfrid Wybergh, on succeeding to the
large estates of Isel and Brayton in Cumberland, which had belonged to the Lawsons, assumed their name, and was created a baronet
in 1831. He married Caroline, daughter of Sir
James Graham of Netherby, and sister to the
Peelite statesman of that name, and was father
of a second Sir Wilfrid Lawson, whom every
one remembers as a Radical M.P. and leader
in the cause of Temperance.

Wilfrid Lawson the younger was born in 1829.
In after-life he was accustomed to say, "I never
had any education," and in the formal sense of
book-learning this was not far from the truth.
The elder Sir Wilfrid had a very bad opinion
of Public Schools and Universities, and his son
was brought up at home and taught by private
tutors. The library at Brayton is large and mis-

cellaneous; and young Wilfrid, ranging at will
through its preserves, lighted on Adam Smith's
Wealth of Nations, which he always regarded as
one of the great books of the world, and which
went far to determine his social and economic
views.

But probably even Adam Smith played a comparatively small part in his education. When a
strong, active, and healthy boy, full of intelligence and life, is brought up by a thoughtful
father in a wild and beautiful country, and
accustomed from his childhood to watch the
sights and sounds of Nature and to note the
oddities of human character, it may be safely
said that he educates himself. Brayton was
essentially a sporting house, and the young
Lawsons were taught to ride, shoot, and fish
from their very earliest boyhood. Wilfrid's first
pony, a gift from his uncle, Sir James Graham,
was called "Diamond," and was the forerunner
of a long line of hunters of which "Radical"
was the most famous. As the boys never went
to school, the whole family lived constantly
together, brothers and sisters sharing the same
interests, pursuits, and amusements. The
youngest of the family records that Wilfrid
was the kindest of elder brothers, always

plotting treats and surprises for the younger
members of the family, and encouraging them
to take their part in whatever fun or frolic might
be going forward. From time to time he accompanied his parents or his tutor on foreign tours
or short excursions to Scotland or the South of
England, but his boyhood and youth were chiefly
spent in Cumberland; and with the Cumberland
Foxhounds his connexion was long and intimate.
The famous John Peel, who is "kenn'd" all over
the English-speaking world, was a master of
foxhounds on a very primitive and limited scale,
and hunted his own hounds in Cumberland for
upwards of forty-six years. He died in 1854.
By this time Wilfrid Lawson was twenty-five
years old, desperately fond of hunting, and well
supplied by his father with the sinews of war.
So on the death of John Peel, with whom he
had hunted ever since he could sit in a saddle,
he bought Peel's hounds, amalgamated them
with a small pack which he already possessed,
and became Master of the Cumberland Foxhounds.

It is easy to conceive the popularity which
now encircled the young Squire of Brayton. In
addition to the more commonplace gifts of wealth
and position, he had unbounded gaiety, the

sweetest temper in the world, and a rich sense
of comicality and absurdity. " He was made
a magistrate when he was quite young. He took
a keen interest in all county business and an
active part in all that was going on. It was
wonderful how he contrived to combine business
and pleasure, and to be at all sorts of meetings
and all sorts of entertainments all over the
county, almost at the same time." Among the
lighter traits of his character which are remembered in his family was an exceptional talent for
mimicry, which enabled him to reproduce in the
domestic circle all the oddities and whimsicalities
which he encountered in the work, and amusement of the day. From early boyhood he displayed that knack of writing rapid, fluent, and
vigorous verse which played so conspicuous a
part in the serious correspondence of his mature
life.

But all this time those who knew him best
were aware that, deep under the superficial
gaiety and exuberance of healthy youth, there
lay a solid vein of resolute devotion to truth and
duty. The elder Sir Wilfrid, a thoroughgoing
and all-round Liberal, cared supremely for two
causes—the cause of Temperance and the cause
of Peace. Happily for him, his son was com-

pletely and enthusiastically at one with him on those great issues.

Sir Wilfrid had never cared to enter Parliament, but he saw in his eldest son some rare and special qualifications for parliamentary life; and, in urging the younger Wilfrid to come forward as Liberal candidate, he was reinforced by the potent influence of his brother-in-law, Sir James Graham, one of the great land-owners of Cumberland. That extremely able man, and very variable politician, was now in his sixty-sixth year. He had represented eight constituencies, and now sate for Carlisle; he had held high office in Whig and Tory Governments, and was one of the strongest Free Traders in the Peelite group. His health was beginning to fail, and he was no longer a candidate for office, but he was still a great parliamentary figure, and Gladstone, to the end of his life, was accustomed to quote him as the greatest administrator whom he had ever known. His political opinions, which were eclectic and to some extent individual, by no means coincided with those of his brother-in-law, Sir Wilfrid Lawson and Sir Wilfrid's son; but he did not shrink from contact with their adventurous Radicalism, and actively promoted the scheme of bringing

the younger Wilfrid forward for West Cumberland.

At the General Election of 1857 Wilfrid
Lawson was duly nominated for that constitu-
ency, and, though declared successful on the
show of hands, was beaten at the poll. His
way of consoling himself for this first defeat
was eminently characteristic. He was so long
and so generally known as the unflinching advocate, in season and out of season, of an austere
and unpopular cause, that some other aspects of
his character have been completely overlooked.
Few, I imagine, think of him as a fox-hunter,
and yet hunting was one of the grand passions
which swayed his earlier and middle life. On
this point his own testimony is conclusive :—

"After being defeated in the Liberal raid on
West Cumberland I consoled myself considerably
by hunting. I do not see anything really noble
in galloping after a fox, but it is undeniably
delightful. The *Saturday Review* once wrote
that no amusement is long popular in England
'which is not either unwholesome or wicked.'
Fox-hunting may be the exception which proves
the rule. I have sometimes said that no man
is likely to be much excited again by anything,
who has killed a fox in the open with his own

hounds after forty minutes without a check, or
who has won a contested election in the open
voting days by a majority of less than two
figures. I suppose hunting has seen its best
days. The fiend who invented barbed wire
struck at it its heaviest blow. But I doubt not
that there are hundreds of young Englishmen
who still feel towards it as I did when I was
young.

"In looking back I think perhaps the keenest
delight which ever thrilled one was to look out
of doors about ten on a winter's night, when
there was a suspicion of frost, and to find that
there was a soft wind blowing, so that one
could hunt the next day. Even now the very
sight of a fox electrifies one, though to fall in
with one casually is almost as rare as to fall
in with a Radical.

"About this time I had more or less acquaintance with the old Cumberland hunter, John
Peel. Some people, I fancy, look upon him as
a myth, or at least as a character about whom
we have no reliable details, any more than we
have about Nimrod. But this is a mistake. I
believe there is some foundation for everybody
who becomes prominent in either national
or local history. At any rate, I have seen

John Peel in the flesh and have hunted with him."

At the General Election of 1859 Wilfrid Lawson returned to the charge, and was elected for Carlisle. I have been told by those who remembered his first appearance in the House that he was a very good-looking young man, smartly dressed according to the fashion of the day, with the "Dundreary whiskers" and peg-top trousers which now only survive in the pages of *Punch*. His maiden speech (in favour of the Ballot) was delivered in 1860, and in 1864, by introducing his "Permissive Bill," he made himself what he remained to the end of his life—the leader of the Anti-Liquor party in Parliament.

The main incidents of his parliamentary career can be briefly told. He lost his seat for Carlisle in 1865, chiefly through the unpopularity of his views on liquor-laws, but regained it in 1868, having in the meanwhile succeeded to his father's baronetcy and estates. He sate for Carlisle till the General Election of 1885, when he was defeated. At the General Election of 1886 he was returned for the Cockermouth Division of Cumberland, which he retained till 1900, when he went down in the "Khaki Election." In

1903 he was returned for the Camborne Division of Cornwall, on the understanding that at the next General Election he should return to the Cockermouth Division. There he was successful at the General Election of 1906, and six months later he died.

All the influences which surrounded Wilfrid Lawson at the age when human nature is

> Wax to receive, and marble to retain,

tended to encourage and develope that Liberal habit of mind which was part of his essential constitution. But Liberalism is a name which, at one time or another, has been stretched to cover a large variety of opinions and beliefs, and young Lawson did not long leave his friends in doubt about the particular type of Liberalism which was to claim his allegiance. It might have been expected that his close association with Sir James Graham (who, when he was not a Tory, was a Whig) would have inclined the younger politician to "the principles of the Revolution of 1688," and to "the cause for which Hampden died on the field and Sidney on the scaffold." But Lawson's ardent and adventurous spirit utterly declined to be "nourished in the creed outworn" of Whiggery, and the only use which he had for " Whigs " was to make them rhyme with " Prigs," whenever their short-comings moved his muse to wrath. His parliamentary record proves beyond doubt or contradiction that he was from first to last, and only more markedly as time went on, a Radical.

In February 1881 I was sitting by Lawson's side on the platform of the Memorial Hall, in Farringdon Street, at a meeting called to support the independence of the Transvaal; and Lawson, in the course of his speech, said, suddenly and emphatically, "I am a Democrat," whereupon a voice from the hall interjected, "Then why don't you drop your 'andle?" Lawson was far too sensible a man to think that he would help his cause by an affectation of singularity in a matter of names or titles; but he showed his contempt—in my judgment excessive—for titular honours when he refused the Privy Councillorship; and he spoke the literal truth when he said to his constituents in 1878 : "A seat in the House of Commons I value as the only honour I have that is worth possessing."

Lawson declared himself a Democrat, but faith in Democracy means a good deal more than a contempt for honours. It means, though in a very different sense from that in which

St. Augustine used the phrase, the conviction that *securus judicat orbis terrarum*. It means the belief, which Gladstone formulated, that " it is in the masses of the People that the deepest fountains of true life reside." A politician who believed, absolutely and without qualification, in Democracy would wish to see Lincoln's great ideal of " Government of the people, by the people, and for the people " applied without stint or reserve to every department of the national life. In the broadest and simplest terms he would trust the people to act wisely and rightly, and would leave them free to work out their own salvation.

Tried by this test, was Lawson a Democrat ? In nine out of ten of those concerns which affect the public good and which form the matter of politics, his democratic faith stood firm and immovable. In the tenth, and that was the main work of his life, it failed. He would not trust the people with the control of the liquor-traffic. He was willing enough that they should abolish it or diminish it. He was unwilling that they should establish or increase it. Here we seem to touch one inconsistency of Lawson's creed ; and, like many another inconsistency in men who have played great parts in history, it displays the intensity of a master-passion, trampling on the obstacles raised by logic and theory. That master-passion was, beyond question, his hatred of an agency which he believed to be fatal to physical and moral health, and of all forces and systems and doctrines which tended to encourage it and give it scope. I do not know who it was that first called Alcohol "the Devil in Solution," but the phrase exactly expresses Lawson's belief, and his belief necessarily governed his action.

In the general field of politics, and outside the special department of the Liquor-Laws, Lawson followed the advanced line of the Liberal party. He was no lover of sects and schisms, plots in the lobby or combinations in the tea-room. His nature was to go straight ahead, turning neither to the right nor to the left, and always in what fox-hunters would call "the first flight." Apart from questions connected with Liquor, he was singularly free from crotchets and "isms"; and, whatever was the policy of the advanced section of the Liberal party, you might be pretty sure that Lawson would be found supporting it. He had absolutely nothing in common with the bureaucratic, imperialist, and warlike spirit which, even before Gladstone's disappearance, began to infect the Liberal party. His hatred of militarism was one of his strongest passions. In July 1882 he consented to make a speech on Local Option at Aylesbury, and I well remember that, in discussing the arrangements for the meeting, he stipulated that he must get back to the House in time for the division on the Vote of Credit for military operations in Egypt. "I would not miss that division," he said, "though it was to be the last vote I should ever give in the House of Commons." Of course he voted against the Liberal government, which was then, in his judgment, violating the first principles of Liberalism. The bombardment of Alexandria moved his liveliest indignation, and on the 12th of July he protested against it with an incisive vigour which was very distasteful to his leaders.

"I say deliberately, and in doing so I challenge either Tory or Liberal to contradict me, that no Tory government could have done what the Liberal government did yesterday in bombarding these forts. If such a thing had been proposed, what would have happened? We should have had my Right Hon. and learned friend, the Secretary of State for the Home Department [1] stumping the country, and denouncing Government by Ultimatum. We should have had the noble Marquess, the Secretary of State for India,[2] coming down and moving a Resolution, condemning these proceedings being taken behind the back of Parliament. We should have had the President of the Board of Trade [3] summoning the Caucuses. We should have had the Chancellor of the Duchy of Lancaster [4] declaiming in the Town Hall of Birmingham against the wicked Tory Government; and, as for the Prime Minister, we all know there would not have been a railway-train, passing a roadside station, that he would not have pulled up to proclaim non-intervention as to the duty of the Government."

This was in July. In the subsequent autumn Gladstone moved a Vote of Thanks to our soldiers for their conduct in Egypt, and Lawson opposed the motion in a speech full of caustic humour and common-sense. "If," he said, "it comes to a Vote of Thanks, it is not

---

[1] Sir William Harcourt.
[2] Lord Hartington.
[3] J. Chamberlain.
[4] J. Bright. (Mr. Bright resigned office on July 17th.)

8

to the English troops that we should have moved it, but to the Egyptians—for running away."

I said just now that Lawson followed the advanced line of the Liberal party. Not seldom he indicated that line as the right policy for the party, long before the leaders had come to recognize its possibility or its expediency. Thus in November 1881, when the Liberal government was imprisoning Parnell without trial, and Gladstone was invoking "the resources of civilization" against its enemies, and Forster was hunting, very unsuccessfully, for the "Village Ruffians" whom he had promised to lay by the heels, Lawson made an emphatic declaration in favour of Home Rule. Addressing his constituents at Carlisle, he spoke as follows:—

"I am convinced of one thing—that, as surely as I stand here, a disaffected nation, hating the rule of the nation that governs it, is not a source of strength to that country, but a source of weakness to every one concerned in the matter. Suppose you had a housemaid who was continually breaking the crockery, who went into hysterics once a week, and had to be put into a strait-waistcoat, and three or four policemen brought in to keep her in order, would you keep her? No; you would say, '*Wayward sister, go in peace.*' (Cheers and laughter.) Or my friend Mr. Howard here. He keeps a pack of foxhounds. Suppose he had one abominable hound, always worrying the other hounds, howling and yelling all night, and flying at the huntsman's throat whenever he went into the kennel, do you think he would keep that hound? Would he say, 'I must not have my pack "disintegrated"'? No, he would write to the master of a pack of harriers, and say, 'I beg to make you a present of the most valuable hound in my pack.' (Loud laughter.)"

There were probably not three other Members of Parliament who at that time would have ventured on that suggestion of Irish policy; and, apart from the singular courage which the speech disclosed, it is worth recalling as a typical instance of the speaker's favourite method. No one ever excelled him in the art of enforcing a serious argument by a humorous illustration; and the allusion to the probable conduct of the disgusted Master of Foxhounds is about as characteristic a touch as any which can be found in all the great array of his collected speeches.

In this particular matter of Home Rule,

Lawson was miles ahead of his party. He thought and spoke and acted for himself, and was indeed a pioneer of the new policy. When the strife raged round more ordinary topics, such as the Extension of the Suffrage, the Ballot, Disestablishment, and resistance to the claims of the House of Lords, he marched in the foremost rank. Perhaps, indeed, he outstripped it when, commending the Burials Act of 1880, he declared that the Act, good in itself, was only an instalment of a larger reform, and that the churches as well as the churchyards ought to be thrown open for Noncomformist rites.

When a man's work in life has been done mainly through public speech, it is interesting to know something about his way of speaking. In this respect, as in so many others, Lawson was quite unlike what people who did not know him expected him to be. There was nothing fanatical, fiery, or excited about his style of oratory. He spoke with perfect ease and fluency, but quietly, deliberately, and with complete self-control. He was the master, not the servant, of his oratorical power. As a rule his speeches were carefully prepared, and he made free use of notes; but he could speak, when necessary, without premeditation; he was always on the happiest terms with his audience; was quick in reply, clever in dealing with an interruption, and successful in turning the laugh against the interrupter.

James Russell Lowell, referring to his own writings at the time of the American Civil War, remarked that he had been "able to keep his head fairly clear of passion, when his heart was at boiling-point." Lawson might have said exactly the same about his political speaking. His heart was always "at boiling-point" when he was pleading for the causes in which he believed; but he contrived to "keep his head clear of passion," and was perfectly prepared to argue the point against adversaries who merely howled and raved.

The aim of Logic, according to the ancients, is to arrive at truth; the aim of Rhetoric to persuade men. In Lawson's speaking both faculties were combined; and, while he was always ready to give a reason for the faith that was in him, he knew as well as any one the value of resonant declamation, and the power of finely chosen words to enforce a moral appeal. It is only natural that his best-remembered speeches should be those connected with the liquor-traffic; for that was the subject which lay nearest his heart, and which inspired his most memorable performances in the way of public speaking. Those speeches will not easily perish, for the various organizations which seek to reform the liquor-laws, and the host of speakers and writers and compilers of extracts who labour for the same end, will long turn to Lawson for their most effective quotations. Even Canning himself, in his great comparison of a nation at peace to a man-of-war riding at anchor,[1] was not happier than Lawson in this description of the tide which was to carry the Permissive Bill :—

"I have alluded to that little sign of progress.[2] I shall be told it is all very well, but you know that all the great statesmen are still dead against your Bill.[3] Of course they are. Why, when the great statesmen have come round, the Bill is as good as carried. Have you seen a flotilla of ships of all sizes riding at anchor in the tideway, and have you seen the tide turn and suddenly begin to flow? Which came round first? The little cock-boats; then the ships a little bigger; then [the three-deckers; and then

[1] At Plymouth in 1823 (vol. vi. of Canning's *Speeches*).
[2] The passing of the Irish Sunday Closing Bill.
[3] The Permissive Bill.

the great man-of-war wheels round along with the others. When the tide is strong enough, the statesmen — the tide-waiters — will come round with it. But don't you hurry these statesmen. They are far cleverer than we are. They won't do the right thing till the right time, and the right time is when you tell them they must do it. Statesmen, indeed! Who pins his faith on statesmen? Not I. I have lived long enough to get over all that." [1]

My own acquaintance with Wilfrid Lawson began, as I said before, when I entered Parliament at the General Election of 1880. He was then fifty, and I was twenty-seven; but it is a pleasant characteristic of the House of Commons that it obliterates all distinctions of age, as well as those of rank and wealth, and puts young and old and middle-aged on a footing of absolute equality. While this is a general law of the place, it is of course illustrated with special force in particular instances. Some of our seniors, with the best will in the world, used rather to patronize us and play the Heavy Father. Lawson's genial spirit, and total freedom from stiffness and pomposity, would have made such an attitude towards younger men

[1] At Manchester, October 1876.

impossible; and I think that we regarded him as a kind of Elder Brother, whom it was particularly easy to approach, and on whose unaffected kindness we could always rely. Though my personal acquaintance with Lawson dated only from my entrance into Parliament, I was of course familiar with his public record; and it is conceivable that one might have formed in one's mind a rather alarming picture of the zealot who, in season and out of season, had so long been preaching the stern doctrine which was masked under the name of the Permissive Bill. But all such apprehensions were dispelled by Justin McCarthy, who, in his *History of Our Own Times* (published in 1878), had written as follows:—

" The parliamentary leader of the agitation [against the Liquor-Traffic] was Sir Wilfrid Lawson, a man of position, of great energy, and of thorough earnestness. Sir Wilfrid Lawson was not, however, merely energetic and earnest. He had a peculiarly effective style of speaking, curiously unlike what might be expected from the advocate of an austere and somewhat fanatical sort of legislation. He was a humorist of a fresh and vigorous order, and he always took care to amuse his listeners, and never allowed his speeches to bore them."

This account of Lawson I found, on personal contact, to be strictly true; and I might have added that, unlike most leaders of great causes, he was perfectly tolerant of those who did not share his faith. In those distant and unregenerate days I had not even become a convert to the principle of Local Control over the liquor-traffic; but this painful fact did not in the least impair the friendliness and good-fellowship with which Lawson honoured me. He knew that I was a convinced and ardent Radical, so that, on nine points out of ten in the Liberal creed, I agreed with him. He seemed content to accept me on that footing, and pleasantly assured me that as regards the liquor-laws I should come right one day. Whether I ever quite fulfilled his sanguine expectations I am not absolutely sure; but I know very well that, in the quarter of a century during which I enjoyed the privilege of his friendship, I learned to regard the nobility and beauty of his character with ever-increasing admiration. His personal attractiveness had always been the same, but our political sympathy grew deeper as time went on. In all those great issues of national policy where questions of right and wrong are concerned, he seemed to find his way, by a kind of intuition, to the right side, long before the public conscience had been enlightened, and even when, as in the case of the South African War, it had been systematically misled. His memory will always abide with me as that of the most unswervingly conscientious politician whom I have ever known.

This seems, in some ways, a hard saying; for it has been my happiness to know, and sometimes to be closely associated with, politicians of the highest character and of unquestionable integrity. But most of these men have been, on one side or the other, members of the government; and it is obvious that any man who joins a government must do so with the full knowledge that he is making himself part of a system in which compromise, adjustment, mutual concession, and give-and-take are the necessary conditions of work; where no one can have everything exactly as he would wish it; and where each man must be content if, in vital and urgent matters, he is sufficiently at one with his colleagues to make combined action possible. Then again some of the most high-minded men whom I have known in public life have been, before and above all else, loyal members of a party. To such men it is the easiest and most natural thing in the world to

put their scruples in their pockets; to sub-
ordinate their special objects, if they have any,
to the general purpose; to stifle all critical
impulses whether in themselves or in others;
and to back their leaders' policy however strange
or inconsistent it may seem. Their motto is,
" My party, right or wrong," and they act up
to what they profess.

With the habits of mind thus indicated Lawson
had no sympathy. He would not have passed
censures on members of governments or devotees of Party, but he himself was built on
different lines. He, instinctively and by habit,
applied a perfectly independent judgment to each
question as it arose. His conscience was, in
Newman's fine phrase, a King in its imperious-
ness, a Prophet in its predictions, a Priest in
its benedictions or anathemas. If the course
pursued even by his political friends deviated
by a hair's breadth from the line which he
thought right, his opposition was a foregone
conclusion. He could never be convinced, or
intimidated, or cajoled. In brief, his was exactly
that type of character and intellect which is
to the political managers a powerful irritant,
and to the hacks whom they manipulate a
sealed and hopeless mystery.

In my estimate of Lawson's character, I have assigned the first place to his conscientiousness; the second, I think, belongs to his benevolence. "Philanthropy" would perhaps be a better word, but it is too much associated with societies and subscription-lists. Those who love a pseudo-philosophical style might prefer to call the quality altruism. But, name it how we please, I mean the quality which impels a man to sacrifice ease, comfort, popularity, if need be health and money; to spend and be spent; to face ridicule and calumny; to risk misunderstanding; to imperil valued friendships, and to brave the alternative reproach of foolery and knavery; in order to serve and save his fellowmen. This impulse always seemed to me the dominating influence of Lawson's life. He had absolutely nothing to gain by entering public life. The accidents of birth and fortune had placed him far above the sphere in which sordid and vulgar ambitions operate. The honourable prizes of parliamentary service meant nothing to a man who would not, for any inducement, have endured the trammels of office. He held tenaciously to the high faith that the chief reward of life is the consciousness of duty done; and to applause, whether of parliaments or mobs, parties or persons, he was as indifferent as he was to calumny and abuse—and one could not express indifference more strongly.

Wilfrid Lawson entered public life solely because he believed that a seat in the House of Commons afforded him a special and privileged opportunity of working for his fellow-men, and of employing his peculiar gifts in the promotion of the great causes which were as dear to him as life itself. Those causes, taken in the mass, coincided pretty closely with those for which the Liberal party has always contended. It has been truly said that Liberalism is not so much a set of opinions as a temper of mind; and the best answer ever made to the question, "Why are you a Liberal?" was, "Because I can't help it." In each succeeding age the Liberal "temper of mind" is brought to bear on the problems, ever fresh yet ever recurring, which concern the public good; and it issues in those practical efforts to find the right solution which we call the "Causes." It is indeed a guess, but a pretty safe guess, that Wilfrid Lawson grew up a Liberal "because he couldn't help it."

As regards the intercourse of private life, I consider Lawson the most purely humorous man whom I ever encountered. Wild horses should not drag me into a discussion of the difference between Wit and Humour; but I shall sufficiently convey my meaning when I say that Lawson woke one's laughter, not by polished epigrams or verbal felicities, or anything which could possibly have been prepared beforehand, but by the spontaneous flow of his mirthful and mirth-making spirit, which saw instantaneously the ludicrous aspect of each incident as it arose, and made the most unexpected turns from grave to gay. His memory was crammed with treasures of fun, which came tumbling out in headlong profusion, but always hitting, as it were by accident, the point of the moment's joke. No ludicrous scene or situation or phrase or characteristic seemed ever to have escaped his notice; and though no human being was far removed from the feebleness of "anecdotage," yet no one told a humorous story with so much pith and point. To hear Lawson talking at his best—and he was almost always at his best—was to enjoy the very perfection of irresistible comicality.

When the gift of humour is so strongly developed in a man as it was in Lawson, it must of necessity appear, not only in his speech but

in his writing. Lawson made no pretensions to
literary culture, and bestowed, so far as I know,
no special pains on his written style. He wrote,
as he spoke, out of the abundance of his heart ;
but his mode of expressing himself, when he
wrote for publication, was singularly racy, pointed,
and effective. Serious, too, in their main purpose and drift were his private letters, of which
he wrote an enormous quantity and to all sorts
of people ; but in these his humour refused to
be suppressed, and bubbled out in happy phrases
and quaint illusions. Almost every letter contained some characteristic touch of good sense
and good feeling made persuasive by good fun.

All through his parliamentary life he kept
a singularly full and accurate diary ; but the
limits of space forbid more than one quotation,
which, though written twenty-five years ago,
has a striking relevance to the circumstances
of to-day.

July 13, 1891.

[*The Kaiser was in London.*] " Some of our party went
to the Wimbledon Review, and said it was good. Some (I
one of them) went to see the finish of the Eton and Harrow
match at Lord's. Harrow was manifestly the stronger, so
the best men won—which is not always the case in this
world. As the battle was over by 4.30, he went off to the
Zoo for a bit. . . . It would be well, perhaps, if Emperors
were kept in cages also. They would do less harm than when
they are loose."

CHAPTER VIII

LORD ACTON [1]

THE portraits which, so far, I have drawn are the portraits of men who were very widely known. Hardly any one, at any rate during the Seventies, knew John Emerich Edward Dalberg-Acton, first Lord Acton. Yet he was a man so remarkable, in many respects unique, that this collection would be incomplete without some attempt to depict him.

We will take physical characteristics first. Acton was of middle height, massive and portly in build, with a broad expanse of forehead from which the dark hair was slowly retreating. Dark too, though latterly streaked with silver, was his abundant beard, whiskers, and moustache. His eyes were bright and searching, but the expression of his face was serious and serene. His bearing was dignified, his dress mid-Victorian,

[1] 1834–1902

LORD ACTON.

To face p. 128.

and his whole aspect, when one saw him in
repose, suggested solidity and even approached
lethargy. This suggestion was dispelled the
moment that he began to speak. He spoke eagerly
and pointedly, and evidently enjoyed talking,
though he did not indulge in monologues but
took his part on equal terms. He was quick
at seizing the point, terse and apt in reply.
He was a close observer of all personal
characteristics; had a keen eye for pretence,
pomposity, and unreality; and was peculiarly
happy when he was leading a vain or shallow
talker to utter absurdities or to reveal ignorance.
To all such offences he was merciless; not then
and there, for his manners were excellent, but
at a convenient season or in a confidential
letter. He was genuinely humorous, but his
humour was almost always sarcastic. Whether
as host or guest, he thoroughly enjoyed society
in every form; ate and drank with a serious
and rather German gusto; and was essentially
a gossip, diligent in collecting information,
social, political, or personal, and eager, when
it was unimportant, to impart it.

I lay stress on "unimportant," for his most
conspicuous trait was a sphinx-like mysterious-
ness, which conveyed the sense that he knew

a great deal more than he chose to impart, and was a walking depository of vital secrets.

That Acton was unknown to the great majority of his countrymen was due to a combination of circumstances. He was a Roman Catholic by religion, more than half a German by blood, born at Naples, and educated at Munich. In early life he had sate in Parliament for two microscopic boroughs, Carlow and Bridgnorth, long since disfranchised; and was raised to the peerage by Gladstone in 1869. From first to last he was a profound Gladstonian, and Gladstone held him in the highest esteem. The two men were drawn together by common convictions in the spheres of religion and morality, and in what Gladstone called "the mixed sphere of religion and the *sæculum*."

Acton was profoundly and essentially a Liberal, in the highest sense of that much-abused word. "Liberty," he said, "is not a means to a higher end. It is itself the highest political end." His politics were part of his religion, and his religion was his master-passion. It was, of course, a religion dogmatic and sacramental, but it was also intensely ethical. "Is this true? Is this right?" were the tests which he unfailingly applied to belief and conduct. "In judging

men and things," he said, "ethics go before
dogma, politics, and nationality." It is obvious
that a man who entertained this sentiment would
be a man after Gladstone's own heart; and, conversely, Gladstone, as being the essentially
ethical statesman, was the idol of Acton's
profoundest worship. After analysing, with all
the apparatus of his historical omniscience, the
powers of Chatham, Fox, Pitt, Canning, and Peel,
he triumphantly affirmed that "the highest
merits of the five, without their drawbacks,
were united in Mr. Gladstone."

Domestic circumstances led Acton to spend
a good deal of his time abroad; but from
Tegernsee or the Riviera he watched English
politics with an anxious scrutiny. His loyal
enthusiam for his political leader rather increased
than declined during the troublous years which
succeeded 1885. He was a staunch Home Ruler,
and of so Gladstonian a type that he approved
of the two capital vices which destroyed the
Irish policy of 1886—the Land Purchase Bill
and the exclusion of the Irish Members from
the House of Commons. Following Gladstone
through evil report and good report, through
honour and dishonour, he persuaded himself that,
when there next was a Liberal government, he

would become Foreign Secretary. When in 1892 Gladstone formed his last administration, there were some who thought that a place might have been found for Acton in a Cabinet which contained Mr. Arthur Acland and Mr. Arnold Morley; but other counsels prevailed. Acton was fobbed off with the offer of some absurd appointment in the Household, which would have obliged him to play at being a soldier, and to wear a brass helmet with a horsehair plume. Even this offer, not far removed from an insult, was, after he had accepted it, withdrawn; and the greatest historian—some said the most learned man all round—in Europe, was made a Lord-in-Waiting. It was reserved, not for his chief and idol, but for a politician with whom he had scarcely an idea in common, to redress this anomaly. In 1895 Lord Rosebery made Acton Regius Professor of Modern History at Cambridge, and so placed him in a position where his unrivalled gifts at last found scope for their exercise.

Here it is necessary to look back a little. From early manhood Acton had devoted himself to a task in which many a noble heart has been broken. He laboured, with amazing industry and with an unconquerable hopefulness, to reconcile Liberalism, spiritual, intellectual,

and political, with the Papal dominion in the
sphere of faith and morals. He failed, as many
good men have failed before him, and the
Vatican Council with its consequences seemed
to emphasize his failure. But he did not, as
so many in like circumstances have done, lose
heart or faith. He pursued his path, "with
his eyes fixed on higher lodestars," and devoted
himself to what he intended to be the main
work of his life—a History of Liberty. Never
was there a more glorious theme; but it was
too vast for individual compass. His time, his
talents, and his fortune were absorbed in the
collection of material for the book—and it never
was written. What he left behind him was a
vast collection of disjointed notes, gathered
from every age and every land and every tongue.
No one had the clue to the labyrinth, or the
secret of the plan which would have woven the
fragments into one. A spiteful commentator
said, when his Letters were published, that
"he won an immense reputation merely by
doing nothing": the truth is that he had set
himself a task too great to be accomplished
within the limits of a human life. I have sometimes thought that George Eliot might have had
Acton in mind when she wrote of the Rev.

Edward Casaubon in *Middlemarch* : " This learned gentleman was possessed of a fortune ; he had assembled his voluminous notes, and had made that sort of reputation which precedes performance—often the larger part of a man's fame."

Acton's appointment to the Professorship of Modern History at Cambridge saved a portion, and indeed a considerable portion, of his life's work from waste and oblivion. If it had not been for the years between 1895 and 1905, his vast knowledge would have profited only a very few. But at Cambridge he was in perpetual contact with fresh minds eager to know and to transmit what they acquired. Every one who came to him for assistance and instruction went away not merely satisfied and enlightened, but moved and touched by the profundity of his learning and by the depth of his moral convictions. He who for so long had been Unknown was here-after to be Well-known ; but he was only preaching from a more exalted pulpit the faith which he had held and taught for fifty years. While it was his fate to be suspected by Catholics as a Liberal and by Liberals as a Catholic, he was deeply convinced that religion lies near the heart of all history. " He never read of an action without appraising its significance and morality, never learnt a fact without fitting it into its environment, and never studied a life or a period without considering its effect upon the progress of humanity." This testimony, rendered by one of his colleagues in the professorial body, is amply justified by his public and private writings. "If," he said, "we lower our standard in history, we cannot uphold it in Church and State." Again: "To develope, and perfect, and arm conscience is the best achievement of history, the chief business of every life; and the first agent therein is Religion, or what resembles Religion." From his professorial chair he addressed to his pupils this noble allocution, pontifical in the best sense of the word:—

"Try others by the final maxim that governs your own lives, and suffer no man and no cause to escape the undying penalty which history has the power to inflict on wrong."

In spite of his eventual appointment to a post where his vast and varied knowledge could be turned to account, Acton left behind him no monumental work to which his friends could point and say, "There; we always told you that he was the most learned man in England." But he left a more valuable legacy. As long as his name is remembered and his words are read, Englishmen will not lack the needful reminder that the Moral Law is supreme in civil and international, as in private and personal, concerns; and that, for men or for nations, Righteousness is the only true glory.

CHAPTER IX

HENRY LABOUCHERE [1]

"WHEN the Grand Old Man goes, our leader must be Le-bowcher." This fervent utterance of a convinced Radical, somewhere about the year 1882, supplies me with a fitting text.

I cannot pretend to write Labouchere's early history, or to describe his habits in private life; nor can I even profess to have ever been an intimate friend. My connexion with him was purely fortuitous; it was confined to the House of Commons, and began with the new Parliament of 1880. The saying which I have inscribed at the head of this chapter sufficiently indicates the position which, quite early in the life of that Parliament, he acquired in Radical circles out of doors. Inside the House, we saw a different side of him; and the contrast between the Labouchere of the House and the Labouchere

[1] 1831–1912.

of the platform was at once amusing and instructive.

As a Harrow boy of fifteen, I had admired the gay audacity with which, at the General Election of 1868, the democratic Labouchere upset the calculations of official Whiggery in Middlesex, though he lost his own seat by doing so; and it may be that some allusion of mine to that "unchartered freedom" first commended me to his kindly regard. At any rate, it is certain that from April 1880 onwards he always showed himself to me in his most accessible and obliging aspect. I will speak first of some slighter traits, and will then pass on to matters more important.

"The Christian Member for N thampton" (as he delighted to call himself in contrast to his colleague, Bradlaugh) was not, at the time of which I speak, much known in general society. His social day was over, and I cannot suppose that he regretted it. He was the oracle of an initiated circle, and the smoking-room of the House of Commons was his shrine. There, poised in an American rocking-chair and delicately toying with a cigarette, he unlocked the varied treasures of his well-stored memory, and threw over the changing scenes of life the mild

HENRY LABOUCHERE.

To face p. 138.

light of his genial philosophy. It was a chequered experience that made him what he was. He had known men and cities; had probed in turn the mysteries of the Caucus, the Green-room, and the Stock - Exchange; had been a diplomatist, a financier, a journalist, and a politician. Under these circumstances, it was not surprising that his faith—no doubt originally robust—in the rectitude of human nature and the purity of human motive should have undergone some process of degeneration. Still, it may be questioned whether, after all that he had seen and done, he really was the absolute and all-round cynic that he seemed to be. The palpable endeavour to make out the worst of every one—including himself—gave a certain flavour of unreality to his conversation; but, in spite of this drawback, he was an engaging talker. His language was racy and incisive, and he spoke as neatly as he wrote. His voice was pleasant, and his utterance deliberate and effective. He had a quick eye for absurdities and incongruities, a shrewd insight into affectation and bombast, and an admirable impatience of all the moral and intellectual qualities which constitute the Bore. He was by no means inclined to bow the knee too slavishly to an exalted reputation, and he analysed with agreeable frankness the personal and political qualities of great and good men, even they that sate on the Liberal Front Bench. As an unmasker of political humbug he was supreme, but his dislike of that vice often led him into unreasonable depreciations. I well remember the peroration of Mr. Gladstone's speech in introducing the Irish Land Bill of 1881; and I think it deserves to be reproduced :—

"As it has been said that Love is stronger than Death, even so Justice is stronger than popular excitement, stronger than the passions of the moment, stronger even than the grudges, the resentments, and the sad traditions of the past. Walking in that light we cannot err. Guided by that light—that Divine light—we are safe. Every step that we take upon our road is a step that brings us nearer to the goal, and every obstacle, even although for the moment it may seem insurmountable, can only for a little while retard, and never can defeat, the final triumph."

When the orator sate down we streamed into the lobby, each man saying to his neighbour : "Wasn't that splendid?" "The finest thing he ever did!" "What a thrilling perora-

tion!" "Yes" (in a drawl from Labouchere),
"but I call it d——d copy-book-y."

I have spoken of the flavour of unreality
which was imparted to Labouchere's conversation
by his affected cynicism. A similar effect was
produced by his manner of personal narrative.
Ethics apart, I have no quarrel with the man
who romances to amuse his friends; but the
romance should be so conceived and so uttered
as to convey a decent sense of probability, or
at least possibility. Labouchere's narratives conveyed no such sense. Though amusingly told,
they were so outrageously and palpably impossible that his only object in telling them
must have been to test one's credulity. I do
not mind having my leg pulled, but I dislike
to feel the process too distinctly.

These arts of romantic narrative, only partially
successful in the smoking-room, were, I believe,
practised with great effect on the electors of
Northampton. Labouchere was never happier
than in describing the methods by which he
had fobbed off some inconvenient enthusiast,
or thrown dust in the eyes of a too curious
enquirer. His dealings with his constituents, as
he narrated them, had, I suppose, a good deal in
common with his experiences as President of a

South American Republic or Commander of a revolutionary force; but they were extremely entertaining. He used to declare that he had originated the honorific title of "Grand Old Man," and his setting of the scene was as follows: Mr. Bradlaugh had been expelled from the House, and straightway went down to Northampton for re-election, his colleague, "the Christian Member" for the borough, accompanying him. What ensued at the first meeting may be told as Labouchere used to tell it. "I said to our enthusiastic supporters: 'Men of Northampton, I come to you with a message from the Grand Old Man. ₁(Cheers.) I went to see him before I left London; I told him of my errand here; and he laid his hand on my shoulder, saying, in his most solemn tone, 'Bring him back with you, Henry; bring him back.' That carried the election." I dare say it did; and the picture of Mr. Gladstone fondling Labouchere and calling him "Henry" can never be obliterated from the mental gaze of any one who knew the two men.

There was a good deal of impishness in Labouchere's nature. He was of the family of Puck, and "Lord! what fools these mortals be!" probably expressed his attitude towards his fellow-creatures. But it was noticeable that his impishness never degenerated into rudeness. There is as clear a difference between gentle-manlike fun and vulgar fun as between cham-pagne and swipes. Labouchere was a gentleman to the backbone, and had all the courtesy which one would have expected from his antecedents. I remember that, in the stormy days of January 1881, when the authorities of the House were obliged to extemporize some rules against disorder, I happened to be crossing New Palace Yard in company with Mr. Herbert Gladstone. We met Labouchere, who chirped, in his cheeriest manner, " Well, has the tyrant made any fresh attack on free speech to-day ? " Herbert Glad-stone passed on, without reply, and Labouchere said to me, with genuine concern, " He can't have thought I meant his father, can he ? Of course, I was thinking of the Speaker." It was interesting to see that he seemed to shudder at the bare notion of having been unintentionally rude.

I remember Gladstone, in one of his odd fits of political speculation, asking if I thought that there was even one man in the House of Commons, however radical he might be, who would vote for unwigging the Speaker. I, rather obviously, suggested Labouchere, and Gladstone replied, "Yes, possibly; but that would be from freakishness, not from conviction." No powers of divination could have ascertained what Labouchere really believed; but I think it was easier to know what he really enjoyed. I suppose he enjoyed his wealth—most people who have it do so—but chiefly, I should think, on rather impish grounds. It was an acute delight to him in early days to know that he was bound to inherit the fortune of his uncle, Lord Taunton, a high-dried Whig, who detested his eccentricities. He took pleasure in saying to casual acquaintances, "You know that my sister married the Bishop of Rochester;" for he felt the incongruity of the fate which had made him brother-in-law to Anthony Thorold, the primmest, correctest, and most stiffly starched of all the Anglican Episcopate. Litigation always seemed to delight him, less for the objects contested than for the opportunity which it gave him of scoring and surprising; and I am sure that I do him no wrong when I say that he found a peculiar zest in buying a freehold house in Old Palace Yard, and thereby impeding the schemes of Mr. H. Y. Thompson for creating a National Valhalla. I feel certain that he thoroughly enjoyed the proprietorship of *Truth*, and not less the reputation (which we are now told was erroneous) of being its editor. I believe that he had a genuine sympathy with all victims of cruelty, fraud, and injustice, and found a real pleasure in the immense service which *Truth* did in unmasking impostors and bringing torturers to justice.

Labouchere made *Truth*, and, in one most important respect, *Truth* made Labouchere. I do not refer to anything in the way of profit or of consideration which it may have brought him, for he was placed by the circumstances of his birth in a position where such things neither make nor mar. I refer to his political career. I do not know whether, when as a young man he flitted in and out of Parliament, he cherished any serious ambitions. I doubt if he had them even when he became M.P. for Northampton. But the events of the Parliament of 1880 brought him rapidly to the front. His valorous championship of Bradlaugh gave him a peculiar position at a moment when the public mind was violently agitated by panic-fears of Atheism. He stood for religious freedom when many of its sworn adherents ran away; and on all the points of old-fashioned Radicalism (before Socialism affected it) he was as sound as a bell. Hence the cry of the London democrat —" Our leader must be Le-bowcher." But before that desirable consummation could be reached, the Liberal majority of Easter 1880 had melted like last year's snow. The Tories took office, and the General Election of 1885 did not displace them. In February 1886 Gladstone, having squared the Irish members, became Prime Minister, and now Labouchere's position was difficult and tantalizing. His party were in office, and the way seemed clear for some radical reforms on which Liberals had long set their hearts. But Chamberlain, and some of the Radical group with whom Labouchere had acted, declined to accept Home Rule, left the government, and created Radical Unionism. If they voted against the Second Reading of the Home Rule Bill, it would almost certainly be thrown out, and the government would follow it into retirement. Here was, indeed, a perplexing situation, and it forced Labouchere into action which must certainly have been uncongenial to him. Four days before the vital division, when argument on either side was exhausted and every one had decided on his course, Labouchere, writing on behalf of a large body of Liberal

M.P.'s, addressed to Chamberlain an earnest
appeal, imploring him either to vote for the
second reading or at least to abstain. He
pointed out that a second General Election within
seven months would be a serious matter for
Liberals, and that an appeal to the country,
without Chamberlain (then at the height of
his popularity) on the Liberal side, might lead
to a Whig-Tory or Tory-Whig Government, and
so " relegate to the dim and distant future"
those measures which they had so long and so
ardently desired. To this appeal Chamberlain
naturally replied that he and his friends would
be stultifying themselves if, after all they had
said and done, they were at the last moment
to abstain from giving effect to their convictions. "I admit," said Chamberlain, " the
dangers of a General Election at the present
time; but I think the responsibility must in
fairness rest upon those who have brought in,
and forced to a division, a Bill which, in the
words of Mr. Bright, ' not twenty members
outside the Irish party would support if Mr.
Gladstone's great authority were withdrawn
from it.' "

I must believe that, when Labouchere penned
the appealing document, he had his tongue in

his cheek. The simple souls in the constituencies, and the not much wiser ones who had just
entered Parliament, may have believed that
Chamberlain, having staked his whole career
on a decisive act, would shrink from it at the
last moment for fear he should embarrass the
Liberal party; but Labouchere, I feel certain,
had no such illusions. Yet the incident was
not without its effect. The championship of
Bradlaugh was now over, for Bradlaugh was
in the House to look after himself. Henceforward Labouchere was one of the most persistent, and, through *Truth*, one of the most
powerful advocates of Home Rule, and a highly
resourceful counsellor in all the plots and
stratagems which made the political history
of 1886–92.

It was at this period of storm and stress
that Sir Frederick Bridge, who was one of
Labouchere's neighbours in Westminster, was
moved to utter his thought in song. The poem
appeared in *Punch*, and is reprinted here by
permission of the proprietors of that journal.

LABBY IN OUR ABBEY.[1]

Tune—"Sally in our Alley."

Of all the boys that are so smart
    There's none like crafty Labby;
He learns the secrets of each heart,
    And he lives near our Abbey [2];
There is no lawyer in the land
    That's half so sharp as Labby;
He is a demon in the art,
    And guileless as a babby.

For Arthur Balfour, of the week
    By far the very worst day
Is that dread day that comes betwixt
    A Tuesday and a Thursday [3];
For then he reads his vile misdeeds
    ("Unmanly, mean, and shabby")
Exposed to view in type so true
    By penetrating Labby.

Our Ministers and Members all
    Make game of truthful Labby,
Tho', but for him, 'tis said they'd be
    A sleepy lot and flabby;

---

[1] Written during the period when Mr. Arthur Balfour was Chief Secretary for Ireland.
[2] Labouchere resided in Old Palace Yard, Westminster.
[3] *Truth* was published on Wednesday.

> But ere their seven long years are out [1]
> They hope to bury Labby;
> Ah! then how peacefully he'll lie,
> But *not* in our Abbey.

What Sir Frederick Bridge wrote jestingly, Labouchere, for once in his life, took seriously. There can be no doubt that by this time he had formed a definite ambition of political office. During the six years of Tory ascendency he fought incessantly, with tongue and pen, for the Liberal cause, and he reckoned confidently on being included in the next Liberal Cabinet. But he had reckoned without his host. The Parliament which had been elected in July 1886 was dissolved in June 1892. The General Election gave Gladstone a majority of forty all told. He became Prime Minister for the fourth time, and formed his last Cabinet. But he did not find a place in it for Labouchere. Before he submitted his list to the Queen, he had received a direct intimation [2] that he had better not include in it the name of the editor of *Truth*. On this point Her Majesty was declared to be "very stiff." Whether that stiffness encountered any corresponding, or con-

---

[1] A reference to the Septennial Act.
[2] Which I have read.—G. W. E. R.

flicting, stiffness in the Prime Minister I do
not know, but for my own part I believe that
"the Grand Old Man" acquiesced in the exclusion of "Henry" without a sigh or struggle.

Displeased by the issue of events, Labouchere
took a mild revenge. He printed in *Truth*
some severe strictures on Gladstone's new
administration, partly because it was too
Whiggish, and illustrated them with a hideous
cartoon, in which all we who had accepted office
were caricatured. Participating in these rebuffs,
and surprised by my friend's lapse from amenity,
I wrote Labouchere a letter of remonstrance,
which proved about as efficacious as his own
appeal to Chamberlain six years before. This
was his answer :—

August 24, 1892.

My dear Russell,

Never be drawn. Let a licentious and scurrilous Press
say what it likes, and sit tight. . . . My Radicalism goes to
the utter destruction of the aristocracy. So, of course, I call
attention to young patricians, and compare them with those
children of the people, Cobb and Channing. This is involved
in being on the side of destruction.

Yours sincerely,

H. Labouchere.

Thus Labouchere's political ambitions came
to an end, unsung indeed, but, I fear, not

unwept. Very soon he developed a new scheme for the employment of his powers, and pursued it with the most untiring industry. He wished to be made Ambassador at Washington, and he wished it with an insistence which people who knew him superficially would scarcely have expected. Lord Rosebery was at the time Foreign Secretary; and if it be true, as I have seen it stated, that he was one of the very few people whom Labouchere hated, I think the reason might be found in the correspondence of 1892–93.

In later years my communications with Labouchere were few and far between. It happened that, towards the end of the year 1906, I had occasion to write to him for some information about a foreign question. He immediately replied, and then turned to current politics :—

"I find it very comfortable being out of Parliament, and reading in the papers what they do—or don't do—in the H. of C. Our pawky friend C. B. seems to be very popular. I am a Radical, but it strikes me that he will upset the apple-cart or create a reaction if he yields so much to the ultra-Labour men of the Keir Hardie type on social issues, particularly if

"Joe" is good enough to remain an invalid, and the Conservative party can free itself of his fiscal "reforms." As for the Education Bill, I do not love Bishops, but I hate far more the Noncon. Popes. Either you must have pure Secularism in public schools, or teach religion of some sort; and, altho' I personally am an Agnostic, I don't see how Xtianity is to be taught free from all dogma, and entirely creedless, by teachers who do not believe in it. This is the play of *Hamlet* without Hamlet, and acted by persons of his philosophic doubt."

So, at least for once in his life, Labouchere was on the same side as the Bishops, and in that good company we may leave him.

CHAPTER X

JOSEPH CHAMBERLAIN [1]

IT was only for six years that I had any close acquaintance with the late Member for West Birmingham. After the great disruption of 1886 our paths diverged, and since that date I only met him in the casual intercourse of general society, and that rarely. But I never had a disagreeable word from him, and, even after the disruption, many kind ones.

I entered Parliament at the General Election of 1880, being just twenty-seven years old. Chamberlain had entered at a by-election in 1876, and was seventeen years my senior. At that time I knew very little about him. After the Liberal defeat at the polls in 1874, he had denounced Gladstone's Election Address, promising to repeal the Income Tax, as the "meanest document ever issued by a public man." He was reported to have said that the Prince of

[1] 1836–1914.

JOSEPH CHAMBERLAIN,

To face p. 154.

Wales would be received in Birmingham with the same sort of curiosity which would be excited by the Tichborne Claimant. In a debate in 1879 he had referred to Lord Hartington as " the late leader of the Liberal party." At the General Election of 1880 Sir William Harcourt described him as having been consecrated by a kind of apostolic succession to take the place long occupied by John Bright, as Chief Bogey of the Tory party. But none of these things affected me. I had entered the campaign with the one object of defeating Lord Beaconsfield's Eastern policy, and my sole leader was Gladstone. If only he became Prime Minister, nothing else mattered. When, on the 23rd of April, 1880, he kissed hands, the victory was won.

The formation of the new Cabinet was not a matter of thrilling interest. " The old familiar faces " turned up in the old familiar places. Dilke was fobbed off with an Under-Secretaryship. Fawcett was disqualified by blindness. Chamberlain was the sole representative of Radicalism in a Cabinet dependent for its existence on Radical support. The victory over Lord Beaconsfield being won, we were turning our thoughts towards those domestic problems which had so long pressed for solution; and Chamberlain, who had taken no great part in the Eastern Question, became interesting, because his presence in a Cabinet stuffed with Whigs seemed to afford our only hope of social reform.

Early in my first session I was introduced to Chamberlain, I cannot remember by whom, but very likely by my staunch friend, Sir George Trevelyan. I was at once and strongly attracted by him. He was wholly free from the stiffness and pomposity which the old hacks of the Liberal Cabinet sedulously cultivated. He received one at once on the footing of comradeship and equality; and he talked with that complete openness which, when displayed by an older to a younger man, is in itself a compliment. But, before I recall his conversation, let me describe his appearance.

He was then forty-three years old, but looked at least ten years younger. Even as late as 1885, when he was in his fiftieth year, I heard him acclaimed by the "voice" at a public meeting as the "Grand Young Man" of the Liberal party. He had the sharply pointed features which we all remember; pale and rather sallow complexion, dark hair, and slight whiskers. The eyeglass and the orchid were conspicuous

appendages. The obvious and universal remark
was that he resembled Pitt; but the resemblance
began and ended with the angle of the nose.
Pitt was tall, gaunt, stiff, and supremely dignified. Chamberlain was rather short than tall;
not the least dignified; singularly pliant and
active. The extreme alertness of look and
manner and movement irresistibly suggested the
associations of the counter, and Gilbert's

> Pushing young particle—
> What's the next article?
> Threepenny 'bus young man.

His whole appearance was conspicuously neat
and glossy. He looked, to use the common
phrase, as if he had just come out of a band-
box—but critics said that it was a provincial
band-box. He wore his tie in a ring, and displayed his handkerchief outside his frock-coat
like a star.

It seems curious, in view of all that has
happened since, to remember that Chamberlain
played very little part in the Parliament of 1880.
From the beginning to the end of that Parliament, Ireland, in one form or another, engrossed
the House of Commons; and Chamberlain very
rarely intervened in Irish debates. He was

more concerned with the affairs of his department, such as bankruptcy and merchant
shipping; and, as they were not of absorbing
interest, he seemed to be much more at leisure
than most members of the Cabinet. It is,
perhaps, due to this circumstance that I enjoyed
so much of his society; for in the lobby and
in the tea-room and on the terrace I seem to
have been very often in his company; and his
hospitality was unbounded. He was a perfect
host, receiving his guests with " that honest joy
which warms more than dinner or wine ";
mixing his parties adroitly, and inciting, though
never dominating, the conversation. He frankly
enjoyed a good dinner. " So many of the
pleasures of life are illusory," he once said to
me; " but a good dinner is a reality; and, by
Jove ! after such a Session as we've been
through, I think we deserve it." In this connexion I recall some words which now have a
pathetic interest. Knowing that I had never
been strong, Chamberlain said to me, with
genuine kindness, " The House of Commons is
rather a trying place for the health, but don't
let any one persuade you to take exercise.
Exercise was invented by the doctors to bring
grist to their mill. They knew that men who

went in for exertion would soon come to them
as patients. When I was a young man, I believed them, and I constantly suffered from
congestive headaches. Now I defy them and
am perfectly well. I eat and drink what I like,
and as much as I like. I smoke the strongest
cigars all day; and the only exercise I take is
to walk up to bed. That is quite enough for a
man who has worked his brain all day—and I
mean to live to a hundred."

His chief interest and enjoyment always
seemed to consist in work, and, rather specially,
in the work of organizing and controlling political
opinion in Birmingham. If he ever needed
relaxation, he found it in very simple forms.
His love of flowers we all know, and he was
fond of collecting black-and-white furniture. He
had some rather elementary views about the
arts—architecture for one—but for literature
(except French novels, of which he had a large
assortment) he had not the slightest feeling.
When I first knew him, he rented from Lord
Acton a house in Prince's Gate, which, as was
natural in a house of Acton's, contained a considerable library. When he left it for Prince's
Gardens, I said, "You will miss the library";
to which he replied, with indescribable emphasis,

" *Library!* I don't call that a library. There isn't a single book of reference in it."

Of course our conversation turned often, though not always, on politics; and, as I joined the government in 1883, we were officially bound to the support of the same policy. But, in questions outside the official programme, I was a keen supporter of Chamberlain, and his schemes of social reform, as against the fatal *laissez-faire* which the Whigs regarded as the only safe statesmanship. Just before I joined the government, I had declared my opinions in an article in the *Nineteenth Century*, and I reproduce a fragment of it here, in order to show the grounds of my sympathy with Chamberlain. The "Unauthorized Programme" appeared in 1885, and exhibited in a detailed and working form the policy which I had thus enounced in 1883 :—

"The high Whig doctrine would limit the functions of the State to the preservation of life and property, and the enforcement of contracts. Modern Liberalism, on the other hand, regarding the State as 'the nation in its collective and corporate character,' sees in it the one sovereign agent for all moral, material, and social reforms, and recognizes a special duty to deal with questions affecting the food, health, housing, amusement, and culture of the working classes."

Holding these views, I was naturally attracted to Chamberlain's leadership. He alone among the Liberal leaders of the time dared to defy the hoary shibboleths of the Manchester School, and to urge the active intervention of the State and the community in matters hitherto left to individual enterprise and competitive selfishness. He alone seemed to understand the troubles of the poor, and to perceive a way of remedying them. But in matters more strictly political we did not always see eye to eye. He was, even in those distant days, something of a Jingo. The bombardment of Alexandria caused deep searchings of the Liberal conscience, but Chamberlain did not share them. "I was sick," he said to me, "of being kicked all over Europe. I never was a peace-at-any-price man. I opposed the Tory government, not because it went to war, but because it always fought on the wrong side." His attitude towards the Irish questions which arose so constantly between 1880 and 1885 varied from time to time; and this he would neither have cared to deny nor to extenuate. He thought political consistency a highly over-rated virtue. "In politics, a year ahead is the

same as eternity. You begin a new day each
morning, and you should do your work in it, as
the occasion arises, neither looking backwards nor
forwards." Feeling was a stronger element in his
nature than reason, and his feeling was rapidly
and powerfully affected by the circumstances
of the moment. In the debate on Forster's
Coercion Bill in 1881, Mr. T. P. O'Connor
reproached him with having had, "if not the
courage of his convictions, at least the silence
of his shame"; and so general was the belief
in his sympathy with the Irish cause that an
Irish member said to him, in my hearing, "We
shall make you a Home Ruler yet, Mr. Chamberlain"; to which he replied, "By Jove! it
wouldn't take much to do that." During the
progress of that Parliament, the reign of torture
and terror which the Land League maintained
in Ireland, the gross misconduct of the Irish
members in the House, and, perhaps, some personal insolence to himself, visibly affected his
attitude. One day he told me, with impressive
earnestness, that the Irish were fools in thus
provoking the English, for nothing would be
easier than to raise an anti-Irish passion in the
English boroughs, which would rival the anti-
Jewish passion in Russia. Though he receded

from the idea of Home Rule—if, indeed, he had
ever entertained it—he still was an advocate for
a thorough reconstruction of Irish Government
on a representative basis; and the contumely
with which Parnell rejected his scheme of
National Councils made him a vehement and
persistent enemy of the Irish cause.

I have spoken above of Chamberlain's humanitarianism, which I have always believed to be
absolutely genuine. He loathed the sight of
curable misery, and longed to remedy it. A
lover of humanity he certainly was—at least in
those days—but was he equally a lover of freedom? I doubt it. Gladstone, in talking to me
once, likened him to Gambetta, as *un homme
autoritaire*; and certainly the love of governance,
of domination, of having his own way, was a
master-passion. He detested and despised administrative feebleness. I remember the keen
admiration with which he described the American way of dealing with a riot. "You sound a
bugle, so as to let the rioters disperse if they
choose; and, if they don't, you shoot." He
gloried in administrative strength; and, even in
the work of social reconstruction, I think he
would have liked to do the reconstructing with
his own hand, much better than to see it done
by the working classes for themselves.

The year 1885 saw Chamberlain at the height of his power. The old Whigs, most of whom had fallen away from the Government, loathed him. His colleagues in the Cabinet were not very fond of him; and Gladstone simply did not understand him. The saying that Gladstone understood Man but not men was never more conspicuously illustrated than in the case of Chamberlain. He only admitted him to the Cabinet because he was forced to do so, and made no use of him when he got him there. He had not the faintest notion of Chamberlain's influence in the country, and did not even realize, till it was too late, his unique power of public speech. That Chamberlain felt this, and resented it, is only to say that he was human. The game of slight was a game which two could play, and in 1885 Chamberlain promulgated his great programme of political and social reforms without the slightest reference to the chief who had ignored him. It had now been settled that the General Election should take place in November 1885, and early in the year Chamberlain opened the campaign with a series of admirably forceful speeches in great centres of population. The defeat of the Government, in June, gave him an extended freedom, and he used it with abounding energy for the furtherance of the objects on which he had set his heart.

The *Fortnightly Review* published a series of articles dealing with the political situation as transformed by the extension of the suffrage and by redistribution; with the machinery, and the measures, which the time demanded; with the Housing of the Poor, the Agricultural Labourer, Religious Equality, Free Schools, Taxation, and Local Government. These were collected in a volume, and issued in August 1885, with a preface by Chamberlain, who, without committing himself to all the proposals, commended the book as " a definite and practical Programme for the Radical party." The least felicitous of the articles was that which dealt with Religious Equality, and which was attributed, with much inherent probability, to Mr.—now Lord—Morley. Of Chamberlain's attitude towards religion at that period I cannot speak from personal experience. Knowing, I suppose, that I was a determined adherent of traditional Christianity, he never approached the subject of religion. I was told by J. H. Shorthouse that the " Chamberlain influence" in Birmingham was not only heterodox, but actively and bitterly secularist; and such was the spirit which seemed to animate the

article on " Religious Equality." To recommend
this separation of Church and State was quite
in accordance with the Radical tradition; but
the article betrayed such a virulence against the
Church which it proposed to disestablish as to
create general disgust. More than anything else
in the book, it kindled hostility to the Radical
cause, and so contributed to the defeat of the
" Unauthorized Programme." Another lapse
which cost us dear was Chamberlain's declaration, in a public speech, that property must be
prepared to pay " ransom " in the shape of
taxation. Now Chamberlain, who had made
money and enjoyed it, was no enemy to property.
He had no wish, as he said in his forcible ver-
nacular, to " drive every one who was worth a
nag out of the Liberal party." But it was a
case of verbal infelicity. The word " ransom "
was enough to stir the furious opposition of every
property-holder; whereas if the word " insurance "
had been used instead, the declaration would
have passed as a statesmanlike platitude.

However, in spite of these indiscretions, when
we approached the General Election of 1885
Chamberlain's was the most popular name in
the urban constituencies. The artisans were
rather tired of Gladstone, though the labourers

justly regarded him as their emancipator. When, on an urban platform, one mentioned the name of "Gladstone," there was a decorous "Hear, hear"; but, when one came to "Chamberlain," the cheering lifted the roof and lasted for five minutes.

Such was the political situation when, on October 2, 1885, I went on a visit to Hawarden. Soon after I arrived, Gladstone took me aside, and began a political conversation. He knew, rather with disapproval, that I was a supporter of the "Unauthorized Programme," and an adherent of Chamberlain. "What," he asked, "is Chamberlain's object?" I replied that, so far as I knew, Chamberlain's object was not to oust Gladstone from the leadership, but to secure the reversion of it when Gladstone should resign it. Above all, he was determined that Hartington should not lead the Liberal party. Some earnest conversation followed; and at length I suggested that the simplest way out of the perplexities would be to invite Chamberlain to Hawarden, and discuss the situation with him. This would be better than negotiation between emissaries, and might avert the disaster which would certainly ensue if the Liberal party went into the Election with two leaders and two programmes.

Eventually I carried my point. I wrote the
telegraphic invitation with my own hand, and
backed it with a letter to Chamberlain. Unfortunately, I had to leave Hawarden before he arrived,
but he wrote to me on his return to Birmingham.
Nothing, he said, could have been socially more
pleasant than the visit, but politically it had
been a failure. Gladstone would not budge an
inch towards the "Unauthorized Programme";
and, said Chamberlain, "If I were to recede, the
stones would immediately cry out." So we
entered the Election with divided leadership,
and the result was nearly, though not quite, as
bad as I predicted. We were saved from
destruction by the agricultural labourers, whom
the policy of "three acres and a cow" had
attracted. Just after the Election Chamberlain
was dining at a house where a silver cow was
one of the ornaments on the dinner-table, and
he apostrophized it with unmistakable sincerity
—"Oh, you blessed animal! Where should we
have been without you?" On December 9th
I called on Chamberlain in Prince's Gardens
and had a conversation which now illuminates
some passages of his later career. Before the
Election, he had always told us that, as Bright
once said, "Birmingham is Liberal as the sea

is salt." But the polling in the redistributed borough showed that in each of the divisions there was a considerable element of Toryism, and in some a very large one. What was the explanation? "*Fair Trade*," said Chamberlain. "You have no notion what a hold it has laid upon the artisans. It almost beat Broadhurst. I had to neglect my own division to fight Fair Trade in his; and it took me all I knew to get him in." I am convinced that this was to Chamberlain a startling revelation; and, though the subject was soon forced out of view by the Irish controversy, I suspect it remained at the back of his mind. When he was President of the Board of Trade, Sir Thomas Farrer, the Permanent Secretary, had always said, " Chamberlain is not a sound Free-trader"; and the new Fiscal Policy, which was promulgated in 1903, probably expressed a conviction which had long been forming in his mind.

But little remains to be told. The "Hawarden Kite" was sent up in December 1885, and the Liberal party learned, to its astonishment, that its venerable leader was committing it to Home Rule. Gladstone formed his Home Rule administration in February 1886, and Chamberlain joined his Cabinet. Immediately afterwards I was laid low by dangerous illness, and saw nothing of politics for the next three months. On May 7th I met Chamberlain (who in the meantime had left the Government) at dinner, and, as we could not then talk freely, he asked me to call on him on the 10th—the day on which the debate on the Second Reading of the Home Rule Bill began. We talked the Irish Question up and down, in all its phases and all its bearings, and Chamberlain concluded the conversation with these emphatic words—" Mr. Gladstone is certainly a wonderful old gentleman ; but he is seventy-six. Do you think that *I* am going to climb down to *him*? "

That was the end of my political intercourse with Chamberlain, and it could not have ended in a more characteristic fashion.

CHAPTER XI

FOUR DEMAGOGUES

———

JOHN BRIGHT

THE four men whom I am now going to describe were, in all respects save one, as dissimilar as men can be. The one characteristic which they had in common was that all were Demagogues; and, though their methods differed as widely as their characters, each had the power of exciting and leading great masses of his countrymen—and this is Demagogy.

From the moral point of view, if from no other, by far the greatest of the four was John Bright. Indeed, with regard to the other three, moral considerations hardly enter into the estimate.

John Bright, who from the time I entered Parliament honoured me with his friendship, and, on some occasions, with his confidence, was a man to whom Right and Wrong were the two great realities of human life. At each fresh turn in public affairs he asked himself, not which course was pleasantest, or most popular, or most likely to be successful, but which course was right; and, when once conscience had answered the question, he saw the path of duty lying straight before him and followed it, turning neither to the right hand nor to the left.

Of course by the time that I had become acquainted with him the great contentions with which his name is inseparably associated lay far back in the past. Church Rates and Corn Laws had only an antiquarian interest. The Crimea and the Mutiny had long been history. The Government of the United States had crushed the Slave-owners' rebellion; the Irish Church was disestablished; and the English artisans had obtained the franchise. Partly because the causes in which he was most keenly interested were won; partly because his physical health had more than once given way; and partly because he was naturally lazy, he had withdrawn from the battles of the platform, and was content with the tranquil life of the House of Commons and

JOHN BRIGHT.

To face p. 172.

an unlaborious office in the Government. When
one looked at his portly and prosperous-looking
person, and " the snows of his venerated head,"
it was difficult to believe that he had been
the most powerful demagogue of his time; but
the power, though dormant, was not dead. In
1882 he retired from the Cabinet sooner than be
responsible for our disgraceful bombardment of
Alexandria ; and for the next two years he dwelt
in ever-increasing isolation from all political
parties. In 1884 the proposal to extend the
suffrage to the agricultural labourers brought
him back to the political platform, and, for the
last time in his life, he felt himself in close
accord with the Liberal party; but the final
severance was at hand.

In December 1885 some indiscreet Glad-
stonians sent up the "Home Rule Kite," which
has now for thirty years been flapping rather
aimlessly in the wind. The Home Rule Bill,
introduced in April 1886, was defeated in June,
Bright voting against it ; and at the General
Election which ensued on its rejection, the
demagogue of the Forties, Fifties, and Sixties
reasserted for the last time his power of agitating his fellow-citizens and leading them whither-
soever he would. In his case was manifested

the enormous potency of the moral element in political character—of that very element which Bright possessed in rich abundance, and which demagogues have generally lacked. His high reputation as a man whose politics were a part of his religion, and who had never turned aside by a hair's breadth from the narrow path of civil duty as he understood it, gave him a weight of moral influence such as few politicians have ever commanded.

E'en in our ashes live their wonted fires;

and, though the fire of Bright's genius had long smouldered out of sight, the General Election of 1886 showed that it was still alive. Pitt, translating Tacitus, said, "Eloquence is like a flame: it requires matter to feed it, motion to excite it, and it brightens as it burns." The admirable simile was never better illustrated than in the case of Bright. The sinking flame of his eloquence found exactly what it wanted in the controversy about Home Rule. The matter which fed it was hatred of lawlessness and outrage. The motive which excited it was the calamitous activity of the Gladstonian fanatics; and it burned its brightest when he addressed his constituents at Birmingham on the 1st of July, 1886. "Every word, as they said of Daniel Webster, seemed to weigh a pound." The speech was scattered broadcast through the constituencies, and an exhortation from John Bright to put the Union above the Liberal party produced an immense effect on men who disliked Home Rule, but were loath to break away from the political associations of a lifetime. To Bright more than to any one man—more than to Lord Hartington, more, even than to Chamberlain—belonged the victory of 1886.

I have spoken so far of Bright's eloquence, for it was in that one particular alone that he attained the rank of genius. For my own part, I believe that his speeches will always be recognized as the finest, of which we have certain knowledge, in the English language. I insert the qualification about "certain knowledge," because the oratory which has come down to us from the seventeenth and eighteenth centuries was subjected to such elaborate revision and correction, that we can form only an imperfect notion of it as it fell from the speaker's lips. With the development of the reporter's art came the possibility of knowing exactly what the speaker said;

and, though a speech can never be adequately reported, inasmuch as it depends for three-fourths of its effect on voice and look and manner and gesture, still the verbal part of it can now be certainly and accurately known. In this, I think, Bright stands supreme. His oratory is literature. It is wholly free from the over-elaboration of Canning and Sheil; from Peel's pomposity, and Gladstone's long-windedness. Every word is drawn from the pure "well of English undefiled"; every sentence, even the shortest, falls in perfect harmony on the ear; every mood of the human spirit—pathos, indignation, sarcasm, humour, sympathy—finds its natural vent in the successive moods of the ever-varying style.

And we, who have the happiness of remembering him, know that his oratorical equipment did not end with verbal perfection. Voice, intonation, manner, gesture—though the gesture was of the slightest—and a presence singularly dignified; all these were component parts of the transcendent spell. His was indeed the "God-gifted organ-voice of England"; destined, I believe, to "resound for ages."

Lord Lytton once drew an admirable distinction between Genius and Talent:—

Talk not of Genius baffled.   Genius is master of man.
Genius does what it must, and Talent does what it can.

Bright's genius did "what it must," and its
achievements are accessible to all who care to
study English oratory; but "Talent" belongs
to men of lesser mould.   Some have, as the
parable teaches us, five talents, and some two;
some have only one.   Yet the possessor of even
one talent will often be more striking, more
conspicuous, in the course of daily life than
the man who has Genius, and finds his outlet
in obeying it.

In daily life Bright was neither striking nor
conspicuous.   He was friendly, accessible, easily
amused, easily annoyed.   He enjoyed the serenity
of his extremely quiet home, and the harmless
tittle-tattle of a scarcely less quiet club.   He disliked society, smart people, hot rooms, elaborate
meals, ceremonious observances.   Though he was
wholly free from modern heresies about meats and
drinks, his natural distaste for all gross enjoyments made him half a teetotaller and three parts
a vegetarian.   And so with literature.   He knew
the Bible as a Puritan should, and quoted it as
only a Puritan dares.   But Shakespeare repelled
him by what he esteemed wanton coarseness, and
he found his highest enjoyment in Milton, whom

he reckoned the chief of English poets. I cannot
imagine that he ever looked at Swift. With Byron
and Shelley and Moore and Swinburne he could
have had only a very imperfect sympathy. Tennyson and Browning he ignored. But Cowper on
the spiritual side, and Wordsworth as an inter-
preter of nature, were dear to him; he enjoyed
Lowell and Lewis Morris; and his love of virtuous
sentiments rhythmically expressed made him painfully tolerant of some very "minor" poets. Those
whom he admired had reason to be grateful for
his admiration, for even the humblest commonplace that rhymed and scanned sounded noble
when he declaimed it.

I have spoken of Bright's accessibility. This,
I suspect, was an attribute of his old age rather
than of his youth or his prime. When a man
is incessantly battling, even for the best of
causes, he instinctively guards himself against
the approaches of casual acquaintance; and when,
as in Bright's case, he has "endured measureless
calumny and passed through hurricanes of abuse,"
his manner naturally assumes a touch of the
defensive. I can easily understand that man who
knew Bright in the Fifties and Sixties thought
him ungracious and stern. But when I came to
know him he was just on seventy. His victories

were won. His fame—if he cared for it, which
I doubt—was secure. Calumny and abuse had
yielded place to honour and admiration. His
manner towards his equals was friendly and cordial, and to men of my age paternal and benign.
I believe that I owed my place in his regard to
the fact that my father had always held him in
high respect, and had constantly protested against
the insolence with which what are called "the
Upper Classes" had thought it fine to treat the
Radical cotton-spinner. A letter of Bright's
which I print on p. 182 suffices to show the terms
on which the two men corresponded. But, whatever was the cause, Bright always treated me
with an almost affectionate kindness. He would
chat with me about all manner of things grave
and gay; he used to recite poetry for my delight;
he gave me some invaluable hints on the way
to prepare a speech. Sometimes he did me the
honour to listen to my counsels. In 1883 the
long and odious controversy over the C.D. Acts
was nearing its climax. James Stansfeld had
given notice of a motion in the House of
Commons for the suspension of the Acts. We
knew that there would be a stiff fight and a
close division. Every vote was valuable. I was
a convinced and vehement opponent of the Acts,

and was collecting all the support I could for Stansfeld's motion. As the day of the debate drew near, it was reported to me that Bright, though he condemned the Acts, did not mean to vote, and I was told that I might be able to persuade him. Of course I unhesitatingly made the attempt, and my old friend listened gravely to my plea. I found that he had what the Friends call " a stop in his mind "; and this " stop " was due to disgust at the language and methods of some of the ladies who were engaged in the agitation for repeal. He loathed all that was indelicate and unfeminine, and had no liking for what John Knox called " the monstrous regiment of women." In those points I sympathized with him; but I urged that the follies and offences of advocates could not make a good cause bad, or justify its supporters in shrinking from the conflict. Bright listened, consented, and voted with us in the critical division which virtually repealed the Acts.

Though Bright was kindliness personified, he had none of that amiable weakness which sometimes makes people pretend to enjoy what really they dislike. I once met him at one of Mr. Gladstone's breakfast-parties, and our host told a story of a Quaker who, living in a place where the

parish church was dilapidated, refused on conscientious grounds to subscribe towards a new
one, but said he would be happy to help towards
pulling down the old one. At this mild pleasantry we all tittered politely, but Bright only
remarked with a touch of acrimony : " The
Friends are made the subject of some very
stoopid stories."

When he was a militant politician, his most
formidable weapon had been, not his invective,
though that was powerful enough in all conscience, but his sarcastic humour. His speeches
are studded with gibes which made his opponents
wince, and exhibited them to the public view as
objects, not so much of detestation as of ridicule. Every one who knows his face, even in a
photograph, must notice the curl of the nostrils
and the downward curve of the mouth. When
the sarcastic vein was uppermost, these traits
became more distinctly marked ; the nostrils
curled upwards towards the eyes, and the mouth
became a bent bow. I have often admired this
aspect when he was speaking in public (for I
remember him in the House of Commons as far
back as 1867) ; and I admired it no less, though
perhaps I did not enjoy it so much, when, during
the controversy on Home Rule, he twitted me

with what he esteemed my vacillations. " Some
of us don't quite know which side we are on ";
and it was true of those who, believing absolutely
in the principle of self-government, resented the
policy, first secretive and then blustering, which
marked the troublous time of 1885–86.

———

March 19, '77.

DEAR LORD CHARLES RUSSELL,

I thank you for sending me the story of that sad day.
I was on the Continent when I saw the announcement of
your loss in *The Times*. I was shocked, and I pictured to
myself your sorrow and that of your circle, and in some
measure I joined in it. I seem never able to dissociate
fear from weddings. I have lost two sisters soon after
marriage—one on the birth of her first, and the other on
the birth of her second child—the succeeding fever was
the cause of death. These events so affected me, that I
never attend a wedding without a feeling of doubt and sad-
ness. Believe me, I sympathize deeply with you in your
affliction, and hope that you may have in it such consolation
as the case admits of.

I am always,
Most sincerely yours,
JOHN BRIGHT.

———

LORD RANDOLPH CHURCHILL

FROM John Bright to Randolph Churchill the
transition is indeed abrupt. They had this in
common—that both were demagogues; but in

every other respect their natures were so dissimilar that they might have seemed to belong to different orders of creation. To dissimilarity of nature must be added dissimilarity of circumstance; for Blenheim is not more unlike Rochdale than the life of the younger demagogue was unlike the life of the elder.

Look here, upon this picture, and on this.

In the preceding section I have attempted to pourtray an old and venerated friend; in this, I must try my hand on one who was not a friend —at most an acquaintance—a political opponent, but one of the most interesting figures of his day.

Lord Randolph Churchill was born in 1849 and died in 1895. He did not emerge into the public view till 1880, and he had faded out of it some years before his death. But it happened that during the brief period of his political importance I had constant opportunities of seeing and observing him. At this distance of time I may, without immodesty, record the fact that my speech in reply to his on the Third Reading of the Irish Land Bill of 1881 gave me that precious asset which is called " the ear of the

House." "Jackdaw," in *Society*, thus described
the scene :—

"Friday, the 29th of July, was a memorable
day in the annals of that assembly upon which
I look down from this perch. First of all the
Irish Land Bill passed the House of Commons
on that day, after a troublesome and tedious
voyage. On the 7th of April the voyage was
commenced, and in Committee Bay—a veritable
Bay of Biscay—it had been tossed about from
the 26th of May till nearly the same day of
July. At length it reached port, and the captain,
whose eulogy I sang last week, was saluted by
all hands for his patience and persistence, his
energy, his pluck, and his courtesy. But events
of importance never happen singly. On that
remarkable day a new hero came to the front.
Lord Randolph Churchill found an opponent
worthy of his steel. For a long time the
Liberal party, as well as the responsible Tory
party, have been very cowardly in their attitude
to Randy. There is a manner about Randy
that is calculated to inspire cowards with
caution and care instead of stimulating them to
boldness. He is a duke's son, and he knows
it. Rank inspires awe in common minds, and

thus at the outset he has a great advantage.
He knows this when he sets the wisdom of
Right Honourables at defiance and determines
to carve out a line for himself. He is young,
too, and—

> Youth has a sprightliness and fire to boast,
> That in the valley of decline are lost.

" He has all the self-confidence of youth, and
sufficient contempt for the opinion of others to
deliver his own with freedom, not to say fluency.
He always flies at high game. There would be
no notoriety, no sport in attacking inferior men;
so Randy, left to choose his own object of
attack, has been left by his pride of birth, and
by all those other qualities which strikingly
adorn his character, to go at the Prime Minister.
His tactics are unquestionably sound from the
point of view of a man with a name to sustain,
and a political reputation to make. Independence, pluck, and spirit are to some extent
necessary to men who choose such eminent
marks for their shafts. These qualities are
admired, whatever be the opinion of the manner
in which they are exercised; and then when
the reply comes, as come it does, it may be
sharp, but it keeps the assailant before the

public. What matter, then, though great men
sneer at an eloquence unrestrained by any
attempt to adhere rigidly to fact? What matter
though contempt is poured upon you, and you
are compared to a 'small animal whose office
it is to bite, but which does not even produce
in the victim a consciousness that he is actually
bitten?' All that is a mere nothing compared
to the éclat of an encounter with the First
Minister of the Crown. So Randy, well knowing that the impulsive temperament of the
present Premier is safe to lead him into the
trap so artfully prepared, takes repeated occasion to hurl his lance at the Treasury Bench.
In these circumstances the interposition of any
one else—the entry on the field of battle of any
unchallenged foe—is not received kindly by
Randy. But it so happens that on Friday it
was precisely the appearance of an unchallenged
foe that was one of the principal events of the
day. Great was the general glee at the dis-
covery that Randy had his match below the
gangway on the Ministerial side; that there
was one exception to the awe-stricken legislators,
and that there was a man in Israel who would
face the bold free-lance in defence of his own
leader. The new and daring champion who

thus challenged Randy to fight one of his own size and years was not the son, but still he was the descendant of a duke. About four years younger than Randy, George William Erskine Russell, grandson of the sixth Duke of Bedford, declined to be overawed by the aspiring youth of the House of Marlborough.

"The spectacle was a pretty one to see. Young Russell, though unawed, was burning with excitement at his own enterprise, and at times was forced almost to stop to wonder at his own audacity. The House cleared a ring, and at every smart blow delivered at Randy cheered and laughed at the thought that the discomfited noble lord was no longer the monopolist of youth's sprightliness and fire. Vigour and sparkle, or force and fancy, characterized the attack on the leader of the Fourth party. The old Premier looked round with pleased surprise to find that after all there was one man below the gangway who could and would interpose with the chivalry of a man in the ranks who wards off and resents an attack offered to his captain. He had believed himself single-handed in all these encounters. Delight now manifested itself in every feature, and no heartier laughter greeted young Russell's sallies than that which

came to him as the Prime Minister's tribute to
their real effectiveness. I am. afraid I must
say that Randy did not look happy at the dis-
covery that there was another clever young
man in the House. If I were to judge of his
feeling by his face I should say that he was
encouraging a naughty jealousy. He did not
look kindly on George Russell. It appeared to
me as if he would not have been sorry to have
seen the aforesaid George at the bottom of the
sea for the time being. He did not appreciate
George's points, and seemed secretly to curse
the light-headedness of a House which could
laugh so consumedly at so little. I question if
he had a moment's satisfaction with the successful speech of his young opponent save when
there was a momentary doubt whether in his
excitement that opponent was not going to
stick in the very climax of his triumph. When
the little obstacle was overcome, and the speech
flowed merrily on, Randy, you were the picture
of gloom. Now there is room enough and to
spare for two clever youths in Parliament.
Why, you can rub up each other and shine
more brilliantly in your competition. Besides,
between clever opponents nothing is so pretty
as chivalrous feeling. So Randy, my boy, be a

worthy Lord Randolph, eschew haughtiness, wish your new political enemy parliamentary success, and above all things, don't be jealous."

Whether Randolph Churchill ever read this advice I cannot tell; but he certainly acted in the spirit of it, for, when I came to know him personally, the remembrance of that encounter seemed to have left no bitterness. While it was still the fashion among Liberals to believe (as they had believed of Disraeli) that Churchill was simply comic, I observed, through my contact with working-men, that he was becoming powerful. I admired his complete independence in parliamentary action, his wholesome contempt for hoary humbug and solemn plausibility; and his style of oratory on public platforms seemed exactly adapted to a certain class of urban voters —the " Rowdy Philistine," the " Tory Bottles," whom Matthew Arnold knew so well—the " lewd fellows of the baser sort " who mobbed St. Paul at Thessalonica and in the Seventies read the *Daily Telegraph*. The spirit to which Randolph Churchill incessantly and successfully appealed was the spirit which a few years later began to utter itself in the verse of Mr. Rudyard Kipling and the prose of the *Daily Mail*.

For a son to write his father's biography is, as a rule, to court disaster. But to that rule a brilliant exception is to be found in Mr. Winston Churchill's *Life of Lord Randolph Churchill*. It is not too long. It is, I doubt not, accurate in detail. It certainly is brisk, bright, and readable. It avoids all approach to the sin of Ham, and yet it is sufficiently intimate to convey the sense of truth. It must be read by every one who wishes to know the circumstances which shaped a strange career, and the tendencies which marred it.

Biographies must begin with Heredity, but every five years the men of science give us a different estimate of its power. Now they tell us that it is everything; then that it is next to nothing; and then again that it counts for a good deal, but that the will is independent of it and can exercise a choice among the elements which heredity transmits. Into that mysterious domain of Will it is best not to enter, lest we should find ourselves sharing Lord Haldane's unpopularity, quoting Hegel, or showing a suspicious affinity

> With the land that produced one Kant with a K,
>   And many a Cant with a C.

It is better to take our stand on experience, and to note the plain fact that drunkenness, debauchery, and insanity are disturbing elements in the blood; and that, when they run together in the confluence of two families, they threaten uncomfortable consequences to unborn and innocent lives. A long line of sober, moral, and hard-working ancestors, who rose early and lived plainly and observed the First Day, transmitted to John Bright a constitution which, in spite of trials, bore him scatheless to his seventy-seventh year. What are facetiously called our "best families" have another kind of inheritance. Now, as of old, the sins of the fathers are visited on the children unto the third and fourth generation; and, when a descendant adopts a line of life which involves great demands on nerve and brain, he often pays the penalty for his ancestors' wrong-doing.

There is no need for a description of Blenheim, for it can be found in any handbook which deals with "the stately homes of England." Other houses may be more beautiful: many are more interesting; there is none more stately. From Blenheim to Eton; and what Eton was when Randolph Churchill was an Eton boy, we know from Lord Rosebery's vivacious account. Oxford for a sporting undergraduate of good family is much the same in one generation as another.

Randolph Churchill entered Merton College in 1867, and took his degree in 1871. His subsequent career was determined by the fact that Woodstock had long been a pocket-borough of the House of Marlborough, and commonly returned a Churchill. The Reform Act of 1867 had increased its electorate from three hundred to a thousand; but the owner of Blenheim still continued to exercise a salutary influence over his neighbours; and at the General Election of 1874 he proposed his younger son for their acceptance. Churchill's success was ensured by the fact that his opponent was George Brodrick —a grotesque pedant, in whom the characteristic absurdities of the Oxford don and the *Times* leader-writer were combined, and who deserves to be remembered as probably the only man who has ever had to make an *affidavit* that he had been joking.[1]

Entrance into Parliament made no very great change in Randolph Churchill's life and pursuits. In 1875 he married; refusing several advantageous alliances which had been suggested, and going to the United States for his bride. Quite

[1] This incident arose during the Parnell Commission, when Brodrick, in a fit of delicate pleasantry, compared the Irish Members to "Jack the Ripper."

possibly, his career would have been as uneventful as that of any other younger son who sits for a family-borough, had it not been for an incident which Mr. Churchill in his Life of his father handles with delicacy and circumspection. It was this: Randolph Churchill was, as he thought, unjustly treated by an illustrious personage, and all the toadies and sycophants who always surround an actual or expectant Court applauded that treatment to the echo. Unless I very much mistake my man, the sense that this was so fired his passionate nature with a desire for revenge. What revenge could be so complete, or so gratifying, as to force himself by his own unaided exertions into a position where he was indispensable; where even the first subject of the Crown could not afford to affront him; and where all baser foes must lick the dust?

To that position the way lay open through the House of Commons, and the most important steps along that way I had the opportunity of observing at close quarters. Randolph Churchill became famous in the first weeks of the Parliament elected at Easter 1880, and his fame advanced by leaps and bounds till that Parliament was dissolved in November 1885. What then ensued must be told later on.

First let me describe his appearance. I have
seen it stated, with some appearance of authority,
that his height was 5 feet 10 inches; but the
caricaturists (who have a strange knack of
getting things wrong) always represented him
as a little boy. The paragraphists took their
cue from the caricaturists, and " Go it, little
Randy!" became a favourite adjuration of his
supporters. The graver newspapers were always
insisting on his youth, though he had turned
thirty. To my eye, he looked about his real
age, perhaps rather older than younger, though
his very slight figure helped the idea of youth-
fulness. His cheeks and chin were shaved, but
he cultivated a ponderous moustache, which he
constantly turned up at the ends; and this ap-
pendage illustrated what Mr. Gladstone always
urged—that to disguise the mouth, which is one
of the most expressive features of the face, is to
obscure the whole expression. If one could have
looked below the moustache, I suspect that one
would have found the mouth very wide; but the
chin was well developed, the eyes were large,
and bulged in a way which gave the effect of a
chronic stare. He was always carefully dressed,
according to the fashion of the day, in a frock-
coat worn open, with a tie neatly bowed; and

LORD RANDOLPH CHURCHILL.

To face p. 194.

his whole appearance might have been described as spruce.

In speaking, he leant forward, emphasizing his points by the movements of his head, and making comparatively little use of his hands. His voice had rather a guttural sound, and his utterances were marked by a decided lisp, and a curious rolling effect, as if his tongue was too big for his mouth.

In social life he was a courteous host and an appreciative guest; but his conversation was curiously uneven. If he was out of temper, either with a political opponent or with some "scrupulous good man" on his own side, he could be extremely rude. But, if things went well, he could be capital company; cynical, in the exact sense of that much-abused word, and excelling in a sarcastic description of a character or a situation. More than any other politician I have ever known, he loved to talk about the House of Commons, its personages, its characteristics, and its doings. He frankly delighted in "shop," and always said that the House was the most interesting place he knew.

Certainly he did a great deal to make it interesting to other people. When he was in the House, there always were the elements of a storm. His extraordinary quickness in seeing the possibilities of a situation, his intuitive sense for what was popular and effective, his total lack of reverence, and his intimate knowledge of weak spots on his own side, made his activities a perpetual joy to those who were not his victims.

Above all he excelled in his management of Mr. Gladstone; and there is something to be said for the theory that, if Gladstone had ignored him, his rise would not have been so rapid. But to ignore an agile, reckless, and sarcastic opponent was a feat beyond Gladstone's powers. His "vulnerable temper and impetuous moods" made such self-restraint impossible; and Randolph Churchill, perceiving this infirmity, played upon it without compunction. To use a boy's phrase, Gladstone "rose freely"; and each time that Churchill excited the leader of the House into indignant activity, a large feather was added to the Churchillian cap.

> Crabbed age and youth
> Cannot live together,

and, though Gladstone was not really crabbed and Churchill was not really young, all the Conservative papers, and the comic papers with-

out distinction of party, fastened on the quaint
contrast between the ruffled dignity of the
Member for Midlothian and the smart irrever-
ence of the Member for Woodstock.

One of the motives which actuated Gladstone
in his attention to whatever Churchill said or
did was his extraordinary veneration for the
aristocracy. He more than once laid it down,
as essential to a true estimate of our national
character, that the English people are confirmed
Inequalitarians. Now "Inequalitarian" says in
seven syllables what "snob" says in one; so I
rather resent my old leader's dictum, and yet I
find it difficult to contradict him when he speaks
of "the distinct undeniable popular preference,
whenever other things are substantially equal,
for a man who is a lord over a man who is not."
Perhaps "preference" is not exactly the word to
describe Gladstone's feeling towards Churchill;
but I feel no doubt that he took a keener
interest in his parliamentary performances than
in those of his untitled compeers.

It should be borne in mind that, though
Churchill was perpetually harassing Gladstone
by his assaults and stratagems, his manner towards the older man was always courteous.
Indeed this habitual courtesy was what lent

its peculiar zest to an encounter, which Mr.
Churchill recalls in his book and which is in-
delibly impressed on my visual memory. It
took place in May 1885, when our crimes and
blunders in Egypt were coming home to roost,
and when even the loyallest Liberals were
sickened by three years' causeless and useless
carnage.

Gladstone, even more attentive and alert than
usual when Churchill is speaking, is sitting
in his accustomed place on the Treasury
Bench. On the opposite side below the gangway Churchill, pale and dangerous-looking, is
on his legs, leaning forward and holding some
notes in his hand. Has the Right Hon. Gentleman read his *Times* this morning? No. Well,
that is a pity, for, if he had read it he would
have found a most interesting review of Lord
Beaconsfield's Letters to his sister. The speaker
must make a brief citation. His utterance becomes slower and clearer; the Prime Minister
looks increasingly stern. The speaker proceeds.
Lord Beaconsfield in his early travels had been
introduced to "a very celebrated Minister,"
called Redschid Pasha; of whom the introducer
said: "he has destroyed in the course of the
last three months—not in war—upwards of four

thousand of my acquaintance." And what was
this Minister like? Now the utterance becomes
still more deliberate. "A very ferocious-looking,
shrivelled, careworn man, plainly dressed, with
a brow covered with wrinkles, and a countenance
clouded with anxiety and thought." Each word
is emphasized in turn; and, as the speaker looks
towards the Treasury Bench, the eyes of the
House follow him, and the resemblance, half-
painful, half-grotesque, becomes irresistible. But
there is more to come. The perpetrator of
these crimes assured Lord Beaconsfield that
"the peace of the world was his only object,
and the happiness of mankind his only wish."
Then a pause: the notes are returned to the
pocket, and the speaker utters his final words:
"There, upon the Treasury Bench, is the resus-
citated Redschid Pasha."

Brutal, but triumphant. Triumphant, too,
and not brutal, was the speech at Blackpool in
1884, when Churchill poked bitter fun at the
persistence of the Gladstonian troupe in adver-
tising the hero at his meals and his exercise,
his work and his recreation—even at his devo-
tions. Brutal, perhaps, in form, but absolutely
true in substance, was the reference to the
Election of 1886, as decreed "to gratify the

ambition of an old man in a hurry." Purely
brutal, yet admirably calculated to please the
mob, was the closing declaration of the same
address : " The negotiator of the *Alabama* arbi-
tration, the hero of the Transvaal surrender, the
perpetrator of the bombardment of Alexandria,
the decimator of the struggling Soudan tribes,
the betrayer of Khartoum, the person guilty of the
death of Gordon, the patentee of the Penjdeh
shame, now stands before the country all alone,
rejected by a democratic House of Commons."

I have quoted this passage to show what
Churchill could do at his worst, when he calculated that the occasion required the exercise
of all his powers of invective ; but, even in
more tranquil times, he relied a good deal on
the power of insolent speech. To him the
estimable leader of the Conservative party in
the House was "The Goat"; two of his
worthiest colleagues were "Marshall and Snel-
grove"; two promising Under-Secretaries were
"Young Taper and Young Tadpole." A leading
occupant of the front Opposition Bench was
"the opulent lord of pineries and vineries." A
Liberal lawyer, when the Chancellorship seemed
likely to fall vacant, was told that he recalled
the very letter of the sentence on the serpent :

"On thy belly shalt thou go, and dirt shalt thou eat."

In this insistent use of invective and sarcasm, as in some other matters, Churchill had no doubt formed himself on Lord Beaconsfield; and Goldwin Smith, who always put things unpleasantly, called him "the spawn and ape of Dizzy."

I said before that Churchill's fame increased from year to year, between 1880 to 1885. My visual memory contains no clearer image than Churchill, dancing a kind of wild hornpipe on the front bench below the gangway when the tellers announced the figures of the division which defeated Gladstone on the 8th of June, 1885. A month later the dancer of the hornpipe was Secretary of State for India, and beyond comparison the most popular figure on the Tory side. At the General Election in November, he was to the Tories what Chamberlain was to the Radicals (barring the fatal folly which Chamberlain committed by his sudden attack on the Church). Churchill made no such blunders; and, not content with his majority of 1,500 in South Paddington, he pulled down Bright's majority in Birmingham to 700, in sheer lightness of heart. Then came the "Hawarden

Kite;" then six months of plotting and counter-plotting about Home Rule; then a Tory majority, a Tory Prime Minister, and Churchill Chancellor of the Exchequer and Leader of the House. In the autumn of 1886 he stood on the very summit of a desperate but gratified ambition. His sudden resignation in the following December remains one of the most extraordinary incidents in English politics. It showed, if nothing else, his absolute confidence in his own power—his conviction that he was the one necessary man. It would scarcely have been an exaggeration if he had applied to himself Byron's words about a greater downfall:—

I have warred with a world which has vanquished me only,
   When the meteor of conquest allured me too far;
I have coped with the nations who dread me thus lonely,
   The last single captive to millions in war.

Lord Salisbury expressed the truth in more homely language when, a little later, some of his friends urged the desirability of asking Churchill to resume his place in the Cabinet: "When one has had a boil on one's neck, and it has burst, one doesn't invite it to return."

CHARLES STEWART PARNELL

WHEN I entered Parliament, Parnell, who had entered it five years earlier, had already established a reputation. It was not an oratorical reputation, for he could scarcely string five words together; it was not a reputation for debating skill, for he had taken little part in legislative business. It was a reputation for inconvenient persistency. " His plan for obstructing the business of the House of Commons caused the House to sit continuously from 4 p.m. till 6 p.m. on the following evening, 31st July, to 1st August, 1877, this being the longest recorded sitting." Obstruction was once defined by Gladstone as an attempt to influence the judgment of the House by other means than argument, and the definition will serve. Obstruction, in this sense, was invented and practised in some rudimentary forms by George Cavendish-Bentinck (1821–91) and James Lowther (1840–1904) in the Parliament of 1868; but it was developed into a fine art by the Irish and the Radicals in the Parliament of 1874, and it culminated in January 1881, when the House sate for forty-one hours continuously. Renowned as an organizer of obstruction, Parnell was also interesting as having deposed Isaac Butt, suppressed "Sober Sensible Shaw," and made himself the undisputed leader of the Irish Party. He was a conspicuous figure in the House, and, sitting opposite to him, I had the opportunity of observing him pretty closely. His appearance was striking. He was tall and well built. His features were regular, the nose being slightly aquiline, with a fastidious curl of the nostril. His eyes, when he was angry, which was not seldom, seemed to emit a kind of red light; and George Howard (afterwards Lord Carlisle) once quoted happily from *The Newcomes* : "The figure of this garçon is not agreeable. Of pale, he has become livid." He had a mass of lightish-brown hair ; beard, moustache, and whiskers, all worn long and rather tangled; insomuch that when his toadies called him the "Uncrowned King of Ireland," his critics substituted "uncombed." His clothes were rough and badly put on, and the whole effect was that of a man who disregarded personal appearances. Yet he was unmistakably a gentleman ; and when seated in the midst of his servile troop, he looked like a being of a different order.

As the Session of 1880 advanced, the true

C. S. PARNELL.

To face p. 204.

inwardness of the man was clearly disclosed. It was evident that he hated England, that he contemned the House of Commons, that he despised the Liberals much more profoundly than the Tories, and that he regarded his followers as merely voters, or, at the best, as fit for work too dirty for a gentleman to undertake.

To me, watching him closely, it appeared that the humiliation of England, and of everything English, was the master-passion of his life. He knew that to circumvent or to defeat the House of Commons was to injure England in a vital point; and to that end he devoted all his powers. He mastered the forms of the House, which in those days, before Procedure had been reformed, could easily be abused for obstructive purposes; he acquired, by constant practice, great skill in debate, and he was as quick as Randolph Churchill in detecting opportunities for damaging attack. As the Parliament of 1880 drew towards its close, and the working alliance between Parnell and the Tories became manifest to all men, I remember the impotent horror with which Liberal fogies regarded the compact between "men of desperate counsels" on different sides for the destruction of Gladstone's government—an end which they triumphantly attained on the 8th of June, 1885, when Irish yells of "Coercion" and "Kilmainham" greeted the figures that announced Gladstone's defeat.

Parnell's public career, from 1880 to 1891, is matter of history, and there is no need for me to recapitulate it here. It is enough for me to record the impression which a close study of that career, combined with my personal observation in Parliament, have left engraved on my mind.

Perhaps the most clearly marked feature of Parnell's character was that form of cruelty which consists in a callous indifference to suffering. Exercising dictatorial authority over Ireland, he never moved a finger to protect the victims of the Land League — ignorant peasants, women and girls, old men, little children, dumb animals. Murder, torture, and the long-drawn anguish of expectant fear he regarded with unpitying eye. The culminating horrors of the Phœnix Park distracted public attention from the sickening series of agrarian murders which had preceded it, and surpassed it in moral heinousness, because wrought, not on the well-protected officials of a powerful government, but on agents and servants and

down-trodden peasants. Parnell's attitude towards agrarian murder may be illustrated by
the following incident. In 1880 a young land-
agent, called Boyd, was murdered in the neighbourhood of New Ross. Shortly afterwards
Parnell, then at the zenith of his popularity,
attended a meeting in the district, and thus
improved the occasion:—

"I do wish," he said, "in reference to a sad
occurrence that took place lately of the shooting
or attempted shooting of a land-agent in this
neighbourhood"—(cries of "Down with him!"
groans and cheers)—"I do wish to point out
that recourse to such methods of procedure is
entirely unnecessary, and also prejudicial where
there is a suitable organization among the
tenants themselves. . . . I believe that if
Kilkenny county had been organized, young
Boyd never would have been shot, because his
father, in the face of a strong and organized
public opinion, would not have ventured to
abuse his rights as a landlord."

Let any one imagine these words applied to
a near kinsman of his own, murdered in the
discharge of his duty, and then let him consider
his estimate of the man who uttered them.
Hardly less remarkable in its cynical disregard

of human misery, was the speech, in the same
year, at Ennis, when in answer to the question,
What should be done to a man who made a
bid for a farm from which another had been
evicted ? Parnell formulated his famous scheme
of social excommunication, and recommended
that any one who was presumptuous enough
to exercise a common right of citizenship should
be treated as "a leper."

But to multiply instances would be needlessly
to elaborate a painful theme. Enough has been
cited to illustrate the temperament of the man;
and, if his callous words of seeming condonation
were culpable, his stubborn silence in the sight
of so much misery, which a word from him
would have allayed, was, if possible, more odious
still.

To cruelty must be added deceitfulness.
Parnell's course in Parliament, his peculiar
methods in debate, his habitual reliance on bare
denials of inconvenient statements, the marked
contrast between his English and his American
utterances, had long created in minds not
prone to suspicion the belief that he was un-
trustworthy. But the traditions of our political
life have taught Englishmen to place a generous
reliance on even the most astonishing statements

of our public men, and suspicion would probably
have never ripened into certainty had not Parnell,
in a strange moment of cynical candour, admitted
the truth that, on a certain occasion, he was
trying to deceive the House of Commons.   If
the   Special   Commission   of   1888–89   had
elicited no other fact it would have justified its
creation.

After   cruelty   and   deceitfulness,   which   are
ethical defects wherever they occur, that passionate and vindictive hatred of England which
inspired   and   regulated   Parnell's   whole   career
may almost be written down as praise.   Con-
sidered   as   a   purely   abstract   question,   love   of
England may not be a virtue nor hatred of her
a vice; but patriotism is, after all, a respectable
prejudice,   and   Englishmen   will   have   to   learn
and unlearn much before they can lavish tears
over the memory of a man who lived and died
the remorseless foe of their country's greatness,
safety, and fair fame.   Hating England as he
did, it was only natural that Parnell should
hate   the   politicians   who   in   turn   represented
her among the nations, and who wielded her
civil and military power.   This particular sub-
division of his animosity was modified by personal
predilections.   As an autocrat by temper, a Tory

14

in opinion, and a landlord by profession, his
natural affinities were with the Conservative
party. Like all despots, he both disliked and
despised those who truckled to him, and which-
ever party was most frightened of him and his
American allies, that party he most cordially
contemned. As regards his relations with individual politicians, some interesting questions
have from time to time arisen. Gladstone once
imprisoned him for six months without trial,
and announced the feat amid the applause of
the Guildhall.[1] In the inner circle of the
Gladstonian mysteries it was held that this
polite attention (like the pickled salmon which
Mrs. Gamp produced when Mrs. Prig was
irritable) "worked a softening change," and
that Parnell emerged from his seclusion in a
chastened and contrite frame, full of sorrow for

[1] "Within these few moments I have been informed that
towards the vindication of law, of order, and of the rights of
property, of the freedom of the land, of the first elements
of political life and civilization, the first step has been taken
in the arrest of the man who, unhappily, from motives
which I do not challenge, which I cannot examine, and
with which I have nothing to do, has made himself beyond
all others prominent in the attempt to destroy the authority
of the law, and to substitute what would end in being
nothing more or less than anarchical oppression exercised
upon the people of Ireland."

his past misdeeds and of reverent admiration
for the fatherly hand which had corrected
them. How far this view tallied with the
truth the last two years of Parnell's life
revealed.

But after Gladstone became a Home Ruler,
his surrender to his former captive was absolute.
As regards Sir William Harcourt, it is but bare
justice to both parties to allow that neither he
nor Parnell ever displayed even a Platonic
affection for the other. Their relations in the
perilous times of Fenianism and dynamite had
been those of mutual distrust tempered by
common apprehension. Each knew the length
of the other's foot, and gauged with perfect
nicety the sentiments with which his friend
regarded him. From Lord Morley Parnell
received that reverent homage which a sedentary
man always pays to a man of action, and
which Lord Morley has himself described—"The
pedant, cursed with the ambition to be a ruler
of men, is a curious study. He would be glad
not to go too far, and yet his chief dread is
lest he be left behind. His consciousness of
pure aims allows him to become an accomplice
in the worst crimes. Suspecting himself at
bottom to be a theorist, he hastens to clear his

character as a man of practice by conniving at an enormity."

Himself one of the most sensitive and emotional of men, Lord Morley was fairly fascinated by that cold, hard, and unrelenting temper. It is to be hoped that Parnell responded to these tender emotions, and reciprocated the goodwill of a man who stood by him through good report and bad; but, if he loved Lord Morley, his affection was of that distressing quality which does not shrink from a very inconvenient candour. Before he died he had made some unpleasant disclosures, and he probably contemplated more.

That Parnell should have established so complete an ascendancy over the Irish people, from whom he was separated by every circumstance of blood, faith, speech, and temperament, is, of course, a striking testimony to what, in the jargon of the present day, is called his "personality." That he should have seemed "majestic," "regal," "prince-like," and all the rest of it, to the rabble of shop-boys, booking-clerks, whisky-sellers, and gombeen-men who formed his political following, is not so remarkable; for at any rate he had the appearance, manners, and bearing of an English gentleman; but the

ensuing tribute is really noteworthy. It was
written in 1889 by an English lady of high
intelligence and Liberal sympathies who had
met Parnell at dinner; and read in the light
of subsequent events it seems prophetically
inspired :—

"Certainly it was one of the most interesting
moments I have ever had, or ever expect to
have, in my life. Parnell was absolutely cool
and natural, and the rest of us all thrilling with
excitement. We had a great deal of talk, he
speaking apparently quite openly about past
and future events in connexion with the Home
Rule movement. Mr. —— talked about Irish
history, of which he knew much more than
Parnell, and then they went on to talk of Mr.
Forster. Parnell said that Mr. Balfour had
been told, like Mr. Forster, that if he only
arrested the ringleaders in each village the
agitation would collapse—only that he must,
when he had got them in prison, treat them ill.
'Instead of well?' I said, forgetting to
whom I was talking, and then, as it flashed
across me, I added: 'If I may say so to you.'
He laughed loudly at this, and said: 'Yes, we
were treated *very* well,' evidently meaning it.
Then he went on to talk of Kilmainham, and

of the unreasonable arrests made in the early
months of 1882 by Forster, and so on, quite
naturally. But it all felt rather mad too, and
I kept on repeating to myself: 'Yes, that *is*
Parnell talking to me across the table.'

" We talked of all manner of things, the Commission amongst them. This was the only
point on which he showed any bitterness at all;
in all other Irish matters he seemed singularly
fair and able to see both sides. I mean he's
quite different from Dillon, and talked like a
man of the world, and not like an oppressed
Celt—which he isn't, of course, so perhaps it's
easily explained.

" I cannot exaggerate the impression he made
on me. I never before felt such power and
force, magnetic force, in any man. As for his
eyes, if he looks at you, you can't look away,
and if he doesn't you are wondering how soon
he will look at you again. I am afraid I have
very little trust in his goodness; I should think
it's a very minus quality; but I believe absolutely in his strength and his power of influence.
I should be sorry if he were my enemy; I think
he would stop at nothing."

CHARLES BRADLAUGH

To quote his own account of his beginnings, this robust demagogue was born at Hoxton in 1833. He was "the well-known Radical Lecturer, and proprietor of the periodical the *National Reformer*; also President of the National Secular Society," and was author of "numerous cheap works on secularism and politics." [1]

Biographers tell us that his father was a solicitor's clerk, and that he began life in the same profession, acquiring thereby some legal knowledge, which he used with great effect in public life, and a skill in the perception of legal points which I once heard Lord Chief Justice Coleridge praise enthusiastically.

When he was only sixteen he became a public lecturer under the name of "Iconoclast," and among the ikons which he essayed to break were the existence of God and the credibility of the Bible. Shocked by these subversive activities, "an officious clergyman got him discharged from his employment." Whereupon he enlisted. He had made his choice for the infantry, but the recruiting sergeant of the foot regiment

[1] *Dod's Parliamentary Companion*, 1880.

which he proposed to join happened to owe a
shilling to the recruiting sergeant of the 7th
Dragoon Guards, and offered him Bradlaugh in
payment of the debt.   Thus "Iconoclast"
became a trooper, and acquitted himself so well
in that capacity that in three years he was able
to purchase his discharge.   He now returned to
his profession as a solicitor's clerk, and to his
activities as a public lecturer and journalist.
He was for some years a moneylender on a
small scale, and, presumably with the money so
acquired, became proprietor of the *National
Reformer*.   He rushed up and down the country,
addressing great audiences in the chief centres
of population : satirizing the " God-idea," " im-
preaching the House of Brunswick," and
preaching the Neo-Malthusianism which was
his social creed. At the General Election of
1868 he stood for Northampton and polled 1,086
votes; he stood there again at the General
Election of 1874 and polled 1,653 votes; at a
by-election in the same year his poll crept up to
1,766; and at the General Election of 1880 he
was returned with 3,980 votes as junior colleague
of Henry Labouchere, who thereby attained the
exquisite felicity of being able to style himself
" The Christian Member for Northampton."

Then ensued a series of events which, while they enormously increased Bradlaugh's popularity out of doors, brought discredit on the House of Commons, humiliation on Gladstone's newly-constituted government, and two most unhappy conflicts—the one between justice and law, the other between justice and religion. As the history of these events is, in its earlier stages, rather complicated, it may best be given in his own words :—

"When elected as one of the burgesses to represent Northampton in the House of Commons, I believed that I had the legal right to make affirmation of allegiance in lieu of taking the oath, as provided by Sec. 4 of the Parliamentary Oaths Act, 1866. While I considered that I had this legal right, it was then clearly my moral duty to make the affirmation. The oath, although to me including words of idle and meaningless character, was and is regarded by a large number of my fellow-countrymen as an appeal to Deity to take cognizance of their swearing. It would have been an act of hypocrisy to voluntarily take this form if any other had been open to me, or to take it without protest, as though it meant in my mouth any such appeal. I therefore quietly and privately notified the Clerk of the House of my desire to affirm. His view of the law and practice differed from my own, and no similar case having theretofore arisen, it became necessary that I should tender myself to affirm in a more formal manner, and this I did at a season deemed convenient by those in charge of the business of the House. In tendering my affirmation I was careful, when called on by the Speaker to state my objection, to do nothing more than put, in the fewest possible words, my contention that the Parliamentary Oaths Act, 1866, gave the right to affirm in Parliament to every person for the time being by law permitted to make an affirmation in lieu of taking an oath, and that I was such a person, and therefore claimed to affirm. The Speaker, neither refusing nor accepting my affirmation, referred the matter to the House, which appointed a Select Committee to report whether persons entitled to affirm under the Evidence Amendment Acts, 1869 and 1870, were under Sec. 4 of the Parliamentary Oaths Act, 1866, also entitled to affirm as Members of Parliament. This Committee, by the casting vote of its Chairman, has decided that I am not entitled to affirm. . . . The Committee report that I may not affirm, and, protesting against a decision which seems to me alike against the letter of the law and the spirit of modern legislation, I comply with the forms of the House."

Acting on this declaration, Bradlaugh presented himself at the Table of the House and proposed to take the oath in ordinary course; but the Speaker weakly allowed some Tory Member to interrupt the proceedings, and the House now forbade him to do that which he had originally declined to do. "If the Hon. Member for Northampton," cried Sir Stafford Northcote, "has no conscience, has the House no conscience?" The House thundered a rather hypocritical assent, and so began a constitutional dispute, embittered alike by theological and by political prejudice, which lasted as long as the Parliament.

It is probable that the squalid scandals of Bradlaugh's case might have been avoided in the first instance by the peremptory intervention of the Chair, or subsequently by a bolder policy on the part of the Liberal leaders; but unquestionably the difficulties were great. The issue before the House was a high trial of the principle of religious liberty; for that sacred

cause was represented by a man who, whether
rightly or wrongly, was reputed to be a re-
publican (which mattered little) and a blasphemer
(which mattered more), and who (and this
mattered most of all) certainly taught a social
doctrine which most decent people hold in
abhorrence. The earliest debates on the question disclosed the fact that a certain section
of the Liberal party had only the frailest hold
on the primary principles of Liberalism, and
were prepared to abandon those principles under
the pressure of social and theological passion.
There was no one in the world to whom
Bradlaugh's doctrines were more abhorrent than
to Gladstone; but that really great Christian
showed, throughout the controversy, a clear
faith in the justice of the case, which no
clouds of prejudice could obscure. In his speech
on the Affirmation Bill (by which in 1883 he
sought, unsuccessfully, to find a way out of
the difficulties) he rose to his highest flight
of eloquence. When Bradlaugh, after one of
his encounters with the authorities of the
House, was excluded from the precincts by
main force, John Bright made, on the spur
of the moment, one of the most moving
speeches which I ever heard from the Treasury

Bench. Among private Members, Wilfrid Lawson was conspicuous for the zeal and force with which he affirmed the right of a duly elected Member to take his seat without inquisition into his religious beliefs, and the great majority of the Liberal party supported Lawson. But all was in vain. A majority of the House would not have Bradlaugh on any terms, and the believers in Religious Liberty and Civil Justice—for both were involved—were beaten at every turn.

I abhorred Bradlaugh's doctrine as profoundly as the best Tory in the House; but I always look back with satisfaction to the fact that I voted for him in every division. To my mind, belief in justice has always been inseparable from belief in God.

What was Bradlaugh like in person? I should say ugly by nature, and made more so by some studied peculiarities. I am not sure about his height, for I never stood close to him; but when he was standing at the Bar he looked tall—thanks, perhaps, to his early drilling; and, as he shouldered his way through the crowded Lobby, he reminded me of Bulwer-Lytton's description of O'Connell:—

With that vast bulk of chest and limb assigned
So oft to men who subjugate their kind;
So sturdy Cromwell pushed, broad-shouldered, on;
So burly Luther breasted Babylon;
So brawny Cleon bawled his Agora down;
And large-limbed Mahmoud clutched a Prophet's crown.

He looked extremely strong, and when wrestling with the officials of the House he seemed equal to half a dozen of them. Bright, seeing him after such a tussle, thought he was in "a deathly faint," but a Tory Member saw only a "theatrical resistance" to superior force.

His forehead was high, and his hair, of a nondescript colour, was brushed straight back and worn extremely long. His face was clean-shaven; and his upper lip the longest that I ever saw, coming down to meet the lower, in that wide mouth which bespeaks the orator. He dressed from head to foot in shining black, with a low-cut waistcoat, and a narrow black tie fastened in a bow. The whole effect of his appearance was absurdly clerical. Barring the black tie, he might have been taken for a Low Church clergyman; with it, he was the exact image of a Dissenting minister. In speaking, his whole style and manner savoured of the pulpit. At once pompous and unctuous, it always reminded

CHARLES BRADLAUGH.

To face p. 222.

me of another celebrated demagogue, Dr. Parker
of the City Temple; and derivatively, through
Parker, of Bishop Samuel Wilberforce, whom I
am convinced that Parker had studied.

But, in spite of clericalism and mannerism,
his style was supremely effective. His speech at
the Bar of the House on the 23rd of June,
1880, was a masterpiece, combining the resolute
assertion of civil right with a dexterous appeal to
generosity. I happened to dine with Gladstone
on the evening of that day, and he pronounced
the speech "consummate," alike in the inborn
quality of the orator and the acquired arts of the
rhetorician. Yet we all are, more or less, the
creatures of convention, and, when Bradlaugh
appealed to the justice of the 'Ouse, the missing
aspirate went far to neutralize the eloquence.

In the following August Dr. Liddon wrote a
letter which deserves attention, alike because it
shows his exemption from the habitual blindness
of clericalism, and because what he predicted
became, six years later, the fact:—

"It seems to me as an outsider, that the
Oath notoriously breaks down if considered as
a protection of the Theistic belief of the House:
and this quite independently of Mr. Bradlaugh.
We both know, or have known, Members of the

House who are not Theists, but who have no scruple about taking the Oath.

"I see nothing to differentiate, e.g. the late Mr. J. S. Mill's doctrine of the categories in his *Logic* from Mr. Bradlaugh's performances in the *National Reformer*, except that the latter is coarse and repulsive, while the former is interesting to every educated man. Our modern society tolerates any amount of blasphemy against the Being and Attributes of God—still more against His revelation of Himself in and through Christ our Lord—if only the blasphemy be thrown into good literary form. Mr. Bradlaugh's real offence is not his Atheism, but the coarseness which accompanies it; and yet this coarseness is surely a service which he unintentionally renders to religion.

"When I say that the religious character of the House of Commons is a 'fiction,' I do not forget that it contains a great many excellent Christians. But it also contains misbelievers and unbelievers in large numbers; and, alas! as matters stand, these latter interest themselves quite as actively as do the Christians in the sacred interests of the Church of Christ. Mr. Bradlaugh's presence in the House will not really add much to the Anti-Christian and Anti-

Theistic elements of it; but it will bring vividly before the mind of the people of this country the unfitness of a legislative body to which he belongs to handle the truths of Divine Revelation and the concerns of the Christian Church. He reduces to a positive absurdity a state of things which for sincere Christians has long been well-nigh intolerable.

"You will say, perhaps, that this is a narrow issue on which to decide a great question. But there is another point, which I own has great weight with me as a clergyman.

"If Mr. Bradlaugh had been admitted to the House of Commons without any delay, he would have found his level, and in all probability his baneful influence with the people would have been materially lessened, as Mill's certainly was.

"But, as matters have gone, he has made himself a name and a power beyond his wildest expectations. He has, as somebody said, become part of the history of England; and he will pose as a Confessor all through this autumn. His wretched books have now an enormous circulation; I have read a great many letters from people who have taken to reading him solely in consequence of the vast advertisement which he has secured for himself and for his produc-

tions. The longer the resistance to his entrance
to the House goes on, the keener and wider will
be the infidel propaganda—a propaganda which
is not less serious from a social point of view
than from a theological and religious one."

What Liddon predicted was exactly what
happened. Bradlaugh was again returned for
Northampton at the General Election of 1885,
and at the beginning of the Session of 1886
Mr. Speaker Peel, bolder than his predecessor,
overruled the attempt to prevent the Member
for Northampton from taking the Oath.

Bradlaugh, who was yet once more elected
at the General Election in the summer of that
year, subsided into a very sober, orderly, and conventional M.P., a moderate Home Ruler, and a
strong anti-Socialist. Having at length secured
the position which rightfully belonged to him,
he ceased to be the least interesting or exciting.
His respectability became even oppressive, and
his influence disappeared.

CHAPTER XII

LORD AND LADY SALISBURY

FROM the days of James the First to those of Queen Victoria, the House of Cecil underwent an eclipse. Robert Cecil, youngest son of Queen Elizabeth's celebrated Lord Treasurer, Burleigh, was raised to the peerage as Lord Cecil in 1603, and died, the first Earl of Salisbury, in 1612. The statesmanship of the family seemed to die with him; for the second, third, fourth, fifth, sixth, and seventh Earls gave politics a wide berth. Possessing the most beautiful home in England, wide estates, abundant wealth, and the social influence which those circumstances bring with them, they lived the patriarchal life of great English noblemen, and left the strifes and intrigues of political contention to those whose taste lay that way. The seventh Earl of Salisbury became the first Marquess of Salisbury, a Knight of the Garter, and a Fellow of the Royal Society; but the political instinct, which presumably Burleigh had transmitted, only revived, and that faintly, in the second Marquess, who was born in 1791, became Lord Privy Seal under Lord Derby in 1852 and Lord President of the Council in 1858, and died in 1868. This Lord Salisbury, though not exactly conspicuous, was by no means an insignificant member of the House of Cecil. His achievement was his marriage. His wife, daughter and heir of Bamber Gascoyne, a great landlord in Liverpool, brought him a twofold inheritance of wealth and talent. His eldest son was an invalid and died before his father, but his second son, Robert Arthur Talbot Cecil —the Lord Salisbury of the Seventies, and of succeeding years—revived the political glories of the family and founded a new dynasty of gifted and public-spirited Cecils.

Lord Robert Cecil was born in 1830, and educated at Eton, where he was miserable, and at Christ Church, where he was undistinguished. His was one of those cases providentially ordained for the comfort of the physically unfit, where an extremely delicate boyhood and youth develope into robust and long-lived age. When he was a boy at Hatfield, the servants

LORD SALISBURY.

To face p. 228.

would come panic-stricken to his elder sister,
Lady Mildred (afterwards Beresford Hope), saying :
"Please come at once, my Lady, Lord Robert
says he's dying"; but he wasn't, and he lived
to be seventy-three. The credit for this victory
over the ills inherent in a frail constitution was
always claimed by Sir Henry Acland, for fifty
years the "beloved physician" of Oxford. Lord
Robert, when an undergraduate, was Acland's
patient, and, as soon as he had got his degree,
Acland advised him to take a long sea-voyage,
and, if possible, to spend some time in the gold-
fields of Australia. Sea-air and an outdoor life
in a genial climate were the best medicines for
a delicate, sedentary, and nervous youth, and
Acland believed that they would build him up
into a strong and useful manhood. But Lord
Salisbury had quite other designs for his son,
and came bustling down to Oxford intent on
counteracting Acland's counsel. "What in the
world have you been doing, Dr. Acland? You
have frightened my son out of his senses.
Australia indeed! He is to enter Parliament
directly. Pray tell him there's nothing the
matter with him, and that the House of
Commons will be the best place for his health
as well as his success."

Acland, in describing this interview, used to narrate his reply with a bland dignity which was eminently characteristic of him. " My Lord," I said, " there are twenty thousand medical practitioners in England, and I have no doubt that any of them would be delighted to give your son the advice you desire, if they knew your Lordship's wishes. I, unfortunately, am the one person who is debarred from doing so, as I have already advised Lord Robert in the contrary sense."

Lord Robert took his doctor's advice, went to Australia, continued his journey to New Zealand, and returned to England in better health than he had ever known. He entered Parliament as Member for the pocket-borough of Stamford at a by-election in 1853, and held the seat without a contest till he succeeded his father as Lord Salisbury in 1868.

But meanwhile he had made another decision, the most important and, as it proved, the most fortunate, of his life. In 1857 he married Georgiana Alderson, of whom it may be truly said that she was for more than forty years the guiding star of his fortunes and the good angel of his house.

Miss Alderson was a daughter of Sir Edward

Alderson, Baron of the Exchequer, an accomplished scholar, a profound jurist, and a high-principled and estimable man. Baron Alderson came of Dissenting ancestry, but he himself was a staunch and zealous Churchman, falling early under the influence of the Oxford Movement and continuing in it to the end. This vein of enthusiastic Churchmanship, approaching what in more recent times would be called Ritualism, powerfully affected the "high and dry" atmosphere in which Lord Robert had been trained, and supplied the impulse which has been seen at work, not only in his own career but in that of his sons. His own attitude towards ecclesiastical parties is well expressed in a letter which he wrote in 1898, when Sir William Harcourt was trying to inflame the public mind against Ritualism. "I feel that the Ritualists are a great evil—not on account of the ritual, which I cannot treat as a matter of first-rate importance, but on account of the anarchy they have introduced into the Church. But Harcourt's objection is pure Ultra-Protestantism. He has held this language for five-and-twenty years. It is too foolish not to be sincere."

It was difficult for any one to be brought into close contact with Lady Robert Cecil, or Lady

Salisbury as she became in 1868, without feeling
the effect of her striking and gifted personality.
She was one of the cleverest women of her
time; many would have said the cleverest.
She had Irish blood in her veins, and it
showed itself in her gaiety, her reckless courage,
her rich humour, and her powers of ready
speech. I do not mean that she spoke in public.
From that form of activity she was restrained
by a curious nervousness which she certainly
showed in no other department of life. Perhaps
it should rather be called emotionalism. She
used to affirm that she could not endure the
sound of her own voice, and that to say "I
thank you for your address," or "I declare this
bazaar open," was a feat beyond her powers.
But in conversation she was prompt, vigorous,
and pungent in an unusual degree; always
seeing the ludicrous aspects of a character or
a situation, but not at all backward in signify-
ing displeasure or satirizing folly. There was
a twinkle in her eye, half-mocking, half-
laughing, which was irresistibly quaint. Her
pen was as trenchant as her tongue, and for
many years she wielded it with great effect in
anonymous journalism. For the first eleven
years of her married life, her husband was still

LADY SALISBURY.

To face p. 232.

a younger son, and Lord Salisbury was not profuse in provision for his family. That Lord Robert Cecil made a good income out of his regular contributions to the *Quarterly* is common knowledge, and the essays on foreign and domestic politics which he contributed to that review were well worth disinterment. Of course this habit of systematic authorship stimulated and disciplined his style, and the trick of writing clearly and humorously never forsook him, even in the busiest days of his official life. He wrote everything with his own hand, and the most ordinary letter and the shortest note always showed the master-touch. It was astonishing to me, when I published the Memoir of Canon Malcolm MacColl, that the purblind critics never discovered the extraordinary merit of Lord Salisbury's letters, with which that memoir abounds.

But Lady Robert's sphere was the *Saturday Review*, then owned by her husband's brother-in-law, A. J. B. Beresford-Hope; and there she merrily plied her pen with advantage alike to herself and to the paper. Perhaps her highest fame as a journalist was attained when the world insisted on attributing to her the authorship of *Frisky Matrons*, and *The Girl of the*

Period, which really were written by Mrs. Lynn Linton.

These literary pastimes were laid aside when Lord Robert Cecil (who had become Lord Cranborne by his elder brother's death in 1865) entered Lord Derby's Government as Secretary of State for India in 1866. Thenceforward to the end of her life Lady Salisbury concentrated all her powers on the furtherance and support of her husband's political career. Her value to him was enormous. His pessimistic spirit, his despondent view of life, his low estimate of the practice of politics even when conducted on a grand scale, found their wholesome antidote in her buoyant temper, her cheery optimism, and the zealous enjoyment with which she played the game. I should think that it is not too much to say that Lord Salisbury's marriage made all the difference between a doleful and a joyous life.

I spoke of the zeal with which Lady Salisbury played the game of politics. Her enemies —and she had plenty—said that she played it too intently, and that it was sometimes allowed to interfere with her natural kindliness, and to bring discord into relations which, in spite of divergence, ought to have been harmonious. Be

that as it may—and it is not for me to pass
judgment—her guiding ambition was to secure
for her husband the national and international
recognition which she knew to be his due, and
to surround him with all those amenities of the
home which count for so much in the lives of
successful politicians.   From that home, as I
remember it, I would not, if I could, raise the
veil.   It must suffice to say that both Lord and
Lady Salisbury pursued in the education of their
children a method highly unconventional indeed,
but founded on the noblest principles; and, in
the event, abundantly justified.

But a Prime Minister and his wife must to
a great extent live their lives in public; and
about the public appearances of Lord and Lady
Salisbury there is no need to be reticent.   We
all remember him in the House of Lords, and
an impressive memory it truly is—the memory of
a very able man with a very high sense of duty,
thinking aloud in the presence of an assembly
with which he did not condescend to argue.
We all remember his majestic appearance, dark
colouring, great stature, and pensive brow—
which the second Lord Lytton described with
admirable fidelity in *Glenaveril* :—

Observe his mien. Above the spacious chest
　　The large Olympian forehead forward droops
Its massive temples, as if thus to rest
　　The crowded brain their firm-built bastion coops
And the large slouching shoulder, as oppressed
　　By the prone head, habitually stoops
Above a world his contemplative gaze
Peruses, finding little there to praise.

Philosopher and Paladin in one ;
　　The soldier's courage and the sage's lore ;
A searching intellect that leaves no stone
　　Unturned in any path its thoughts explore ;
A rush of repartee that, not alone
　　Dazzles, but scathes—like lightning flashing o'er
The loaded fulness of a brooding mind,
Scornful of men, but studious of mankind.

On the sixtieth anniversary of Queen Victoria's
accession, the House of Lords attended Divine
Service in Westminster Abbey. Lord Salisbury
sate in the Sub-dean's seat, where, wrapped in
the scarlet and ermine of his degree, and framed
by the time-stained oak of the stall and canopy,
he looked indeed a worthy representative of the
greatest empire in the world. A busybody (I
think a bishop) once came bustling to Lord
Salisbury about some projected appointment.
" You must forgive my worrying you, but the
office is supremely important." To which the
philosophic statesman replied, " There are only

two supremely important offices in England—
the Premiership and the Foreign Secretaryship,
and at the present moment I happen to hold
them both."

Prime Ministers lead a public life, even in
circumstances which, for lesser people, would be
private. Both at Hatfield and in Arlington Street
Lord and Lady Salisbury entertained on a scale
which gave their hospitalities the character of
public ceremonies. Gladstone, after visiting
Hatfield in 1868, told Bishop Wilberforce that
he had "never seen a more perfect host."
On 15th February, 1878, there was a ball in
Arlington Street at which the Prince and
Princess of Wales were present. I well remember that, when Lord Salisbury led the
Princess to supper, Lady Margaret Beaumont,
by whom I was standing, said, "There's a
splendid couple! The finest man in the room
and the prettiest woman."

CHAPTER XIII

THE DUKE AND DUCHESS OF WESTMINSTER

HUGH LUPUS GROSVENOR,[1] third Marquess and first Duke of Westminster, married in 1852 his cousin, Lady Constance Leveson-Gower, daughter of the second Duke of Sutherland. The Duchess died in 1880; but in the Seventies she and her husband were the most brilliant and conspicuous couple in the social world of London.

The Duke was of middle height, rather above than below, thin and almost shrivelled-looking, with black hair and a sallow complexion. He carried himself very gracefully, with his chin elevated and his head rather thrown back. His bearing was full of natural dignity; but he was light in hand, entirely free from formality and pose, and delightfully courteous. He

[1] 1825–99.

LADY CONSTANCE GROSVENOR.

(Duchess of Westminster.)

LORD GROSVENOR.

(Duke of Westminster.)

To face p. 238.

knew—and it is a rare gift—how to be easy
and free without being free-and-easy. His courtesy was as conspicuous in the hunting-field as
in the drawing-room, and, when he was Master
of the Cheshire Hounds, I have known him jump
off his horse, in the middle of a fine run, in
order to help an older man in difficulties. In
his personal life he was simple, almost austere;
but in everything that pertained to his station
and its responsibilities, stately, profuse, and
grandiose. Though not artistically educated,
he had a genuine sense for art in general and
architecture in particular. He harboured large
designs for the reconstruction of his London
property, which reached from Oxford Street to
the Thames; and had he lived he would have
made the great district which he owned a city
of palaces.

One of his most amiable traits was his love
of animals, which made him, among other things,
a vehement foe of bearing-reins, and helped to
make him a consummate horseman, for there can
be no true horsemanship where the rider does
not feel himself in sympathy with his mount in
the hunting-field. Bend Or, the famous Derby
winner of 1880, was so completely a member of
the family at Eaton that his name became the

pseudonym of his inseparable companion, who is now (1916) the second Duke of Westminster.

The first Duke, of whom I am now writing, was a model country gentleman, the friend of all his neighbours, high and low, and intimately versed in all the duties and interests which belong to an agricultural property—in his case not a very large one, for the 20,000 acres of the Grosvenor Estate in Cheshire and Flintshire are few when compared with the domains of the Tolle-maches and Cholmondeleys and Egertons. Of course the Duke's great wealth was derived from the farm-lands which his ancestress, Mary Davies, brought into the family in 1677, and which now are covered by Grosvenor Square and its adjacent streets, and retain traces of their origin in Green Street and Farm Street and Park Lane; but this is a digression.

The Duke was a man of keen intelligence and impetuous temper. He had a strong sense of public duty, and took an active part in politics, though, except during the five years when he was Master of the Horse in Gladstone's govern-ment, outside the official ring. Indeed he was exactly the type of politician that is the despair of Whips and wire-pullers. By birth and training he was a Whig of the Whigs; yet he first sprang into prominence by helping to defeat Lord Russell's Reform Bill of 1866. He supported the disestablishment of the Irish Church, but he was an even fanatical opponent of Home Rule. He abhorred Lord Beaconsfield and all his works and ways, and was an enthusiastic champion of the Christian cause in Eastern Europe. Throughout the Eastern Question of 1876-79 he supported Gladstone through thick and thin; and, though he had sold Millais's picture of his former leader rather than keep a Home Ruler on his walls, yet Gladstone chose him as the most suitable recipient of his Open Letter on the Armenian Massacres in 1907.

I turn from the Duke to the Duchess—" the bride and the pride of the *Gros-veneur*," as the enthusiastic Egerton - Warburton called her in a song of welcome to Cheshire, adding this chivalrous defiance—

> So I lower my lance,
> And I challenge all France
> To outvie the bright eye of the Lady Constance.

The Duchess of Westminster was one of the most beautiful women in Europe. Certainly France could not have produced her equal. Her profile, slightly aquiline, was absolutely perfect, and her hair, light gold in tint, fell in waves over a noble forehead. Her charm of manner is difficult to describe, but was impossible to resist. It was the perfection of naturalness, gaiety, and welcoming grace. Though she entertained incessantly and on the largest scale, she greeted each guest with a lustrous smile and a genial word which made him feel that, however insignificant he might be, his glorious hostess was pleased to see him.

Although the Duchess's health failed prematurely, and she died quite early in middle life, in her heyday she had a physical vigour, an almost romping activity, and a joy in living, which made her society irresistibly exhilarating. "My dear, I only wish I could get a new pair of feet," was her rapid ejaculation to a girl young enough to be her daughter, in a pause in the dancing at Grosvenor House; and when she could dance no longer, she would stand by with her jocund smile while others danced, and would incite her juniors to renewed activity. "Oh! Lord Lothair, how lazy you are! Keep him up to it, Corisande. You young people don't half waltz. I've a good mind to come and give you a lesson."

As I look back upon "the passing show" of

society in London between 1870 and 1880, the parties at Grosvenor House stand out conspicuous, marked off from all the rest by their magic combination of jollity and splendour. It required Lord Beaconsfield's pen, unequalled at that kind of work, to describe those radiant festivals, and beyond doubt they would have figured in *Lothair*; only, when that great book was in writing, Lord Grosvenor had not succeeded to his hereditary honours, and "The Lady Constance" had not begun her famous reign at Grosvenor House.

CHAPTER XIV

THE DUKE AND DUCHESS OF SUTHERLAND

IN my last chapter I expressed my regret that Lord Beaconsfield, whose sketches of character and life in London were unerring, had never described a ball at Grosvenor House. He did, however, the next best thing, by laying the scene of Lothair's entrance into society at what is palpably meant for Stafford House, now the London Museum, but in the Seventies the abode of the third Duke of Sutherland and his wife, in her own right Countess of Cromartie.

"It was a sumptuous festival. The palace, resonant with fantastic music, blazed amid illumined gardens, rich with summer warmth. The bright moments flew on. Suddenly there was a mysterious silence in the hall, followed by a kind of suppressed stir. Every one seemed to be speaking with bated breath, or, if moving, to be walking on tiptoe. It was the supper-hour—

Soft hour which wakes the wish and melts the heart.

Royalty, followed by the imperial presence of ambassadors, and escorted by a group of dazzling duchesses and paladins of high degree, was ushered with courteous pomp by the host and hostess into a choice saloon, hung with rose-coloured tapestry and illumined by chandeliers of crystal, where they were served from gold plate.

"But the thousand less favoured were not badly off, when they found themselves in the more capacious chambers, into which they rushed with an eagerness hardly in keeping with the splendid nonchalance of the preceding hours. 'What a perfect family!' exclaimed Hogo Bohun, as he extracted a couple of fat little birds from their bed of aspic jelly. 'Everything they do in such perfect taste. How safe you were here to have ortolans for supper!'"

George Granville William Leveson-Gower, third Duke of Sutherland, was born in 1828, and died in 1892. He was essentially, in all his tastes

and feelings, a great aristocrat, as that word is
used in vulgar parlance; but his humour was to
affect, in speech and aspect and bearing, a rough
and ready independence of convention. His tow-
coloured hair and beard were tangled; his clothes
looked as if they had been stuck on with a
pitchfork; he held himself ungracefully, and his
manner was abrupt. His favourite amusements,
apart from the inevitable sports of the field, were
such as to astonish the multitude. He delighted
in navigating yachts, driving locomotives, and
in helping, when he did not hinder, the operations of the Metropolitan Fire Brigade. But
these idiosyncrasies were merely affectations,
and did not conceal, from those who could look
below the surface, his strong common-sense and
his generous instincts. Apart from his paternal
property, he had inherited from his grandmother, in her own right Countess of Sutherland, much more than a million acres in the
Highlands; and he always seemed more at home
on the moors and lochs of Sutherland and Ross-
shire than amid the rococco splendours of Trentham or Stafford House. He liked to fancy
himself a chief, and found enjoyment in kilts
and bagpipes.

The second Duke had been a principal sup-

porter of the London and North-Western Railway,
at a time when railways were still unfashionable ;
and, following the example so set, the third Duke
contributed more than £226,000 to the formation
of the Highland Railway. An even larger sum
he bestowed on the reclamation of waste lands
and the development of Scottish agriculture. He
had by nature a shrewd instinct for business, and
this assured him that before many years were
over Staffordshire would become uninhabitable;
and, although he could scarcely have foreseen
that a time would come when Trentham would
be so polluted that no public body would accept
it as a gift, he seemed to realize that his successors would make Dunrobin their headquarters,
and arranged his affairs accordingly.

In politics the Duke was an hereditary Whig,
and in his youth was esteemed a Radical. Here
is his portrait as he appeared in those distant
days to a close and sarcastic observer—

" He was opposed to all privilege, and indeed
to all orders of men, except dukes, who were a
necessity. He was also in favour of the equal
division of all property, except land. Liberty
depended on land, and the greater the land-
owners the greater the liberty of the country.
He would hold forth on this topic even with

energy, and was amazed at any one differing from him; 'as if a fellow could have too much land,' he would urge with a voice and glance which defied contradiction."

Apart from questions of land, the Duke's politics were distinctly Liberal. When Garibaldi visited England in 1864, the Duke met him at Nine Elms Station, conveyed him in triumph to Stafford House, lodged him there with a degree of magnificence which the hardy leader of "The Thousand" found rather burdensome, and, when the visit came to its abrupt and mysterious end, carried him back to Caprera in his yacht. In Parliament he voted steadily for all such measures as extension of the Franchise and Irish Disestablishment; but when Lord Beaconsfield became Prime Minister, and the great controversy of the Eastern Question arose, the Duke was a renegade, and arrayed himself against Gladstone's crusade, taking his part with the Turk, the Tories, and the *Times*.[1] From this great apostasy he never rallied, and in his later years he disappeared completely from political life.

[1] A fund for wounded Turkish soldiers was opened at Stafford House, and the hall-porter, replying to a journalist who asked how it was doing, said, " Not very well. There's a terrible deal of Christian feeling about in the country."

In 1849 Lord Stafford (whom as third Duke of Sutherland we have just been discussing) married, before he struck twenty-one, Anne Hay-Mackenzie. If she had wedded any one else, this young lady would have been esteemed a great heiress, for she represented the Earls of Cromartie (who were attainted for their participation in the rising of 1745), and inherited from them some 150,000 acres in Ross-shire. She had also considerable beauty, remarkable health, and unbounded activity. She rode and danced and swam—in those days ladies did not shoot—with a zest which lasted at least into middle life. In 1861 Lord Stafford succeeded his father as Duke of Sutherland, and Lord Palmerston, always susceptible to female charms, induced Queen Victoria to reinstate the Duchess in her hereditary honours, making her Countess of Cromartie in her own right, with remainder to her second son, and to heirs female as well as male. When asked why he had advised this startling use of the prerogative, " Cupid," as his friends called him, could only reply, " A cause de ses beaux yeux."

As mistress of Stafford House the Duchess had a brilliant reign. The house had been built by Frederick, Duke of York, on land mysteriously acquired from the Green Park, and was leased from the Crown by the first Duke of Sutherland. Its famous hall and staircase, designed by Sir Charles Barry, perfect in proportion and singularly harmonious in their tints of purple and grey, are the triumph of scagliola, and always deceived the onlooker into the notion that they were marble, until he inadvertently touched them and found them warm. The house was admirably adapted for entertaining on the largest scale, and the third Duke and Duchess habitually threw open its wide doors to the whole world of London. Lord Beaconsfield, in the passage which I quoted above, did not exaggerate the splendid appearance of a ball at Stafford House; but appearances, in balls as in life, are not everything, and Stafford House always lacked the peculiar sense of personal welcome and hospitable delight which marked the related and rival house in Upper Grosvenor Street. At Grosvenor House a ball was a party; at Stafford House it was a mob.

On New Year's Day, 1870, the Duchess wrote thus to a friend : " I am to be the new Mistress of the Robes. I could wish it had not been through Mr. Gladstone; but he has very prettily expressed the personal wishes of the Queen in his letter to me, which he might not have done. It will make me very happy to have oppor-

DUCHESS OF SUTHERLAND.

To face p. 250.

tunities of seeing more of the Queen, for whom
I have always had such admiration and devotion."

This letter was highly characteristic of the
writer. A warm heart, when it accepts a boon,
does not gird at the giver; and a wise head
knows how to restrain its feelings when they
go astray. But though several good fairies had
assisted at the birth of Anne Duchess of Sutherland, some had been conspicuously absent, and,
as years went on, the effects of their absence
became increasingly evident. She was still,
when dressed in black, with a great cross of
diamonds at her throat and a firmament of
diamond stars in her dark hair, an impressive
figure; but her face acquired a look of settled
melancholy, which contrasted even painfully with
the glittering scenes through which she moved.
She gradually retired from London and society,
forsook Dunrobin and Trentham, and established herself at Torquay, where she lived surrounded by an obsequious clique, which had
all the foibles, though none of the interest, of
a Court. She passed through many phases of
religion, from Dr. Cumming's prophetical ministry
in Crown Court, and the fervent Evangelicalism
of Miss Marsh's faith, to the mild Anglicanism

of Bishop Wilkinson, and the florid Ritualism of later guides. Roman proselytizers, who are fond of fishing in troubled waters, marked her as their prey, but never succeeded in landing her. She died, unexpectedly, in her sixtieth year. Of her five children none survive.

CHAPTER XV

THE DUKE AND DUCHESS OF ABERCORN

WHEN one is arranging a gallery of portraits, relationship to the subject does not by itself justify the inclusion of a particular picture; but, if the subject was in any way remarkable, relationship does not forbid one to include his or her portrait. The Duke and Duchess of Abercorn were so noteworthy—indeed, so unique—a couple, that a Portrait-Gallery of the Seventies which lacked their pictures would be glaringly incomplete.

James Hamilton,[1] tenth Earl and first Duke of Abercorn, and Duke of Chatelherault in France, was all that his name suggests; and from first to last he was one of the handsomest men of his generation. Among his contemporaries at Oxford there were only three who could be bracketed with him—Henry Edward

---

[1] 1811-85.

Manning, Sidney Herbert, and Lord Douglas, afterwards eleventh Duke of Hamilton. I have heard Gladstone, who was a contemporary of all four, discuss their respective charms. Douglas was a Greek statue; Herbert was too tall for perfect beauty; and Manning too short. Abercorn's defect was an over-refinement of feature which suggested effeminacy. By the time that the four rivals had attained middle life (and two of them did not live beyond it) Abercorn's supremacy was assured by a change in fashions. The return of the bearded heroes from the Crimea made beards fashionable; and Abercorn was one of the first to follow the new mode. Never was that hazardous translation from *tonsus* to *barbatus* so strikingly successful. The beard, of the same rich brown as the curling hair, was trimmed and pointed and kept with scrupulous care; and, blending with the whiskers and moustache, gave a picturesqueness and virility to the appearance which redeemed it from insipidity. Those who saw Abercorn dressed for a fancy ball, in black velvet with a point lace collar and the blue ribbon of the Garter round his neck, saw Vandyke's picture of Charles I step out of its frame; and the resemblance was heightened by the narrowness

DUKE OF ABERCORN.

DUCHESS OF ABERCORN.

To face p. 254.

of the forehead and the singular dignity of
bearing. Even as a boy at Harrow, Abercorn
had been a conspicuous dandy, and the habit
never forsook him; but he always dressed, not
in strict conformity to the rule of the moment,
but with a certain elasticity in the matter of
fabric, colour, and art, which added greatly to
the distinction of his appearance. He was in
all respects a great gentleman; and, in some
senses of the term, a man of fashion and of the
world : but he was a good deal more than this.
He had excellent abilities, which an almost
morbid shyness prevented him from displaying,
but which he cultivated by much more reading
than his friends ever suspected. It was not a
little remarkable that for the greater part of
his life he took scarcely any part in public
affairs. He had succeeded to his title while
still a boy, and entered the House of Lords in
1832. The texture of his Conservatism was
above reproach, and he had very considerable
advantages of person and address. But, beyond
an ornamental post in the Household of the
Prince Consort, he held no public office till
Lord Derby formed his last administration in
1866. Then the hour struck and the man
arrived.

Lord Abercorn was the heaven-sent Viceroy
of Ireland. He arrived at Dublin at a critical
moment. The embers of the Fenian conspiracy
were still smouldering, and there were signs
which showed that the long-threatened attack
on the Irish Church was not far off. Over all
difficulties Lord Abercorn triumphed by probity,
courage, and a wise employment of social splendour. Of all the men who have ever filled the
Viceregal throne, he was the best qualified by
appearance and manner to play the part of a
Vice-King. "Give me Abercorn," cried an enthusiastic Irishman, "that looks at ye over his
bird as if ye was the dirt beneath his feet."

The General Election of 1868 decided the fate
of the Irish Church, made Gladstone Prime
Minister, and sent Abercorn back to the private
and domestic life which he so thoroughly enjoyed. Disraeli had rewarded his services by
making him a duke, and now conferred on him
immortality by drawing his portrait as "The
Duke" in *Lothair*. Though he was the head of
a great Scottish house, his main possessions lay
in the North of Ireland, where he owned some
eighty thousand acres in Tyrone and Donegal;
and there were some who thought that he might
have been Duke of Ulster; but the Queen was

reminded that this was a royal title, and Lord Abercorn became Duke of Abercorn in the peerage of Ireland. Till this new dukedom was created, the Duke of Leinster had been the sole duke in the peerage of Ireland, and was playfully known as "Ireland's Only." When the newly created Duke of Abercorn wrote a mock apology for thus invading his monopoly, the elder duke responded, gracefully and appositely, that, though he was no longer "Ireland's Only," he was quite contented to be "Premier Duke of Ireland."

When Lord Beaconsfield formed his last Administration, at the beginning of 1874, the Duke of Abercorn accepted the Viceroyalty; but his health was not quite what it had been, and the burdens and formalities of viceregal life were becoming irksome. He therefore resigned in 1876, and for the remainder of his days lived a life of patriarchal state and tranquillity, mainly at Baron's Court, in County Tyrone, surrounded by his descendants to the fourth generation. So much for a rough sketch of the Duke of Abercorn : I now attempt a more finished portrait of the Duchess.

Lady Louisa Jane Russell, daughter of John, sixth Duke of Bedford, by his second wife, Lady

Georgiana Gordon, was born in 1812. As she
advanced towards girlhood, many a fond remin-
iscence and many a daring prophecy gathered
round her. Old stagers saw reproduced in her
the magical charm by which her grandmother,
Jane, Duchess of Gordon, had raised the Gordon Highlanders. More modern observers recognized the brilliant grace which had nearly made
Lady Georgiana wife of Eugène Beauharnais, and
Vice-Queen of Italy. Her line of feature was
marked and aquiline—a legacy from the "Gallant
Gordons"; her figure was extraordinarily slight,
and every movement, posture, and gesture was
the very perfection of girlish grace.

One of the few redeeming features in the
character of George IV was his kindness to
children; and it was at a children's ball at Carlton House that little Lady Louisa Russell first
encountered the future partner of her brilliant
life. James Hamilton (afterwards Duke of Abercorn) was a year and a half older than his
partner, and a singularly handsome boy. The
children were mutually attracted to each other,
danced together, went to supper together, and
(it is believed) made arrangements for a matri-
monial alliance later on. But the idyll was
rudely broken by the imperative necessity that

Lord Abercorn should return to Harrow and Lady Louisa to the schoolroom; nor was it renewed till 1832, when the "young man of great possessions"—beauty, rank, and fortune—re-encountered the heroine of the children's ball. "Lady Louisa, do you remember what I said to you at Carlton House when we were boy and girl?" "Yes, I think I do." "Well, I haven't changed my mind."

So all went merry as a marriage-bell, and Lady Louisa Russell became Marchioness of Abercorn on the 25th of October, 1832, she being twenty and her husband nearly twenty-two years old; and in due course the mother of fourteen children,[1] and the ancestress of a family so numerous that 160 survived her.

The position which Lady Abercorn—for such was her style during the central part of her life—occupied in society was quite unique. She was an hereditary favourite at Court, a personal friend

[1] James, second Duke of Abercorn; Lord Claud Hamilton, M.P.; Lord George Hamilton, M.P.; Lord Ronald and Lord Cosmo Hamilton, who both died young; Lord Frederick Hamilton, M.P.; Lord Ernest Hamilton, M.P.; Harriet, Countess of Lichfield; Beatrix, Countess of Durham; Louisa, Duchess of Buccleuch; Katherine, Countess of Mount Edgcumbe; Georgina, Countess Winterton; Albertha, Marchioness of Blandford; and Maud, Marchioness of Lansdowne.

of Queen Victoria (who wished her to be Mistress
of the Robes in 1841), the mother of charming
and beautiful daughters, and the head of an
establishment, conducted, first at Dudley House,
Park Lane, and afterwards at Chesterfield House,
on a profuse and splendid scale. Yet, though
essentially "in the world," Lady Abercorn never
was "of" it. A strong strain of Evangelical
piety, which had reached her in early life indi-
rectly from Charles Simeon, blended itself har-
moniously with the Presbyterian traditions of
the Hamiltons, and Lady Abercorn lived in
a circle—not small—of intimate and devoted
friends, but was curiously aloof from the excitement, the ostentation, and the moral pliability
of what was then called the "Beau Monde,"
and is now the "Smart Set." At one period
of her life she was strongly addicted to the prophetical ministry of Dr. Cumming, and the
current joke was that, whereas other mothers of
marriageable daughters invited desirable young
men to their opera-boxes, Lady Abercorn would
ask them to share her pew in Crown Court.

The appointment of Lord Abercorn to the Irish
Viceroyalty necessarily changed, for a while, the
tenour of his wife's life; and the success of his
Administration was in part due to the winning

charm and gracious dignity by which his Vice-Queen swayed the Irish heart.   Ireland had been the adopted home of her married life, and it is worthy of note that in the short Parliament of 1885–86 she had all her five surviving sons battling for the Union, the eldest in the House of Lords and his four younger brothers in the House of Commons.   Perhaps even more remarkable is the fact that at a by-election in 1904 she was still able to take a keen interest and a prominent part in the election of her grandson, Lord Turnour, for the Horsham Division of Sussex.   She died on the 30th of March, 1905, in her ninety-fourth year.

To draw what I promised—a finished portrait of Louisa, Duchess of Abercorn—is, I find, no easy task.   A keen sense of humour, natural grace of speech and bearing, a wealth of warm affection, merry interest in her friends' concerns —all these attributes were joined in her with a dignity which belonged to a bygone generation, and an eager piety which, amidst the abounding distractions of a brilliant and crowded life, never for an instant lost sight of " the one thing needful."   Ben Jonson may have had some such image before his mental gaze when he wrote his address to Lucy Harington, Countess of Bedford.

To Lady Louisa Russell this portrait of her ancestress must have been familiar from her childhood, and it may have helped to shape, by some undetected influence, the lines on which her own character developed.

> This morning, timely rapt with holy fire,
>   I sought to form unto my zealous muse
> What kind of creature I could most desire
>   To honour, serve, and love, as poets use.
>
> I meant to make her fair, and free, and wise,
>   Of greatest blood, and yet more good than great—
> I meant the day-star should not brighter rise,
>   Nor lend like influence from his lucent seat.
>
> I meant she should be courteous, facile, sweet,
>   Hating that solemn vice of greatness, Pride;
> I meant each softest virtue there should meet,
>   Fit in that softer bosom to reside.

Those who had the privilege of knowing Louisa, Duchess of Abercorn, saw in actual life what the poet imagined.

CHAPTER XVI

LORD AND LADY SPENCER

DURING the period which we are now considering there was no more conspicuous couple in London than Lord and Lady Spencer. Theirs was one of those marriages in which, to quote a phrase of Gladstone's, "the union of thought, heart, and action both fulfils the ideal and brings duality near to the borders of identity."

John Poyntz Spencer, sixth Earl Spencer, was born in 1835, succeeded his father in 1857, and married in 1858 Charlotte Frances Frederica Seymour. Three sisters, all pretty, close to one another in age, constantly seen together, must always attract attention; and the three Miss Seymours who became respectively Lady Clifden, Lady Charles Bruce, and Lady Spencer, were very bright stars in the social firmament. Lady Spencer was not faultlessly, but splendidly, beautiful; with a truly noble brow, and a general effect of radiance which seemed to surround her like an atmosphere. When, in 1868, her husband was made Lord-Lieutenant of Ireland, every one felt that "Spencer's Fairy Queen" was the ideal occupant of a Viceregal throne. Those were the halcyon days of Liberalism, but in a later and more dangerous Viceroyalty Lady Spencer's high courage and steady nerve did much to steady the social fabric of Ireland, which Fenianism was shaking to its base.

As mistress of Spencer House, the most beautiful though not the most grandiose house in London, and of Althorp, where the high traditions of hospitality were scrupulously observed, Lady Spencer naturally had a great position in society; but she always seemed to have a soul above her surroundings and a mind which appraised state and splendour at their proper worth. She was by conviction a strong and steady Liberal; and long before "slumming" became a fashionable game, she had shown a generous and a wise insight into the problems of poverty.

After what I have said in praise of Lady Spencer, perhaps I can best introduce Lord Spencer by saying that he was worthy of his wife. He was one of the greatest gentlemen I ever saw, with that absolutely perfect manner,

LORD SPENCER.

LADY SPENCER.

To face p. 264.

both dignified and gentle, which no one nowadays
can even imitate. He rode as became a Master
of the Pytchley, with that "noble horsemanship" which in all generations has "witched"
the English "world." His face was far from
handsome; but his great height, his willowy
figure, and his stately bearing made his presence
peculiarly effective. To my eye he was the most
conspicuous man at the Coronation of King
Edward VII. He was one of the four Knights
of the Garter chosen to bear the canopy above
the King at his anointing; the splendid dark
blue velvet mantle of the Order sate on him as
naturally as a frock-coat on Mr. Chamberlain,
and combined with his grey-red beard and
stately figure to give the effect of a portrait by
Vandyke.

Lord Spencer was an Englishman to the backbone; Harrow and Cambridge and Althorp had
only developed his natural bias. He loved a
country life, field-sports, agriculture, county business. He was typically English in this—that
he disliked social changes. All his domestic
apparatus, though handsome, was old-fashioned.
He liked to have the *Times* delivered at
Althorp in the evening, as it had been in his
boyhood. When he went abroad an English

breakfast of eggs and bacon, eaten at half-past nine, was an essential feature of his holiday.

He was also an Englishman—and an Englishman of the best type—in his devotion to public duty. There could never have been a man (unless it was his uncle, Lord Althorp, of the Reform Bill) to whom the drudgery of political office, and platform oratory, and ceremonious pomp, were less congenial. But he was the head of a great family which had long played its part in public life; alike his personal convictions and his hereditary associations bound him to the Whigs; and when Mr. Gladstone asked him to be in turn a Lord-Lieutenant of Ireland, Lord President of the Council, and First Lord of the Admiralty, he never let ease and enjoyment stand in the way, if his leader thought he could possibly serve the State.

I said just now that he was a Whig; but he was a Whig with a difference, and that difference was a life-long devotion to Gladstone. In him Whiggery became Liberalism; and in some notable respects—as in his views of the Eastern Question—his Liberalism was not distinguishable from Radicalism.

Of course the most notable incident in his life was his conversion to Home Rule. When

the Liberal Government of 1880, represented in
Ireland by Forster and Lord Cowper, had failed
ingloriously in its contest with murder and
outrage, Gladstone turned for help to Spencer;
and Spencer, with characteristic self-forgetful-
ness, undertook at a moment's notice as formidable a task as could be offered to an English
statesman—the Viceroyalty of a rebellious Ireland.
A week later, the Irish troubles culminated in
the murders of the Phœnix Park, and "The
Irish Question" entered on the most dangerous
phase that it had ever known. Spencer's simple
sense of duty, his persistent courage, and his
strong common sense, bore him safely—nay,
triumphantly—through all perils and perplexities.
Between 1882 and 1885 he abolished agrarian
murder, broke the tyranny of the Land League,
and re-established social order.

Then, on the 8th of June, 1885, came the
defeat of Gladstone's second administration,
over an amendment to the Budget, and Lord
Salisbury became Prime Minister.

The fall of the Liberal Government involved,
of course, Lord Spencer's return from Ireland,
and some of his friends resolved, after the
manner of admiring Englishmen, to give him
a public dinner. The current phrase, not

perhaps scientifically accurate, was that we were to "Dine Spencer for coercing the Irish." As he had done this thoroughly for the space of three years, and at the risk of his own life had destroyed a treasonable and murderous conspiracy, he was well entitled to all the honours which we could give him. So it was arranged that the dinner should take place at the Westminster Palace Hotel on the 24th of July. Shortly before the day arrived Chamberlain said to me : " I think you had better not attend that dinner to Spencer. I am not going, nor is Dilke. Certainly Spencer has done his duty, and shown capital pluck ; but I hope we should all have done the same, and there's no reason to mark it by a dinner. Besides, coercion is not a nice business for Liberals, though we may be forced into it." However, as I had greatly admired Lord Spencer's administration and as his family and mine had been politically associated for a century, I made a point of attending, and a capital evening we had. There was an enthusiastic and representative company of two hundred Liberals. Lord Hartington presided, and exalted Lord Spencer to the skies ; and Lord Spencer justified the Crimes Act by saying that, when it was passed, there was an organization of thirty thousand Fenians, aided by branches in Scotland and England, and by funds from America, defying the law of the land in Ireland. Not a word in all this about Home Rule, or the Union of Hearts; but we cheered it to the echo, in happy ignorance of what the next six months had in store for us.

When, in the following December, it became known that Gladstone had accepted Home Rule and had thereby split the Liberal party in two, one of the first questions was: "What will Spencer do?" and the general answer was that he would stick to the Union. But those who answered thus ignored two or three forces to which Spencer was specially amenable. One of these was the Whiggish spirit. Spencer was, as Acton said of himself, "possessed by a Whig devil"; or, to put the matter more attractively, he held that people had the right to be governed according to their own wishes. Another force was Gladstone's influence, to which Spencer had always been particularly sensitive; and, though Gladstone always denied that he had converted Spencer, I feel pretty sure that the younger man would have found it extremely difficult to withstand his chief's deliberate judgment. But there was in Spencer's case a third influence,

less palpable, perhaps, than the other two, but
powerful. Here I concur with Lord Morley:
" Lord Spencer knew the importance of a firm
and continuous system in Ireland. Such a
system he had inflexibly carried out. . . . But
the Government was turned out and the party
of 'law and order' came in. He saw his firm
and continuous system, at the first opportunity,
flouted and discarded. He was aware, as officials and as the public were aware, that his
successor at Dublin Castle made little secret
that he had come over to reverse his policy."
The mortification of a brave and conscientious
man who sees his work contemned and undone
by the very people who ought to have valued
it the most highly, may well account for unexpected decisions.   But, whatever was the cause
of Spencer's adhesion, he was by far the most
important ally whom Gladstone acquired.   As
Lord Morley says, he " was hardly second in
weight to Mr. Gladstone himself.   His unrivalled
experience of Irish administration, his powers of
firm decision in difficult circumstances, and the
impression of high public spirit, uprightness and
fortitude, which had stamped itself deep upon
the public mind, gave him a force of moral
authority in an Irish crisis that was unique."

All through the troublous years of 1886–92
he was active in the propagation of the new
policy; and it was a source of amusement to
his friends to see this intensely old-fashioned,
and socially conservative, Whig, trying to adapt
himself, graciously indeed but with palpable
effort, to the exigencies of the platform in great
industrial centres, and to the social environment of such as Matthew Arnold's friend, Mr.
Bottles.

The least happy portion of Lord Spencer's
political career was that which was spent at the
Admiralty, between 1892 and 1895. For the first
time in his active life he found himself out of
sympathy with Gladstone. He yielded to the
demands of the Sea-Lords in the way of Naval
expenditure, and forced on the Cabinet some
Naval Estimates which Gladstone pronounced
"mad and drunk." In truth those Naval Estimates applied the final push which drove Gladstone
for the last time out of office. How, he asked
himself, could he turn his back on his former
self by becoming a party to swollen expenditure? "My name," he said, "stands in Europe
as a symbol of the policy of peace, moderation,
and non-aggression. What would be said of my
active participation in a policy which will be

taken as plunging England into the whirlpool of militarism ? "

So he retired, laying down for ever the burden of power, and on the 3rd of March, 1894, he formally placed his resignation in the Queen's hands. A friend of mine, not a politician, once said to the Queen: "Does an outgoing Prime Minister recommend his successor to your Majesty ? " and the Queen replied, with characteristic distinctness, "Not unless I ask him." She did not ask Gladstone ; but the following note in Lord Morley's Life is interesting : "He said that, if asked, he should advise her to send for Lord Spencer." It would have been an admirable choice, and might have averted the ruin which overtook the Liberal party in 1895.

N.B.—The late Mr. S. H. Jeyes in his excellent monograph on Lord Rosebery [1] made the strange mistake of saying (page 103) that the Queen chose Lord Rosebery as Prime Minister, " on the advice of Mr. Gladstone." I have repeatedly called attention to this error. The author, unhappily, has gone hence ; but surely the publishers might venture to correct a proved and palpable blunder.

[1] In *The Prime Ministers of Queen Victoria*. J. M. Dent & Sons.

CHAPTER XVII

LORD AND LADY MOUNT-TEMPLE

WILLIAM FRANCIS COWPER [1] was the second son of the fifth Earl Cowper, who died in 1837. Two years later, Lady Cowper, who was a sister of Lord Melbourne, married Lord Palmerston, and became one of the most famous figures in the social and political world. By the circumstances of his early home, William Cowper was initiated from his childhood into the innermost circle of Whig society, which was refined, intellectual, and luxurious, but not the least religious. He went in due course to Eton, where he was popular and happy. "From the first," so wrote Gladstone, who was his school-fellow, "he left very marked and clear recollections. Even from Eton days, the stamp of purity, modesty, gentleness was upon him in a peculiar degree." But neither

[1] 1811–88.

at home nor at Eton was he brought in contact
with religion. "No serious thought," he said,
"was ever presented to my mind." But the
wind bloweth where it listeth. After leaving
Eton, William Cowper went as a private pupil
to a famous Evangelical, James Anderson, of
Brighton; and there he made his First Communion, "experiencing intense delight in devot-
ing himself sincerely to God."

According to the almost invariable law of
young and ardent natures when they first give
themselves consciously to the sacred cause,
"Billy Cowper," as he was always called, felt a
longing for Holy Orders, and expressed it in an
enthusiastic letter to his father, "quoting from
South and Bourdaloue, with phrases about fighting against the world."

The announcement of Billy's desire filled his
parents with dismay; but, like wise people, they
merely said that he might do as he liked, and
recommended him to see a little more of the
world before he decided. They called into
council some friends of the family, including
Lord John Russell, and the upshot of the
conclave was that Billy became a cornet in the
Blues. His good looks, his charming manners,
his social connexions, combined to make him a

LADY MOUNT-TEMPLE.

To face p. 274.

LORD MOUNT-TEMPLE.

universal favourite. The famous and formidable
Lady Holland wrote to a friend : " I have made
acquaintance with the fascinating Billy since I
saw you. I only wonder you have not lost your
heart to him. I am sure I should had mine
been disengaged."

Billy's friends were surprised when he forsook
the delights of London to become aide-de-camp
to the Lord-Lieutenant of Ireland. The duties
of his new post left him plenty of leisure for
study and meditation, and he dated a distinct
advance in his religious life from a solitary visit
to Killarney in 1833. A servant of God he had
long been, but now he resolved to be *servus
inutilis* no longer. Henceforward, to the end
of his life, he was active in that service of God
which expresses itself in the service of man. In
this dedication of his powers he was encouraged
by the example and influence of the great Lord
Shaftesbury, who had married his sister, Lady
Emily Cowper, in 1830.

At the General Election of 1835 William Cowper
was returned in the Whig interest for the borough
of Hertford, which he represented till 1868. In
that year he was returned for South Hampshire,
and retained the seat till 1880, when he was
raised to the peerage.

In 1885 he made this confession of his political faith. "I am," he said, "a Liberal, because I believe that God has sent me into the world to do my best to improve it; and because I cannot rest satisfied with the defects and deficiencies of the political and social condition of my country. My disposition is to hope and trust that legislative remedies may be found for much of the suffering and error that now afflict the people, and I do not share with the Conservatives their distrust of the benefits of change, and their fear of failure in attempts at improvements. Though I perceive the use of the man who sits on the hinder dickey of the coach to put on the drag when the coach is going too fast down a hill, I prefer sitting in front, to help the coachman drive steadily in the right direction."

Soon after William Cowper entered Parliament he was made private secretary to his uncle, Lord Melbourne; and characteristically noted the event as "removing me at once from frivolous and dangerous companionship, and filling up most of my time with prescribed rules and occupations." From 1830 to 1874 the Whigs were seldom out of office, and Lord Palmerston's stepson was not likely to be over-

looked. In 1841 he was made a Junior Lord
of the Treasury; in 1846, and again in 1852, a
Junior Lord of the Admiralty; in 1852 Under-
Secretary for the Home Department; in 1855
President of the Board of Health; in 1857
Vice-President of the Committee of Council in
Education, and in 1859 of the Board of Trade;
and in 1860 he became First Commissioner of
Works. In this last capacity he rendered an
essential service to London by the pains which
he bestowed on the floral and arboreal decoration
of the parks, on both sides of the water. "He
rejoiced that he had been able to make for the
poor of London a garden more beautiful than
that of any rich man in the land."

Lord Palmerston died in 1865, having be-
queathed his estates to Lady Palmerston and,
on her death, to her son William Cowper, who
thereupon assumed the name of Temple. When
Gladstone formed his Government in 1868 he
offered the Chancellorship of the Duchy of
Lancaster to William Cowper-Temple, who
declined it, but as a private member secured
himself a questionable fame as author of the
"Cowper-Temple Clause" in the Education Act
of 1870. This date brings our narrative into
the Seventies, when, as again in the Eighties,

Cowper-Temple played an active and most beneficent part in all forms of philanthropy and social service. As President of the Board of Health he had been a pioneer of sanitary reform, and now he busied himself in the application of sanitary science to domestic life. His keen sympathy with all forms of suffering led him to abandon field-sports, and to become a leader of the crusade against vivisection. In compassion for drunkards, he gave up wine, which he liked and understood, and adopted the " Blue Ribbon." His zeal in the cause of abstinence gave point to Lord Houghton's joke about the title which he assumed when he was raised to the peerage. " Do you know the precedent for Billy Cowper's new name ? You'll find it in *Don Juan*—

> "And Lord Mount Coffee-House, the Irish peer,
>   Who killed himself for love, with drink, last year."

The religious fervour which had marked William Cowper from the early days at Brighton seemed to grow and expand every year; and his name will long be remembered in connexion with the religious conferences which, beginning in the year 1874, he used to assemble at his beautiful house, Broadlands, near Romsey, where seekers after truth, of all denominations and none, used to meet for the consideration of the things which really matter.

Vividly stands out in memory the figure of the beloved and gracious host who presided over these gatherings. Lord Mount-Temple was about the middle height, slender in form, and singularly graceful in form and bearing. His hair and moustache were grey, but he had no other signs of age. His blue eyes were generally half-closed in a fashion which gave an expression of quaint fun to his face. His firmness was as notable as his gentleness; and his friends and family sometimes chaffed him for his charming trick of bowing in complaisance, if something was suggested to him that he did not mean to do, and yet pursuing his way unhindered without jar or discussion. His voice was soft and beautifully modulated, and in power of public speaking he was far above the average of public men, with a peculiar sweetness and winningness. His manners were perfect, and he delighted in a refined and graceful hospitality. He was one of the last people who habitually went about London on horseback; he rode admirably, and seemed thoroughly to enjoy the rather vivacious antics of a favourite mare ominously named "Hysteria."

The saints of the earth are not always agreeable, and not always wise. Sometimes they are neither. Sometimes they are saintly but unwise; sometimes saintly and disagreeable. When we find a saint who is both agreeable and wise, the threefold character is irresistible; and such was the character of William Francis, first and last Lord Mount-Temple.

It is now time to recall the other member of this remarkable partnership. In 1848 William Cowper married Georgina Tollemache, the youngest and most beautiful of nine beautiful sisters; daughters of Admiral Tollemache and sisters of the first Lord Tollemache of Helmingham.

Mrs. Cowper-Temple, to call her by the name which she bore in the Seventies—Lady Mount-Temple as she was from 1880 till her death in 1901—was one of the most remarkable women of her time. She had, beside an almost faultless beauty, an extraordinary dignity of presence and bearing, which was the outward and visible sign of a nature singularly noble and elevated. Ruskin described her as "eminent in her grace

above a stunted group of Roman worshippers."
He tells us in *Præterita* how he spent the
winter of 1840 in pursuing her—" a fair English
girl, who was not only the admitted queen of
beauty in the English circle of that winter in
Rome, but was so, in the kind of beauty which
I had only hitherto dreamed of as possible, but
never yet seen living: statuesque severity with
womanly sweetness joined. I don't think I ever
succeeded in getting nearer than within fifty
yards of her; but she was the light and solace
of all the Roman winter to me, in the mere
chance glimpses of her far away, and the hope
of them."

The dominant note of Lady Mount-Temple's
character was her passionate indignation against
cruelty and injustice. She had a genuine love
of the outcast and down-trodden, a chivalry of
spirit which always instinctively allied her with
the weaker side, with " lost causes and for-
saken beliefs"; and which made her the champion
of people whom the world casts out of its
synagogue, and of enterprises which it regards
as offensive insanities. Her husband shared to
the full her zeal for social service; and, as this
zeal was allied with an absorbing interest in
religious, ethical, and psychological problems,

the result was that Broadlands became the
scene of strange gatherings. Thither came the
High Priestess of the Shakers when she was
evicted from her dwelling for refusing to pay
rates; and Pearsall Smith the American
evangelist, and Richard Booth the inventor of
the "Blue Ribbon," and Lord Shaftesbury,
and Archbishop Benson, and Burne-Jones, and
Antoinette Sterling, and preaching negresses,
and Ritualistic curates, and vegetarians, and
clairvoyantes, and "spiritual wives"; all these
have I met in that beautiful house, amid
an unequalled environment of Italian pictures
and of gardens where the saints seemed to
walk under trees of Paradise by the crystal
river.

It is almost impossible to avoid transcen-
dentalism when one thinks of Broadlands and
the company which gathered in it. I do not
think that the host and hostess would have
harboured a vivisector, for cruelty was the one
sin with which they could make no terms. But
with this sole exception it mattered not how
low one had sunk in social disgrace, how far one
had wandered from the paths of sane thinking
and the jog-trot customs of the world; the
doors of Broadlands were always open wide,

and the wanderer passing through them found himself in a circle where natural dignity and courtly manners were mingled with an openness of mind to which no conceivable aspect of truth was unwelcome, and a largeness of heart to which no experience of humanity appealed in vain. In that atmosphere nothing that was mean or base or cruel could live. Truth and love, mercy and self-sacrifice, were the vital air. Of that strangely unworldly society—unlike anything in the whole of my social experience—Lady Mount-Temple was the soul and the sun. For twelve years she was a widow, and death came as a merciful deliverance to a soul too sensitive to know happiness in a world where others suffered. It was an event of which the general world took very slight notice; but in the hearts of those who knew her it has awakened thoughts too deep for tears. She was a woman on whom Nature had lavished gifts—beauty, grace, intellect, character, position, influence; but all these were qualified—should we not rather say enhanced?—by a sympathy with suffering so keen that she could never be happy in a world where others were miserable. To her all the cruelties and tyrannies that are done under the sun, all the pangs and tears of a groaning and travailing creation, were

> Desperate tides of the whole great world's anguish,
> Forced through the channels of a single heart,

and the problem of pain was one of the unsearchable mysteries of God.   To know the truth about Him, and to lessen the load of earthly suffering, were the two objects to which her long life was unbrokenly devoted.

CHAPTER XVIII

A GROUP OF POETS

THE centre of the group must, of course, be Tennyson. It is true that, when the Seventies began, some rivals had sprung up to dispute the universal sway which he exercised in the Sixties; but, for all that, he was still the most commanding figure in English poetry. He was seldom to be encountered in society, but spent his time between his two beautiful homes in Sussex and the Isle of Wight. Is there in the English language a more exquisite fragment of landscape-painting than his description of the view from Aldworth?—

> You came, and looked, and loved the view,
>   Long known and loved by me—
> Green Sussex fading into blue,
>   With one grey glimpse of sea.

Now and then one caught sight of him in London, and he certainly looked the poet to perfection. His long dark hair, mingled with the untrimmed luxuriance of beard, whiskers, and moustache, his soft hat of Spanish mould, his loose cloak and his clay pipe, all combined to give the world assurance of a "Bard": for so 'twas the mode in Tennysonian circles to style him. His manner was abrupt, his voice gruff, his vocabulary borrowed from the eighteenth century, and his whole demeanour that of a man who expected, and was accustomed, to be worshipped. Once a lady, who profoundly admired his genius, ventured to remonstrate with him on what she thought his undue eagerness for a peerage. He replied in a document called *My Wrath*. The entreaties of his friends prevented him from despatching it; but he kept it handy in a drawer, and, if a visitor chanced to mention the lady's name, he would rejoin: "Oh, do you know that woman? then you shall hear what I think of her," and would read the document, "mouthing out his hollow oes and aes," with much "deep-chested music," while his hearers listened and trembled. Some similar ebullitions, reported to me by disciples who sate at his feet, warned me that, though Tennyson was one of the chief divinities of my poetical heaven, my safest course was to worship him at a distance.

LORD TENNYSON.

To face p. 286.

For the second figure in the group it is obvious
to recall Robert Browning. "Meredith," said
Oscar Wilde, "is a prose Browning—and so
is Browning." For my own part, I should
rather put it that Browning was the poet of
unpoetical people. Conscientious souls, who
felt that they ought to like poetry and did not,
found relief in Browning. This, their friends
told them, was poetry. It was really prose,
broken up into lines of irregular length; and as
it was very ugly, and very unmusical and quite
unintelligible, it suited them a great deal better
than Keats or Shelley, Milton or Shakespeare.
Especially did such clergymen as ensue culture
love their Browning. Like Mr. Thomas Bowdler,
of Expurgative memory, they thought Shakespeare a little coarse. They suspected Milton
of Socinianism, and Wordsworth of Pantheism;
while Tennyson's championship of "honest
doubt" as against "half the creeds" jarred
their professional susceptibilities. But they got
Browning from the Public Library, and found
passages which seemed to be attempts to turn the
Thirty-nine Articles into very blank verse; and
then their hearts beat high with joy. Here, they
said within themselves, is poetry, and orthodoxy
too! A dozen lines of this stuff, interpolated

into the undisguised prose of the sermon, will
give it a literary flavour; and the cultivated
layman in the pew will think: "This is a
preacher worth listening to."

Socially Browning was delightful. Tennyson
was reported to have said, "Browning, you will
die of apoplexy in a stiff choker at a London
dinner-party"! and the picturesque prophecy
conveyed a truth. Browning was thoroughly
at home in society; enjoyed his dinner; shared
Tennyson's appreciation of port; was bright,
cheerful, and quite unaffected. No slouch hats
or conspirators' cloaks for Browning. He was
neat and even dapper in dress; bore himself
gaily; moved alertly; and stood on happy
terms with all the world. He might have passed
for a politician, or a financier, or a diplomatist;
or, indeed, for anything except a poet. In conversation he was sprightly, energetic, and entertaining—never the least rapt or mystical. One
story about him, which I have told elsewhere,
I cannot forbear to repeat. He sometimes
honoured me with his company at dinner, and
once I had collected a group of eager disciples
to meet him. As soon as dinner was over one
of these enthusiasts led the great man into a
corner, and began cross-examining him about such

ROBERT BROWNING.

To face p. 288.

topics as the identity of *The Lost Leader* and
the meaning of the one hundred and fifth line
of a *Death in the Desert*. Browning, who had
never meant the Lost Leader for any one in
particular, and had forgotten all about Theotypas,
was bored to the last extremity, but, for a
space, endured the catechism with admirable
fortitude; then, patience being exhausted, he
laid his hand on the questioner's shoulder, saying, "But, my dear fellow, this is too bad. *I*
am monopolizing *you*," and skipped out of
the corner.

To the same period belongs another memory
which has always gratified me. *Robert
Elsmere* was published in 1888, and as we had
been told in the Puffs Preliminary that it
was going to overthrow the tottering fabric of
traditional Christianity, every one was very
eager, if not to read it, at least to talk about
it.[1] "Have you read *Robert Elsmere*, Mr.
Browning?" asked an eager admirer. "No, I
haven't, and what's more I don't mean to!
I like religion to be treated seriously; and

[1] "I found Lady Charles Beresford enthralled by *Robert
Elsmere*. . . . Goschen had read only one volume yet. The
rest at Wilton had not begun it, but were all meaning to
read it" (Matthew Arnold, April 10, 1888).

I don't want to hear what *this* curate thought about it, or what *that* curate thought about it. *No, I don't.*" Surely the secret thoughts of many hearts found utterance in that emphatic cry.

I know a minor poet who vehemently resents the appellation. "A poet," he says, "is a poet, and these distinctions are offensive"; and he refuses to be comforted by the parallel cases of the Major and Minor Prophets. I therefore shrink from calling the second Lord Lytton ("Owen Meredith"), a minor poet, and prefer to state the case by saying that he was so many other things—diplomatist, viceroy, politician, romancist, country gentleman, and member of society—that the poetical aspect of his genius was sometimes obscured.

That the man who wrote "Last words of a sensitive second-rate poet" was himself a poet, whether major or minor, seems to me indisputable; but "Marah" has always left on my mind the impression that Lord Lytton's was one of those cases in which, to use Swift's phrase, the life is "*blasted* with poetic fire"—not warmed or cheered.

Though the greater part of his time was spent

LORD LYTTON.

To face p. 290.

abroad, he was often to be met in the society
of London, where he was always a brilliant
and a conspicuous personage. He was short,
with a slight, graceful, and pliant figure, and
though, as far as I know, he had not a drop
of foreign blood in his veins, he looked thoroughly
un-English. He had an aquiline nose, a dark
complexion, and abundance of dark hair and beard,
with full, deep-set, blue eyes. He was always
rather elaborately dressed, with stars and ribbons
in the evening, and fur coats in the daytime,
and apparently paid much attention to the processes of the toilet.

He was a professed admirer of beauty, and
displayed his admiration more openly than is
common in our frigid and conventional society.
But he admired other things besides beauty.
Cleverness, originality, aloofness from the
common throng, always seemed to attract him;
and he had acquired in foreign experience that
truly un-English habit of mind which prompts
the question, "What has he done?" rather than
"What has he got?"

In conversation he always struck me as actuated
by a vivid curiosity. As he lived so much out
of England, every visit which he paid to London
seemed to interest and even excite him. He

had begun life early (for he was an Attaché at Washington when he was eighteen), and had seen it in great variety, and in some of its most gorgeous aspects—did he not preside over the great Durbar of 1877, when Queen Victoria was proclaimed Empress of India? But he never appeared satiated or wearied or bored. Every new face he saw attracted his notice and prompted his brisk questionings. Though he was expert in gastronomy, had glorified dinner in oft-quoted verse,[1] and had coined a famous epigram about the comparative merits of hunger and greediness, he would ignore the most savoury messes if he caught sight of an unknown figure among his fellow-guests. "Who's that opposite? Taper? Oh, the new Under-Secretary? I wanted to see him—I've heard a good deal about him. That's a clever-looking fellow at the end of the table. St. Barbe, is it? How good that last book of his is! What has become of Matthew Arnold's friend Adolescens Leo, whom I met here two years ago? I never saw a fellow get through so much

---

[1] You can live without love—
    What is passion but pining?
  But where is the man that
    Can live without dining?

champagne in a short time; but certainly there was some excuse for him in this house. Our host's Perrier Jouet is irresistible." And so he would run on, till he knew the name and achievements of every one at table, had speculated on the future of newcomers, and had recalled the upward or downward career of old acquaintances. Of course it often chanced that he found himself in the society of a friend from whom he had been separated for years, and then the rencounter was always interesting; for he was instantly back among the scenes and associations which he had once enjoyed, and his "picturesque sensibility" and vividness of speech made them real to the younger generation. If it were not for my rule of using only English words, I should say that "élan" was his distinguishing characteristic; and, in social intercourse, one never could discern a trace of the bitterness, the disillusionment, the jaded epicureanism, which pervaded his poetry. Indeed, the Man and the Poet seemed to be two different people.

My fourth poet is Matthew Arnold, of whom I have often said that, if one could fashion oneself, he is the person whom I should most wish to resemble. He was indeed the most delightful of companions; a man of the world entirely free from worldliness, and a man of letters without the faintest trace of pedantry. What was he like outwardly? There can be no disloyalty to his dear memory in quoting a description which he enjoyed so much that he printed it in the last paper which he ever wrote—his account of his lecturing tour in America.

"I proceeded to Chicago. An evening paper was given me soon after I arrived; I opened it, and found the following picture of myself: 'He has harsh features, supercilious manners, parts his hair down the middle, wears a single eye-glass and ill-fitting clothes.'"

"Harsh" is not the word which I should have applied to Arnold's features, although they were strongly marked. His nose was long and his mouth wide, but both were well shaped and were exaggerated rather than harsh. Dizzy said of John Wilson Croker that "baldness perhaps contributed to the spiritual expression of a brow which was, however, essentially intellectual." Arnold's brow, both high and wide, owed nothing of its character to baldness, for his hair, to the very end, was thick, glossy, and black as a raven's wing. When American scribe said

MATTHEW ARNOLD.

To face p. 294.

that Arnold's manner was "supercilious," he went astray; but if for "manner" he had said "aspect," he would have been nearer the mark. In the strict sense of the word, as given in another chapter,[1] Arnold's aspect was supercilious, because his black eyebrows arched themselves in the sort of curve with which one regards some surprising object; while the corners of his mouth turned down with that other curve which implies disapproval. In fact his face was exactly that of a critic; regarding all phenomena with his interest, but finding in them not much to praise.

He was tall and strongly built, with a body well framed for exercise, and a natural dignity of bearing. That he looked remarkably unlike one's notion of a poet was due to the fact that, as the American observed, he parted his hair down the middle, which in those days was thought the sign of a fop, and that he cultivated large, black, mutton-chop whiskers, which of all hirsute adornments are the least romantic-looking.

If Arnold entered a company in which he was not known, the first impression would be that the newcomer was a man of high distinc-

[1] See p. 355.

tion, though in what direction it might have been hard to guess; the second, that he was conscious of his eminence. In half an hour's time the first impression would have been intensified, but the second would have been dissipated by the charm of his address, his fun, his affectionateness, and his eager interest in his friends' concerns.

A well-arranged dinner, great or small, is a conspiracy to promote enjoyment and goodwill; and in such an enterprise Arnold was an invaluable ally. He enjoyed both his food and his wine, but was as happy with roast mutton and light claret as with quails and Roman punch. He entered with perfect ease and naturalness into the habits and interests of his fellow-guests; and, even if absurdity or ignorance chose to air itself, his amenity always made the best of a situation. Can I ever forget an evening when he was dining with me, Mr. George Buckle and Mr. Herbert Paul being of the company, and George Augustus Sala announced, for Arnold's gratification, that he had just been reading the *Georgics*. "They've given me," he said, "quite a new idea of Virgil. I take it that he was a rough kind of farmer-fellow, with leather leggings and a billhook. Wasn't that about it, Mr. Arnold?" Arnold "hesitated" dissent from this startling view with a delicacy which was all his own. "Well, my dear Mr. Sala, somehow I did not think Virgil was quite like that. But your view of him is very interesting."

These personal sketches are not intended to convey, except quite incidentally, my judgment on the work of the poets whom I have described. But I cannot finish my sketch of this loved and honoured friend without saying that, though the world paid more heed to some of his contemporaries, he alone was of the house and lineage of Wordsworth.

CHAPTER XIX

SOME MEDICINE-MEN

FOR my sins, I suppose—to my advantage, I am sure—I have had a vast experience of doctors; and it seems to me that the doctors of the present day scarcely fill the conspicuous place in the public eye which was filled by the "Medicine-men" of my youth.

In those days people ranged themselves under the names of their respective doctors, with a strenuous exclusiveness which recalled the rivalries of apostolic days. *I am of Gull, and I of Jenner, and I of Clark,* were the cries of the contending parties; and the adherents of each were not content with extolling their own oracle, but were contemptuous or even angry with those who professed a different faith. "It really makes me quite unhappy to think of poor old Lady Twitterton being in the hands of such a charlatan as X." "How the Duke of

Omnium can endure Y.'s vulgarity is more than
I can understand." " Z. calls himself a doctor,
but he really is a preacher, and a very dull
preacher too."

In this group of portraits I must assign the
first place to Sir William Jenner (1815–98), if
only because for five-and-thirty years he was
the trusted friend and adviser of Queen Victoria.
He had early devoted himself to the study of
fever, and was the first man in England, though
not in Europe, to diagnose the difference
between typhus and typhoid. In February
1861 he was appointed Physician Extraordinary
to the Queen, and in the following December
he attended, together with some more antique
practitioners, the death-bed of the Prince
Consort. The Prince died of a fever vaguely
described as " gastric ": and there were those
who thought that, if he had been from first to
last under Jenner's exclusive control, the fatal
issue might have been averted. As it was, Jenner's
ability, carefulness, and force of character profoundly impressed the Queen, and in January
1862 he was gazetted Physician in Ordinary.
This appointment of course made his future;
and from thenceforward he exercised an authority,

alike over doctors and over patients, which was possessed by none of his contemporaries. Something of this authority was due, I think, to his appearance, which was eminently calculated to overawe the timid. He was very far from beautiful. His eyes was heavily lidded, and he looked at one, so to say, through a slit. In middle life he developed a moustache, which, in those days, was considered a highly irregular adornment for a doctor (and was commonly attributed to a Royal hint). It detracted from his professional aspect, and made him look something like one of those ruthless old Prussian generals with whom we have lately been made familiar in the illustrated papers. His authority was enhanced by his manner, which was rough ; and his voice, which was gruff. He cultivated the bearing of the "man who will stand no nonsense" ; and appeared to fashion himself on the traditions of Abernethy, who bullied his patients as freely as he physicked them. Jenner was said by his admirers to carry the kindest of hearts under the most rugged of exteriors ; but to those who came only into contact with the exterior he was distinctly alarming. The antithesis between him and his most eminent rival was stated, I know not with what

SIR WILLIAM JENNER.

To face p. 300.

justice, thus: "Jenner says that it is a very serious case, and frightens every one to death; but the patient recovers. Gull says that there is nothing to be anxious about, and the patient dies next day."

Sir William Gull (1816–90) was decidedly more popular than Jenner, though he had little more in the way of personal beauty to recommend him, being heavy-looking, unkempt, and farmer-like. Jenner was pre-eminently the doctor of serious people, from the Queen downwards: Gull's followers were of a livelier and more mundane type. Fashionable ladies, for whom Jenner was a good deal too rough, thought Gull quite charming. One of these I remember saying, "Instead of disgusting medicines, he orders me strawberries and cream." He also was very popular with City men, stock-brokers, financiers, and the like; for whom he prescribed much in the fashion of Dr. Jobling, sometime Medical Officer to the Anglo-Bengalee Disinterested Loan and Life Insurance Company: "How are you? A little worn with business, eh? If so, rest. A little feverish from wine, humph? If so, water. Nothing at all the matter, and quite comfortable? Then take some lunch. A very wholesome thing at this time of day to strengthen the gastric juices with lunch."

But Gull's chief hold upon society resulted from the fact that he was Physician in Ordinary to the Prince of Wales. Courtiers, not least the courtiers of an heir apparent, very readily take their cue from the potentate whom they surround, and the circle which had its centre at Marlborough House made it a point of allegiance to consult Gull whenever they had a headache.

At the close of 1871 Gull's popularity reached high-water mark. On the 22nd of November it was known that the Prince of Wales was suffering from typhoid fever, and the course of the illness was watched by the nation with ever-increasing concern till the 14th of December, when an improvement was announced. All through those anxious weeks, Gull's name was four times a day in the public eye, for four bulletins were issued daily; and, as hope began to return, the man in the street heaved a sigh of relief, and said, "This is Gull's doing." But, as regards medical personalities, the case was complicated, for Queen Victoria had insisted that Jenner should be summoned to reinforce Gull, and the rival schools of Jennerites and Gullites waxed warm in dispute. "If Jenner

had been called in at first, all this anxiety would
have been avoided." "If Gull had been allowed
a free hand without Jenner's interference, the
Prince would have recovered weeks ago." Such
were the asseverations of the two parties, but
both were nonsense. Typhoid will run its
course in spite of all the doctors in Harley
Street; and it is probable that the Prince's life
was saved by the immense improvement in nursing which even then had been effected. Exactly
ten years before, the Prince Consort had died
of exactly the same illness. "Ah," said the
Queen to Sir Theodore Martin, "had *my* Prince
had the same treatment as the Prince of Wales,
he might not have died." But "treatment"
in such a context means nursing rather than
physicking.

On the happy conclusion of the illness,
honours were divided. Gull was made a baronet,
and Jenner, already a baronet, received the
K.C.B. Neither could be said to have laboured
in vain, for Gull left £344,000, and Jenner
£385,000.

Junior to these great men, but in his own
sphere not less influential, was Sir Andrew
Clark (1826–93). Clark was a Scotsman, in the

fullest sense of the term; and knew the value, as well as the interest, of theology and metaphysics. As Physician at the London Hospital, he made acquaintance with Mrs. Gladstone, who was working at the East End during the outbreak of cholera in 1866. Through her he came to know her eminent husband; and, in the great days of Gladstonian ascendency, to have written a book which Gladstone admired, or imported a wine which Gladstone liked, or prescribed a medicine which did Gladstone good, was a stepping-stone to fame and fortune. Clark knew his patient through and through; and played on his idiosyncrasies with admirable skill. When Gladstone, having drunk champagne at dinner, crowned the banquet with port, a less eupeptic friend suggested doubts about the wisdom of mixing wines, but the defence was at hand: "Clark assures me that, if I allow ten minutes to elapse between the two kinds of wine, there is no mixture." The great man's theological palate was similarly gratified. Once he said to me, "Have you ever heard Clark talk about the relation between natural and revealed religion?" Yes, I had; and I confess that the discourse seemed less impressive on the second or third, than on the first, hearing,

But Clark had another patient who, I suspect, was even more profitable than Gladstone, and this was G. H. Wilkinson, Vicar of St. Peter's, Eaton Square, and eventually Bishop of St. Andrews. Wilkinson had learned by his own experience that religion and health are closely connected. He knew that spiritual depression is often due to bad digestion or agitated nerves, and he knew also that religious work, if it is to be efficiently performed, requires habitual obedience to the laws of healthy living. As Vicar of St. Peter's, Eaton Square, a pioneer of religious revival, and a spiritual guide, he lived a life which made peculiar demands upon nervous energy; and, through Clark's help, he lived it for fourteen years without a breakdown. In matters of exercise and sleep, eating and drinking, arrangement of hours, amount of holiday, and every other detail of a busy man's existence, he followed Clark's rules; and, profiting by them himself, he advised his followers to consult the same oracle. If one of his curates complained of that highly theological disease *accidie*, he was sent to Clark for a tonic. If a district-visitor was tempted to despair, she was advised to consult Clark about her liver. The same spirit, at once devout and sensible, animated

20

both the confessional and the consulting-room,
and its effects, though always salutary, used
sometimes to make scoffers smile. "I can recommend that claret—it is what the Vicar drinks;
Andrew Clark told him that really good claret is
the best wine to work on." "My daughter is
paying some visits in Northamptonshire. She had
rather overdone herself this Lent, and the Vicar
said that nothing would set her up again so well
as a week's spring hunting with the Woodland
Pytchley—and Clark quite agreed."

I spoke just now of the confessional and consulting-room, but really it was a false antithesis;
for Clark's consulting-room was quite as much
a confessional as Wilkinson's study. It was so
arranged as to have a rather ecclesiastical appearance; and, whereas most of the great doctors
sought to impress their patients by signed
portraits of the Royal Family, Clark relied on a
huge triptych published by the Arundel Society.
He was rather a good-looking man, with a fine
brow, bright eyes, grey hair and beard, and he
had successfully cultivated a semi-clerical
manner. Seated with his back to the window,
he let the light fall on his patient's face; heard
the confession, and put appropriate questions.
" You complain of dyspepsia—what do you eat

for breakfast?" "Oh, the same as other people
—fish and eggs." "*I hope not.* Your breakfast must be, not fish and eggs, but *some* fish,
or, not *and*, *an egg*—not eggs."

As every doctor who aims at social fame must
have a "note" or token to distinguish him
from his brethren, Clark enforced abstinence
from soup at dinner; and, looking round a
London dinner-table, you would detect Clark's
influence in the number of diners who waved
away the "consommé" and shuddered at
"bisque." He assumed his most impressive
air, when, having enjoined a rule of diet, he
dismissed the awe-stricken patient with the
Scripture-like formula, "I seek to impose a yoke
upon you that you may be truly free." Really
St. Paul himself never framed a better sentence.

Turning from Medicine to Surgery, we at once
encounter the stately figure of Sir James Paget
(1814–99). He was tall and spare, with a
manner at once dignified and courteous. There
is no need to describe his face, for (like Mr.
Bardell), "some time before his death, he had
stamped his likeness upon a little boy." Nay,
on four little boys, who all rose to some eminence
in the world, and all bore a striking resem-

blance to their distinguished father. Whoever
has seen the present (1916) Bishop of Stepney,
or the late Bishop of Oxford, has seen Sir
James Paget.

Of Paget's proficiency in his profession I am
not competent to speak. It is enough to say
that his grave aspect and attentive way of listening inspired that strong feeling of confidence
which helps alike the patient and the practitioner. There is less room for humbug in
surgery than in medicine, as no Pauline formula
will mend a broken leg.

But in one particular, quite outside his
profession, Paget excelled. He was one of the
best speakers in England. Not an orator,
for I believe that his speeches were written
and committed to memory; but they were
delivered faultlessly, without note or hesitation
or verbal slip; and their effect was enormously enhanced by his dignified bearing and
carefully measured utterance. The *Spectator*,
under the editorship of Hutton and Town-
send, long ago acquired among its attached
readers the nickname of the *Grandmother*;
and in nothing was it more grandmotherly
than in its love of doctors and doctor-
ing. One of its prime favourites was Paget,

SIR JAMES PAGET.

To face p. 308.

and, though it had the anile quality of over-emphasis, yet I remember no emotion of dissent when it attributed to an after-dinner speech of Paget's, "Baconian strength and insight."

Sir John Russell Reynolds (1828–96) was pre-eminently "a physician of the old school." This by no means conveys that he was medically out of date, for he was a pioneer of neurology, and, till his pupil, Sir William Gowers, arose, its most authoritative exponent. But he was "of the old school" in his courtly manner, his wide culture, and his tendency to quote. His grandfather had attended George III, and the fact that he did not attend Queen Victoria was attributed to professional jealousy in some of those who had the Royal ear.

Wilson Fox (1831–87) died all too young for the public recognition that was his undoubted due; but not too young to have won the lively affection of his patients, who mourned for him as for a brother. Since the days of St. Luke, no one ever better deserved the title of "The Beloved Physician."

Sir Henry Thompson (1820–1904) was a specialist, whose name first became widely known in connexion with the last illness of Napoleon III. Apart from his surgical skill, he acquired a social fame as a teacher and practitioner of dietetic reform. In several brightly written and readable treatises he laid down the doctrine that a great deal of ill-health is directly attributable to our national habit of devouring what Harold Skimpole called "legs of sheep and oxen." He urged the wholesomeness and nutritious properties of a diet partly French and partly Italian, and what he taught he illustrated in a systematic hospitality. "Thompson's Octaves" were dinners of eight—eight guests and eight dishes—I am not sure whether eight kinds of wine were added; but I know that his guests came away with a diminished faith in the Roast Beef of Old England, and a conviction that the Church's rule of abstinence, if scientifically managed, was probably not such a bad thing after all.

One word should be added about Homœopathy, though even in the Seventies it was an expiring heresy. People who had never been ill in their lives professed themselves homœopathists; but the moment they were alarmed sent surrep-

titiously for the allopathist, who prescribed what
the æsthetes called "two nocturnes in blue and
an arrangement in black," and so vindicated
the claims of orthodoxy. On the borderland of
homœopathy and orthodoxy, with one foot in
each world, dwelt, and I believe still dwells,
Dr. Joseph Kidd, and what Clark was to High
Church people, that was Kidd to Plymouth
Brethren—physician and minister in one, "guide,
philosopher, and friend."

But Kidd had at any rate one eminent patient,
who knew nothing of "Bethesda" or "The
Priory." [1] Lord Beaconsfield, in his late years,
suffered grievously from a gouty kind of asthma.
The orthodox faculty having prescribed in vain,
Dr. Kidd became his physician in 1877; and, by
reversing all the treatment previously pursued,
gave his patient certainly an easier, and probably
a longer, life than he would have otherwise
enjoyed. The proceedings at the Berlin Congress of 1878 were interrupted by Lord Beaconsfield's untimely illness. Dr. Kidd was summoned
to Berlin, and the plague was stayed. In the
following year, Lord Beaconsfield said to his
friend Bernal-Osborne, "I owe the health and
comfort of my life, and my fitness for work, to

[1] Two centres of contrariant Plymouthism,

his care." On April 19, 1881, the great man died, with his hand in Dr. Kidd's; and Dr. Kidd wrote an interesting account of his patient's long struggle with death in the *Nineteenth Century* for July 1889.

CHAPTER XX

THREE CARDINALS

CARDINAL HOWARD

IT is seldom that the Sacred College numbers at the same time three Englishmen; but this was the case at the close of the Seventies. The three English Cardinals formed an interesting group; but they were men of very different degrees of importance; and I will describe the least important first.

Edward Henry Howard (1829–92) was a cousin of the twelfth Duke of Norfolk, and obtained his commission in the 2nd Life Guards in 1850. As the most striking figure in the Household Cavalry, he was chosen to lead the Duke of Wellington's funeral procession in November 1852. For three years he was one of the most brilliant and popular members of the gay world, at a period when Society was still aristocratic, and unvulgarized either by shekels or by dollars.

But a change was at work in the young Life-guardsman, of which not his closest friends had a suspicion. "To his young soul diviner promptings came," and he responded to them with startling suddenness. In November 1853 it happened that he was engaged to dine with his cousin, Mrs. Hoare (mother of the late Sir Henry Hoare), at her house in St. James's Square. On the morning of the dinner a note arrived from him saying that he was unable to fulfil his engagement, as he was forced to leave London. Mrs. Hoare supposed that the regiment had been suddenly ordered to Windsor, and thought no more of the matter till a letter arrived from Rome saying that Edward Howard had realized his vocation to the priesthood, and was studying Theology at the Accademia Ecclesiastica.[1] His progress in his new career was rapid. Having only received Minor Orders and the Diaconate, he was ordained priest in 1854, and was made a Domestic Chamberlain to Pius IX three years later.

In those days, when the Temporal Power

[1] Where, curiously enough, he had Henry Edward Manning, born in 1808, for a fellow-student.

CARDINAL HOWARD.

To face p. 314.

was still unabolished, the official service of the
Papacy offered many opportunities to a young,
eager, and well-connected ecclesiastic. Edward
Howard, who, though extremely bright and
popular, had never been suspected of cleverness,
was found to have a special gift for acquiring
languages, and therefore chose a Diplomatic
career. After serving in various posts he was
sent, in 1862, to India to arrange the pending
difficulties between England and Portugal, in
regard to the ecclesiastical government of the
Province of Goa. In this task he acquitted
himself so well that he was created a Prelate,
and was made Archbishop of Neo-Cæsarea in
1872. In 1877 he was raised to the Purple,
which Manning had attained in 1875. Newman's
belated elevation came in 1879, and so the trio
of English Cardinals was complete.

Having retired from the Diplomatic Service,
Cardinal Howard resided principally in Rome;
but he paid frequent visits to England, making
his headquarters, as was natural, at Arundel,
and often appearing in general society. Wherever
he went he was a striking and impressive figure.
His smooth and inexpressive, almost childlike,
face, with its innocent blue eyes, reminded one
of Lord Rosebery, but the resemblance ended

with the face. Cardinal Howard was tall—well over six feet, I should think—with a singularly dignified appearance and a soldier-like air. To the end he walked like a dismounted cavalryman, and, as he swept along the nave of St. Peter's in his crimson soutane, he might have passed for one of those cloaked troopers of the Life Guards who adorn the streets near Knightsbridge Barracks on a winter evening.

In society, Howard was perfectly easy, genial and unaffected; and though he was rightly conscious of his official dignity, he was far too great a gentleman to give himself any airs or graces; and his conversation, though perfectly decorous, was quite unecclesiastical. His closing years were spent in England, where he died after a long and distressing illness, tended to the last by the affectionate devotion of his kinsman and fellow-Catholic, the present Duke of Norfolk. He rests in the Fitzalan Chapel at Arundel.

CARDINAL NEWMAN

JOHN HENRY NEWMAN (1801–90) joined the Church of Rome in 1845, and from that time forward lived a life so completely secluded that

CARDINAL NEWMAN.

To face p. 316.

the world outside the Oratory had few opportunities of knowing him by sight. I have traced in
another book [1] the history of his life in the Roman
Communion, and it is a sorry story of ungrateful
handling, frustration, and defeat inflicted by the
Roman authorities on the most valuable recruit
whom they had ever won from the Church of
England. If Newman had been less of a Christian he might well have adopted Mirabeau's
motto, "Kill your conscience, for it is the most
savage enemy of every one who wants success."
His supreme disappointment was the dogma of
Papal Infallibility, defined by the Vatican Council
of 1869–70. To use his own phrase, he "bowed
his head" beneath this final blow, and for the next
nine years he remained buried in his Oratorian
home, emerging only to cross swords with Gladstone over the question of the civil allegiance of
Roman Catholics. During this period of what
looked like final retirement he wrote a solemn
testament for the use of his friends after his
death, and from it I quote these words: "I have
before now said, in writing to Cardinals . . .
when I considered myself treated with slight and
unfairness, 'So this is the return made to me for
working in the Catholic cause for so many years,'

[1] *Literary Essays.*

i.e. to that effect. I feel it still, and ever shall ; but it was not a disappointed ambition which I was then expressing, but a scorn and wonder at the injustice shown me, and at the demand of toadyism on my part if I was to get their favour and the favour of Rome."

Those words, and others revealing " the real state of my mind, and what my cross has been," were written in 1876 ; but now a startling change was at hand. Pius IX died in 1878, and Leo XIII succeeded him. Newman had loved Pius personally, but had notoriously dissented from some parts of his policy, and had suffered for his dissent. The sentiments of Leo were believed to differ materially from those of his predecessor; and " the natural reaction of opinion —the swing of the pendulum from one Pontificate to another—seemed to some of Newman's friends a golden opportunity for securing for his great work for the Church the formal approval from Rome itself which had been so long delayed."

So says Mr. Ward, and the Duke of Norfolk adds : " It appeared to me that in the cause both of justice and of truth it was of the utmost importance that the Church should put her seal on Newman's work." That "seal" could only

take one form—the Cardinal's hat. The Duke
of Norfolk, in a private interview with the Pope,
made the suggestion; and it was graciously
received. After various delays, some of which
bore a suspicious resemblance to former frustra-
tions, Newman received the supreme honour in
May, 1879. To the journal of 1876, from which
the foregoing confession of disappointment is
cited, he now appended this significant note :
"Since writing the above I have been made a
Cardinal!"[1]

The world of London now had an opportunity
of seeing Newman in the flesh ; and for those who
remembered, or were interested in, the Oxford
Movement of 1833–45, this was a thrilling experience. In May 1880 the newly made Cardinal paid
a visit to the Duke of Norfolk at his house in St.
James's Square, and the Duchess gave an evening party in his honour. On the 15th of May
Matthew Arnold described this party in a letter
to his sister :—

"I met A. P. S.[2] at dinner at the Buxtons'
before I went, who was deeply interested and
excited at my having the invitation to meet the

[1] For Cardinal Manning's share in the transaction, see Mr.
Wilfrid Ward's *Life of Newman*, vol. ii. ch. xxxiii.
[2] Dean Stanley.

Cardinal; he hurried me off the moment dinner
was over, saying, 'This is not a thing to lose.'
Newman was in costume—not full Cardinal's costume, but a sort of vest with gold about it—and
the red cap; he was in state at the end of the
room, with the Duchess of Norfolk on one side of
him and a chaplain on the other, and people filed
before him as before the Queen, dropping on their
knees when they were presented and kissing his
hand. It was the faithful who knelt in general,
but it was in general only the faithful who were
presented. That old mountebank Lord H——
dropped on his knees, however, and mumbled
the Cardinal's hand like a piece of cake. I only
made a deferential bow, and Newman took my
hand in both of his and was charming. He said,
'I ventured to tell the Duchess I should like to
see you.' One had to move on directly, for there
was a crowd of devotees waiting, and he retires at
eleven."

The privilege of seeing Newman, which was
so sparingly permitted to Londoners, was easily
attained by people, whether dons or undergraduates, who lived in Oxford. It is a very
short journey from Oxford to Birmingham, and
Newman was easily accessible to all whose motives
in seeking an interview he thought sincere. Many,

of course, there were, who, fascinated by the
apparent candour of his reasoning, wished to converse with him on religious subjects, and, more
particularly, to consult him on the exclusive claim
of Rome. This was all honest and gentlemanlike ;
but there were a good many who were quite undis-
turbed by religious qualms, and who merely wished
to see Newman as a man who had played a leading part in an important controversy, or as the
greatest living master of the English language. I
am afraid that these enquirers were apt to invent
scruples which they did not the least feel, and to
seek an audience on false pretences; for it was
known that Newman would not have allowed
himself to be treated as a show, and would have
repressed all gossip and idle curiosity. But,
whether the motive of the visit was conscientious
or fraudulent, men always came back to Oxford
with the same account. They had found Newman
most gracious, kind, and sympathetic ; gentle
towards doubts, encouraging towards aspirations,
and patient with difficulties ; moderate, cautious,
yet clear in counsel. His personal charm consisted in a supreme degree of delicacy. He did
not look like a ghost, for every glance and every
gesture showed that he was very much alive ; but
he seemed to have attained the most absolute

refinement of face, feature, and voice, which is compatible with a corporeal frame. "To look at or to listen to," said one of these admirers, "he is like the most delicious old lady." But assuredly there was nothing effeminate in the spirit which for thirty-five years had braved the wrath of the Curia, and by a master-stroke of righteous indignation had crushed the insolent and clumsy calumnies of Charles Kingsley.

It once happened, before he was raised to the Cardinalate, that Newman, who seldom went much beyond Edgbaston, found himself in one of the slums of Birmingham. The gutter-children, seeing something unfamiliar in his garb and appearance, pursued him with yells and mud. When he regained the Oratory the devoted brethren thronged round him, with loud protestations against the profanity of the children who had ventured to throw mud at the dear Father Superior. But the protestations were checked by Newman, who said, with his peculiar blend of playfulness and pensiveness, "If I thought a Catholic priest was what they think he is, I should throw mud at myself."

CARDINAL MANNING

WHEN John Henry Newman was seven years
old, there occurred an event of which he could
have no cognizance, but which was destined, in
the long run, to exercise a decisive influence over
his working life. This was the birth of Henry
Edward Manning (1808–92).

In 1808 the Mannings were wealthy people,
though afterwards they lost their fortune ; and
" Harry Manning " (as his old friends called him
to the end) began life with some signal advantages. He was educated at Harrow (where he
was Captain of the Cricket Eleven), and at
Balliol; and, though not a particularly accurate
scholar, his general cleverness and resolute will
got him a First Class in Classics, at Christmas
1830. According to the testimony of his contemporaries, Gladstone among others, he was
exceptionally good-looking, beautifully dressed,
full of self-confidence, and loving to have the
pre-eminence. His father had destined him for
Holy Orders, but his own inclinations turned in
a different direction, and he determined to enter
Parliament. In old age he said to the present
writer, who was then in the House of Commons,
" As I go to bed, I look out and see the light

on your Clock-Tower, and I say to myself, 'If I had been able to have my own way, and to go *there*, what a rascal I should have been by this time!'"

The event which changed the current of his life was his father's bankruptcy, which occurred in 1831. Of course all parliamentary dreams were instantly dispelled, and his father could no longer even make him an allowance. He took a supernumerary clerkship in the Colonial Office; but, as this was a terminable appointment, he wisely entered for a Fellowship at Merton College, Oxford, which he won in 1832. He now returned to the abandoned project of seeking Holy Orders, and was ordained to a curacy in Sussex. He soon began to rise in his profession. At twenty-five he was a rector; at twenty-nine rural dean; at thirty-two archdeacon; at thirty-four Select Preacher at Oxford. From 1840 to 1850 he was one of the most considerable figures among the English clergy, and during the last five years of that time, after Newman had seceded, he was commonly regarded as the main strength and stay of those earnest Churchman who had been scandalized by Newman's fall and had no confidence in Pusey's leadership.

CARDINAL MANNING.

To face p. 324.

We now know, what at the time was never suspected, that during these latter years he was tormented by grave doubts about the position and claims of the Church of England. He yearned for "authority," and could not find it in Anglicanism. His misgivings came to a head when the Judicial Committee pronounced in favour of the Rev. G. C. Gorham, who seemed to have committed himself to a denial of the Catholic doctrine of Baptism. Suddenly, as it appeared to the world, but deliberately, as we know from his writings, he resigned his preferments in the Church of England, and was received into the Church of Rome in April 1851.

Three years later he wrote in his journal : "I am conscious of a desire to be in such a position as I had in time past"; and his heart's desire was not long denied him. Nothing can be more instructive than the difference between the treatment accorded to Newman and the treatment accorded to Manning by the Church to which they submitted both themselves. What Rome did for Newman the first section of this chapter has already set forth. Manning's career was strikingly dissimilar. Newman was received into the Church of Rome in October 1845, and was not ordained priest till

May 1847. Manning was received in April 1851, and was ordained priest on the Trinity Sunday next ensuing. He was made D.D. by the Pope in 1854; Superior of the Oblates of St. Charles at Bayswater in 1857, and Provost of the Chapter of Westminster in the same year; Domestic Prelate to the Pope, Protonotary Apostolic and "Monsignore" in 1860; and in 1865, in spite of the fact that he had not been elected by the Chapter, he was made Archbishop of Westminster by the sole act of Pius IX. "Searle, and a hundred other poor devils," pleasantly said Herbert Vaughan, afterwards Cardinal, "will think you are come to torment them before their time." Perhaps they did; but their thoughts could not impede Manning's progress. He was Archbishop in spite of them, and ten years later he was raised to the Purple. It is matter of common knowledge that Manning's early and conspicuous ascendency in the counsels of the Papacy rested on the intimacy of his personal relations with Pius IX; although it is not necessary to give literal credence to that account of those relations which Bishop Wilberforce in his diary repeated from my cousin Odo Russell. Manning was, indeed, a man after the Pope's own heart. There never lived

a stronger Papalist. He was more Ultramontane
than the Ultramontanes. Everything Roman
was to him divine. Rightly or wrongly, he
conceived that English Romanism was practi-
cally Gallicanism; that it minimized Papal
Infallibility, was disloyal to the Temporal Power,
and was prone to accommodate itself to its
Protestant and secular environment. Against
this temporizing policy he set his face as a flint.
He believed that he had been divinely appointed
of Papalize England. In Cardinal Wiseman he
found a chief like-minded with himself, and they
worked in perfect accordance for an end equally
dear to both. Here comes the tragedy of
Newman's life. Manning thought him a half-
hearted Papalist. He dreaded alike his way of
stating religious truth, and his practical policy;
and he regarded it as a sacred duty to frustrate
his designs.

To Newman, with his abnormal sensitiveness,
the situation must have been galling beyond
endurance. Here was Manning, seven years
his junior, in every gift of intellect immeasurably
his inferior, and a convert of five years later date
than himself; and yet Manning, through his
relation with Rome and his ascendency over
the aged and decrepit Wiseman, was in a

position where he could bring all Newman's
best-laid plans to naught. They had begun
as good friends, though never intimate; for
Manning in his Anglican days had kept clear
of Tractarianism. Newman offered Manning
the post of Vice-Rector in the Irish University,
and Manning declined it, as he was at the
moment entering on his three years' residence
at Rome. When he came to live in London,
he passed instinctively into the innermost circle
of that Ultramontane sentiment which surrounded
Wiseman, which preached by the mouth of Faber,
which intrigued at the Vatican through Monsignor
Talbot, and which wrote with the powerful pen of
W. G. Ward.

The time, as we have already seen, was full
of stress and strain; and some controversies, which
had hitherto belonged to the region of theory, were
forced into practical action by the developments
of European politics. Manning thus summed
up the points at issue : "During these years
three subjects were uppermost: (1) the Temporal Power; (2) the Oxford Question; and
(3) The Infallibility. On all these Newman was
not in accordance with the Holy See. I am
nobody, but I spoke as the Holy See speaks."
When Manning spoke he also acted, and through

his instrumentality Newman was forced to resign the editorship of the *Rambler*, which had taken a line hostile to the Temporal Power. It was easy to offend Newman, and Newman did not readily forget. It is significant that in the *Apologia*, which contains such generous references to friends, both Roman and Anglican, Manning's name never appears: and Manning actually denounced "this Kingsley affair," as he called the *Apologia*, as tending to "make Anglicans remain where they are." This was written on the eve of Manning's elevation to the Archiepiscopate, and from thenceforward his power of frustrating Newman was, of course, increased tenfold. Newman wrote this in the following year: "I think this of Manning: he wishes me no ill, but he is determined to bend or break all opposition. He has an iron will and intends to have his own way. . . . He has never offered me any place or office. The only one I am fit for, the only one I would accept, he is doing all he can to keep me from."

The other side of the case is thus stated by Manning: "I was and am convinced that no Catholic parents ought to send their sons to the national universities; and that no Catholic can be there without danger to faith and morals."

It was an unequal contest. Manning was all-powerful at the Vatican, and Newman was defeated. When the contest was over, Manning suggested an interview, and explanations; but Newman icily declined: "I do not trust him, and his words would be the cause of fresh distrust. . . . I could not in my heart accept his explanations."

Any one who wishes to know what Manning could be and do when his heart was set on a great object should study those chapters in his Life which describe the suppression of Archbishop Errington, his own elevation to the Archiepiscopate, and the Vatican Council. With reference to this last his biographer says :—

"It was the event of his life. . . . For years he had made the question of Papal Infallibility his own. He was identified, whether for good or for evil, with the mysterious dogma, by the popular mind of England. He had preached about it; had worked for it; and in tones and terms of infallible certitude had predicted its definition."

He went into the Council under a solemn vow to do all in his power to obtain the definition. He used all conceivable means to secure his end. He wrote, and talked, and plotted, and canvassed. He avoided argument and appealed to passion and terror. The Church, he said, was in her last struggle with the powers of darkness, and here was the opportunity of striking the blow which should make her victorious. His intensity, his rhetorical skill, his inexhaustible activity, inspired his friends and produced a palpable effect upon the waverers; but, all the time, there was the other side, and on it were ranged Darboy and Dupanloup, Strossmayer and Haynald, Ketteler, and Hefele, and Deschamps; "and a greater name by far than theirs was on their side and in sympathy with them—John Henry Newman."

When the battle was over, and Newman again defeated, Manning wrote, with unmistakable reference: "They were wise, and we were fools. But, strange to say, it has turned out that the wise men were always blundering and the fools were always right. At last the wise men have had to hold their tongues, and, in a way not glorious to them, to submit and to be silent."

Eight years passed. Pius IX died, and Leo XIII, acting on suggestions from England, made Newman a Cardinal, and so affixed the seal of Infallibility to principles and methods against which Manning had waged a thirty years' war.

In 1883 he said to me, pointing to two pictures on the wall : " That is Pio—history will pronounce him to have been a very great Pontiff. Yes, and that is Leo—*hum, hm, h——,*" but I find it impossible to express in letters the curious *diminuendo* of depreciatory sound.

Seven years later Newman was in his grave, and his brother Cardinal talked of him and of their mutual relations with impressive candour. One saying must be recorded. " I suppose you have heard that I tried to prevent Newman from being made a Cardinal. Yes—of course you have. Every one has. But it is not true. Indeed, it is the reverse of the truth. The Duke of Norfolk and Lord Ripon came to me and said, 'We have been to Rome. We have urged Newman's claim to the Cardinalate. We have done as much as laymen can do—and we have made no impression. We come back having accomplished nothing.' I said, 'Leave it to me.' I wrote to Rome, and it was done in three weeks. *Very few people know that.*" Very few indeed !

Why in the long duel, which I have now described, was Newman always defeated, and Manning (except in the last tussle about the Cardinalate) always successful ? Something may, no doubt, be ascribed to training and environ-ment. Manning had all the advantages of mind and body (though they may sometimes be dis-advantages for the soul) which belong to an opulent home and a great Public School. New-man was brought up in a Calvinistic seclusion, varied by eight years at a private school where he never played a game. At Oxford Manning was popular and fashionable; Newman lived, from first to last, like a Seminarist, hampered, as he himself says, by "extreme shyness" and "vivid self-consciousness." Manning went freely into Society, more than once fell in love, and married early. Newman went from his Scholar-ship at Trinity to his Fellowship at Oriel, regarded himself as divinely called to celibacy, and seems to have had no ambition beyond a curacy in a suburb of Oxford.

Temperament co-operated with environment. If one may borrow the title of a famous novel, Manning, already a man of the world, and knowing how to deal with men, may stand for "Sense": Newman, the shrinking and ascetic student, for "Sensibility." He said of himself that he had a "morbidly sensitive skin," and that is about as bad an equipment for active life in a world of struggle as nature can bestow.

That a pre-eminently sensitive man tastes more keenly than others the choice delights of life is probably true; but it is certain that he suffers a thousand miseries which tougher natures never feel. An acute sensitiveness may be allied with, though it is by no means a synonym for, keen sympathy with the sorrows of others, and so may gather round a man a band of grateful friends; but it will never disarm an opponent, or turn a foe into a friend. Still less will it enable a man to force his way through clenched antagonisms, or to crush resistance as he marches towards his end. Then again a sensitive nature is

> Wax to receive and marble to retain.

It may forgive, but it cannot forget, slights and injuries, buffets and bruises. Forgetfulness of injuries is the blessed lot of those who have inflicted them.

"Poor Newman!" said Manning to me, when talking of his deceased colleague—"my Brother of Birmingham," as he used to call him in moments of genial expansion—"he was a great hater." And though the phrase had something of controversial rancour, it expressed a kind of truth. When Newman had been injured, he did not expose himself to a repetition of the injury. When he had been deceived, he did not give the deceiver a second opportunity. When he had been offended, he kept the offender at arm's length. There are curious traditions of personal estrangements, lasting through years, between him and members of his own house; and there is on record a letter in which he told Archbishop Whately, with agreeable frankness, that, though he had not purposely kept out of his way when Whately lately was paying a visit to Oxford, he was glad of the accident which prevented them from meeting.

I question if Manning was very sensitive. No doubt he felt a knock, as we all feel it; but with him it was only a reason for hitting back again; and when he hit he showed both strength and science.

And, yet again, Newman was too much of an Idealist. He idealized the Calvinism in which he had been brought up, but soon found that it was hopelessly inadequate to the demands of intellect and the broad facts of human life; and in his reaction from it he went perilously near the ways of thought which a few years later were stigmatized as Liberalism. When he had adopted the Tractarian position, he idealized

the Anglican bishops; and the dissipation of
that ideal by contact with Episcopal realities
is the history of his submission to Rome. As
a Roman Catholic he found even larger and
more promising scope for Idealism; and the
disillusionments were profounder and more
grievous. That to the end he idealized the
Church of Rome—" the one oracle of truth and
the one ark of salvation "—I cannot doubt;
but he soon ceased to idealize Roman bishops
as he had before ceased to idealize their
Anglican brethren; and to these must be added
cardinals and Jesuits, and politicians and
editors, and, in short, all the agents by whom
the Church of Rome does its practical work.
To say that he was ever disillusioned about the
Pope would be offensive and might be mislead-
ing; so let his own words stand. "I had been
accustomed to believe that, over and above the
attribute of infallibility which attached to the
doctrinal decisions of the Holy See, a gift of
sagacity had in every age characterized its
occupants. I am obliged to say that a sentiment which history has impressed upon me,
and impresses still, has been very considerably
weakened as far as the present Pope (Pius IX)
is concerned, by the experience of the result

of the policy which his chosen councillors have led him to pursue." From first to last Newman idealized the systems to which for the time he belonged, and when in their working they proved to be quite different from what he dreamed, the blow fell with a disabling force ; and the people who wished ill to his schemes " grinned demnebly."

Among those who grinned was Manning, of whom it may, I think, be said without breach of charity, that, willing the end intensely, he also willed the means ; that he was entirely free from what Bishop Wilson called " the *offendiculum* of scrupulosity " ; and that, where a cause was at stake, he did not shrink from crushing an opponent.

I have already described Newman's personal appearance. Manning's I described, with some precision, in another book,[1] and I will not repeat what is so easily accessible. But fortunately Manning made a deep impression on one of his contemporaries, who never was excelled in a personal description—Lord Beaconsfield. What he was like in his younger days may be read in *Endymion*, but in *Lothair* we see him as he was after he had become the

[1] *Collections and Recollections.*

22

official head of the Roman Catholic Church in England. His appearance, his bearing in society, and his methods of proselytization are there drawn by the hand of a master.

"Above the middle height, his stature seemed magnified by the attenuation of his form. It seemed that the soul never had so frail and fragile a tenement. He was dressed in a dark cassock with a red border, and wore scarlet stockings; and over his cassock a purple tippet, and on his breast a small golden cross. His countenance was naturally of an extreme pallor. His cheeks were hollow, and his grey eyes seemed sunk into his clear and noble brow, but they flashed with irresistible penetration."

One slight inaccuracy I detect in this description. Manning was not "above the middle height," but rather below it. His extreme attenuation gave him the appearance of being taller than he was. The "clear and noble brow" is a true touch, and yet it elicited from an Anglican ecclesiastic a characteristic outbreak of professional jealousy. Artists, fascinated by Manning's aspect, were constantly asking him to sit for his portrait, and the portraits often found their way into the Academy. There, one day, as I was looking at a picture of the Cardinal, I chanced to find Archbishop Benson by my side. "What a fine head it is!" I exclaimed. "No," replied the rival practitioner. "Not a fine head—*only no face.*"

Cardinal Manning was fond of society, and excelled in it. He had never forgotten the associations of his Anglican days; and he repined at purely ecclesiastical surroundings. "I live," he once said rather peevishly, "among sacristans." From that meritorious but unexciting company he gladly emerged. He loved the Athenæum, frequented the Lobby of the House of Commons, and enjoyed the platforms of philanthropic and humanitarian societies. He would occasionally drop into evening parties, even in non-Catholic houses, and he sincerely deplored the delicacy of his digestion, which made it impossible for him to dine out. "'I never eat and I never drink,' said the Cardinal; 'I am sorry to say I cannot. I like dinner society very much. You see the world and you hear things which you do not hear otherwise. For a time I presumed to accept invitations, though I sate with an empty plate; but, though the world was indulgent to me, I felt that my habits were an embarrassment to the happier feasters ; it was not fair, and so I gave it up.' " [1]

It was with reference to this part of Manning's social life that the late Lord Coleridge once said to me, " There Manning used to sit, dallying with a biscuit and a glass of soda-water, till one really felt ashamed to eat or drink in the presence of this Saint—*who had dined at two.*"

[1] *Lothair,* vol. i. ch. vi.

CHAPTER XXI

THREE ARCHBISHOPS

ARCHBISHOP TAIT

A RCHIBALD CAMPBELL TAIT (1811–82) was the youngest child of Craufurd Tait by his marriage with a daughter of Sir Ilay Campbell, Lord President of the Court of Session. On both sides his descent was purely Scottish. The Taits belonged to the middle classes, but had gradually risen to the rank of lairds. The parents of the future Archbishop were strict Presbyterians; and, as the Kirk baptizes its infants in private and keeps no register of baptisms, it was suggested, in later years, that Archbishop Tait had never been baptized. As this would have been a fact of serious import to the Episcopal Succession of the Church of England, careful enquiries were set on foot, and the result, which was satisfactory to the enquirers, is, I believe, deposited among the muniments at Lambeth. Young Tait was educated at the University of Glasgow, where he won a "Snell Exhibition" which carried him to Balliol. He resolved to make his career in England, and, as he idolized the principle of religious establishment, he joined the Church of England, being confirmed by the Bishop of Oxford, and so decided his whole subsequent life. His Ordination followed as a matter of course, for, after obtaining his First Class in Classics, he was elected to a Fellowship of Balliol; and as such he was bound by law to take Holy Orders within a given time from his M.A. degree. He had not the least desire to do otherwise—indeed he felt that the clerical character would help him in his tutorial work; and, when once ordained, he became an active clergyman; but, as far as one can judge, he would have been quite as much at home at the Bar or in the Civil Service.

In 1842, on the sudden death of Dr. Arnold, he was elected to the head-mastership of Rugby, and soon afterwards married Catharine Spooner, the daughter of a neighbouring clergyman. As a head-master he was not successful. His scholar-

ARCHBISHOP TAIT.

To face p. 342.

ship was stiff and ungraceful; his preaching was dull; and, owing to the circumstances of his own education, he was entirely out of sympathy with that peculiar temper of mind which, for want of a better name, is called "The Public School spirit." His head-mastership did not last very long. In 1848 he had a desperate attack of rheumatic fever, which crippled him for life; and in the following year he thankfully escaped from the uncongenial toils of Rugby to the Deanery of Carlisle. In 1850 and 1851 he served on the Universities Commission, and was thereby brought into close relations with the Whig Government. In 1856 his home was devastated by the deaths of five little daughters, and this tragic circumstance brought his name under the sympathetic notice of Queen Victoria. Immediately afterwards, to the unbounded surprise of the Church and the world, he was nominated by Lord Palmerston to the See of London; but he really owed this remarkable elevation to Lord Shaftesbury, who "thought that the Broad Church ought to be represented, and selected Dr. Tait as the mildest among them."

In 1868 Bishop Tait was called by Disraeli (after a tussle with the Queen) to the See of

Canterbury, and so became a very conspicuous figure among the men of the Seventies. Let me attempt to describe him.

He was tall, and in later life was inclined to be portly. He bore himself with a very remarkable dignity; and, though he was the least ecclesiastically minded of men, his clean-shaven face and long hair gave him a distinctly ecclesiastical appearance. The Episkopos was declared in every attitude and gesture, and this stately demeanour was all the more effective because palpably unstudied. In private life he was a lovable man, a devoted husband, a tender father, a staunch friend. "Under that stately and reserved demeanour," said Dean Church, "there was really great warmth of heart, and great kindness. Where he loved, he loved strongly." His friend Bishop Ewing described him thus: "Exactly the same as ever, good, humorous, and Scotch, with gravity." Of course the humour was dry and "pawky"; but it was there, and sometimes you found it twinkling quaintly amid grave surroundings.

In 1877 the *Church Times*, representing an ecclesiastical party with which the Archbishop was always at loggerheads, made this remarkable statement :—

"What music is to a man with no ear, that religion is to Archbishop Tait; and it is as idle to argue with him on religious questions and on religious grounds as it would be to play a pathetic composition of Mendelssohn's to a musically deaf person in the hope of softening his temper and extracting a boon from him."

Such are the amenities of theological controversy; the truth was something quite different. We know from Tait's Life, even if we had not gathered it from personal contact, that he was a profoundly religious man; but unfortunately his religion was of a type which is neither understood nor liked in the Church over which he presided. He was not an Evangelical. He had nothing of what friends call "unction" and foes call "gush"; and he differed from the Evangelicals on such points as the doctrine of conversion, the inspiration of the Bible, and the precise method and nature of the Atonement. On these and kindred points he inclined to "liberal" views, though on the central verities of the Christian Faith he was absolutely and exactingly orthodox.

That great party which used to be called "High Church," and which, in Tait's lifetime, acquired the nickname of "Ritualistic," he never understood; he cordially disliked and consistently persecuted it. From 1841, when he drew up and signed the famous "Protest of the Four Tutors" against the teaching of "Tract 90," till 1882, when on his death-bed, he began to show signs of a better mind, he was engaged in unrelenting conflict with a religious party which sturdily withstood and ultimately overcame him.

While he persecuted Ritualists, he tolerated Evangelicals, and patronized Broad Churchmen —until they became too broad. From first to last he was a Liberal Presbyterian, whom circumstances had transplanted to the Church of England, and to the highest place in it. Sincerely religious, consistently orthodox he was, but no impartial critic could say that he was in any intelligible sense a Churchman. He was an Erastian to the backbone. After 1882 Sir William Harcourt used to say, half in jest and half in earnest, "Now that Stanley and Tait are gone, I am the last of the Erastians." Of the Church as a spiritual society, with duties, powers, and rights of its own, quite apart from anything that the State could give or take away, he had positively no conception. He considered the Episcopal office a convenient form of ecclesiastical government, and that was all. "Tait was a very considerable person; but I doubt if he ever read a theological work in his life." This was Gladstone's judgment on a man whose ecclesiastical qualifications he had abundant means of testing.

But, though Tait was essentially untheological, he had other qualities which made him "a very considerable person." Foremost among them I should place his courage. This was a most conspicuous quality, and it was of two kinds, not always found in conjunction. He was as courageous physically as morally. His physical courage was specially displayed in connexion with his health, which, for the last thirty years of his life, was in a most uncomfortable and often a most threatening state, and yet was never permitted to interfere with his work or affect his cheerfulness. After his great illness in 1848, he was permanently disqualified for any violent exercise, hurry, or exertion.[1] He was liable to sudden fits of fainting, giddiness, and internal pain. Soon

---

[1] In spite of some infirmity and much awkwardness, he persisted in riding; and his appearance on horseback was so odd that it suggested a new meaning for the phrase *Tête Monté*.

after he became Archbishop of Canterbury he
had a seizure which all but destroyed him and
which affected him to the last day of his life.
When he preached at St. Paul's, at the Thanks-
giving Service for the recovery of the Prince of
Wales, Sir William Gull, who had doctored the
Prince and the preacher, declared that Tait's
was the more wonderful recovery of the two.

One evening in 1880, after dinner at Lambeth,
conversation drifted towards the subject of
health, and its bearing on usefulness; and the
Archbishop said to me, in his quiet, impressive
manner, "When I got about again after my
illness in '48, I made up my mind that there
were certain things which I must never again
attempt—such as hurrying to catch a train,
walking up steep places, and so on. I kept
to my resolve, and in consequence I have been
able to work as hard as most men. The
heaviest work of my life has been done since
I had an incurable heart-complaint." Certainly
in this calm, patient, and resolute temper, the
Archbishop set an edifying and encouraging
example to all like sufferers.

Not less marked was his moral courage. He
was essentially and absolutely self-reliant. He
thought out his own beliefs, principles, and

rules of conduct for himself. He "conferred
not with flesh and blood." He relied very little
on authority, and was quite unaffected, in the
sphere of opinion, by the influences of private
friendship. He knew his own mind and acted
on it, without losing the good-will of friends
from whom he differed. After a deputation of
excited clergymen had come to address him on
some controversial issue, his account of the
interview was characteristically calm. "I
thanked them for their advice and promised
to act on so much of it as commended itself
to my judgment." His habitual, though not invariable, calmness of speech was allied with
great tenacity of purpose. Dr. Liddon said to
me, "His will is like a great steam-engine"; and
weak-kneed, timid, and episcopolatrous people
fell down flat under its pressure.

It was commonly said that Tait was a "great
statesman," but perhaps "a dexterous politician"
would be nearer the mark. He was capable of
taking a wider view than is common with
clergymen; he was entirely free from professional prejudices; his deference to lay opinion
erred on the side of excess; and he was keenly
alive to the greatness and importance of the
secular power, and the place which it is

appointed to fill in the providential order. Much of his most effective work was done behind the scenes and out of sight—one might almost say underground. When any legislation affecting the Church, such as the Irish Church Bill, the Public Worship Regulation Bill, or the Burials Bill, was before Parliament, the Archbishop was in a chronic state of interviewing, wire-pulling, secret correspondence, attempts to bring pressure on this public man and that, carrying messages from one great person to another, trying to extort conditions, to smooth difficulties, to arrange compromises. This manœuvring was, perhaps, carried to excess ; and, though the real strength of the Archbishop's nature, and his long intercourse with great people and great affairs, enabled him to carry on this kind of work without loss of dignity, it is a dangerous example for weaker and lesser successors to follow. " How soon pluck in some people degenerates into pertness ! " said Bishop Wilberforce of Lord John Russell. " How soon statesmanship in some people degenerates into intrigue ! " is the reflection likely to be suggested by the manœuvres of any who should endeavour to perform the delicate and peculiar negotiations in which Archbishop Tait excelled. . The courage, self-reliance, and persistence of the Archbishop's character, his skill in public affairs, and his inveterate taste for managing and arranging, were closely connected with a very marked feature of his character—his love of power. An early and faithful friend told me that his snare was ambition, and that he would have been the last to deny it. He loved power, knew himself fit to exercise it, sought it, attained it, and used it freely. When Gladstone appointed Dr. King (afterwards Bishop of Lincoln) to the chair of Pastoral Theology, Archbishop Tait, horrified at the elevation of a Ritualist, wrote a letter of urgent remonstrance. Gladstone's reply did not encourage a repetition of the attempt.

If I were asked to single out the most conspicuous service which Tait rendered to the Church of England, I should say that it consisted in his having, by the combined force of personal character and of a deliberate policy, asserted and maintained, at home and abroad, the historic grandeur and the practical importance of the See of Canterbury. " The greatest Archbishop since Laud" was the judgment of a theological opponent; and, though in theology he was more akin to Prynne than to Laud, great he certainly was in this—that he made the office which he filled and the institution over which he presided loom large in the public eye. He reminded men that the Church of England was still a force in the world, and that those who, on whatever grounds, love and serve her must be reckoned with in the deliberations of statesmen and Parliaments. Even those who most profoundly mistrusted his theology and abhorred his Erastianism recognized with pride the position which he had made for himself—for assuredly he did not inherit it from Sumner or transmit it to Benson—in the House of Lords; the anxiety on the part of the secular peers to hear his judgment, the respect with which his interventions in debate were received, and the practical effectiveness of his weighty and commanding speech. Though a dull, and a very dull, preacher, especially when "confined to the paper," he was an admirable speaker. At a conference of clergy, at a public meeting, at a City dinner, he was equally at home; but it was in the House of Lords that he was seen at his best. He "spoke as one having authority."

His last speech in the House was delivered in the Session of 1882, in reply to a proposal by the Duke of Argyll for an alteration of the Parliamentary Oath. The hand of death was already on him, and he spoke with painfully abated force. After the debate he said to his chaplain and son-in-law (now his successor), "They didn't listen to me. It is the first time for twenty years. My work is done."

ARCHBISHOP THOMSON

"Not the vulgar Thompson with a *p*," was the explanatory note of a lady who loved the Archbishop and his family. No—not the vulgar Thompson with a *p*, but the superior Thomson without a *p*, whom *Vanity Fair* described, at the foot of an admirable cartoon, as "The Archbishop of Society."

William Thomson (1819–90) was born at Whitehaven, and educated at Shrewsbury and Queen's College, Oxford. He was a Scholar of his College, and great things were expected of him in the Final Schools, but he only got a Third. The College showed its unabated faith in him by electing him to a Fellowship, and he showed his own robust confidence in himself by publishing, when he was twenty-three, a treatise on *Outlines of the Laws of Thought*.

But undergraduates have uncomfortable memories of the shortcomings of their elders. When Thomson was tutor at Queen's, he heard one night an unseemly noise in the Quad, and went out to investigate it. The list of Honours in the final Schools had just come out, and a Queensman, whose name had unexpectedly appeared in the First Class, was making merry with his friends. The tutor's majestic remonstrance was met by the genial reply: "Ah, old fellow, you little know a man's feelings when he gets his First." But in spite of jeers Thomson, who was ordained in 1844, became Provost of Queen's, Bampton Lecturer, Preacher at Lincoln's Inn, and Chaplain to the Queen. When *Essays and Reviews* threw the Church into commotion, and the arithmetical Colenso perturbed the faithful with his calculations about the cubic content of the Ark and the width of the door of the Tabernacle, Thomson, rightly reading the signs of the times, came forward on behalf of imperilled orthodoxy, published *Aids to Faith*, contributed to *The Speaker's Commentary*, and had his reward by being made Bishop of Gloucester and Bristol in November 1861. And now a greater opportunity was at hand. A Royal death is, of all events, that which most profoundly stirs the emotions and inspires the eloquence of the Anglican Episcopate. The Prince Consort died one month after Thomson was consecrated; and, though all the bishops on the Bench, and all the clergymen who aspired to the Bench, vied with one another in suitable rhetoric, the newly appointed Bishop of Gloucester out-preached them all. In September 1862 the metropolitical See of York became vacant by the promotion of C. T. Longley to Canterbury, and William Thomson ascended the throne which he filled and adorned for twenty-eight succeeding years.

He looked the part to perfection. He was tall and heavily built, but carried himself well; had a trenchant nose and a strongly marked mouth, with dark hair and abundant whiskers. His eyebrows were noticeably arched, and this peculiarity of his face led one of his clergy— C. J. Vaughan, then Vicar of Doncaster and afterwards Master of the Temple—to ask a friend, " Have you ever observed how exactly the Archbishop's eyebrows express what is meant by the word *supercilious* ? "

It must be confessed that Thomson's clergy did not love him. Some of them suggested an alteration in the accustomed form of the archi-episcopal style, and amended " William, by

Divine Providence, Lord Archbishop of York"
into "William, by Divine connivance." Nor
were his episcopal brethren more cordial.
Bishop Samuel Wilberforce (whose curate Thomson once had been and who had earnestly desired to be made Archbishop of York in 1862)
said that Thomson's extreme self-importance
made it difficult for him to understand that
one differed from him unless one convinced him
by rudeness; and, describing Magee's consecration, which occurred just when Tait had been
nominated for Canterbury, Wilberforce genially
observed in his diary : "Archbishop of York
chagrined manifestly."

Of course the curates of Yorkshire believed
in him, and trembled; and, if one exception to
this trembling is recorded, it only heightens the
general consternation. A sporting deacon—a
curate at Doncaster—possessed a large and
savage retriever, and, just as he was starting
for Bishopthorpe, where he was to be ordained
priest, his landlady declined to have the dog
left in her charge. What was to be done?
There was no time to waste, for the last train
was starting directly, and it would not do to be
late; so the curate bundled the dog into the
cab with his portmanteau, and dashed off.

When he alighted, dog and all, at the stately portals of Bishopthorpe, a solemn horror spread itself over the face of the purple-liveried footmen, but the curate pushed on undauntedly to his room. There he unpacked his portmanteau, dressed for dinner, and left the dog in charge of his day-clothes, recommending the footman not, at the peril of his life, to disturb him.

After dinner, the Archbishop, looking several sizes larger than life, came sailing round the drawing-room, and addressed a few appropriate words to each of the pavid ordinands. Arriving at the owner of the dog, he said, with all due solemnity, " I understand, Mr. Auceps, that you take an interest in Natural History." " Yes, your Grace, a great interest." " And you have a remarkably intelligent dog." " Yes, remarkably intelligent ; he can do so-and-so," and went off into an enumeration of the retriever's accomplishments. During this narration the Archbishop looked more than usually supercilious, and the chaplains, curates, and candidates, taking their cue from the Archbishop's eyebrows, sniffed sycophantically. Nettled by this incredulity, young Auceps said : " I know it sounds as if I was drawing the long bow ; but I'm not. The dog is upstairs ; I'll fetch him down, and put him through his tricks." . . . And so he did; and the rest is silence.

But, though Thomson was not beloved by clergy of any age or rank, he was popular with the laity. He was a welcome guest at all the great country houses in which Yorkshire abounds, and in all public gatherings where laity predominate he was acceptable and effective. One of his admirers said : "He was a King of Chairmen," and, in presiding over a Diocesan Conference or a public meeting, he could keep both himself and others in hand. In spite of his pomposity, there was something manly and vigorous about him, which endeared him to Yorkshiremen, and gave rise to stories which were passed with favour from workshop to training-stable. One of these stories ran as follows :—

One night, returning from a meeting in York, he discovered that the coachman was half-seas over; so he made him get into the carriage, and, mounting the box, drove back to Bishopthorpe. When he arrived in the stable-yard, one of the stablemen, who was a friend of the coachman and knew his convivial habits, uttered a cheery shout of welcome : "Eh, Tommy lad! Thoo ist bad to-neet! Why, thoo's gotten t'owld bloke's hat on!"

In great centres of population, more especially at Sheffield, Thomson was seen to the best advantage. Thoughtful artisans, and even the rougher working-men, listened with close attention to his words, whether delivered from the platform or from the pulpit. He had, what certainly no one would have suspected from his bearing in society, a keen sympathy with the struggles of industrial life, and it is to his permanent credit that at the Church Congress of 1865 he introduced, in spite of alarmed remonstrances, the "Working Men's Meeting," which has been a conspicuous feature of all subsequent Congresses. In all public gatherings his commanding presence attracted attention, and he had the charm of a really fine voice. As Fellow of Queen's, he had been chosen to sing that famous song of the Boar's Head with which the College celebrates Christmas, and he was the only bishop on the Bench who at an ordination could sing his part in the *Veni Creator*.

But his gifts did not end with presence or voice. Though not very spiritually minded, and though wholly devoid of unction, he was, in the argumentative way, a striking preacher. "No man," said Archbishop Benson, "was surer of Christ's revelation," and he knew how to state the grounds of his belief in a way which enforced thought and commanded respect even if it did not win assent.

During the parliamentary season he preached constantly in London, and after one of his sermons at the Temple an old Bencher remarked to a fellow-worshipper: "I shouldn't like to tackle the Archbishop of York on the scientific side of Christianity." It was a wise judgment.

In Yorkshire the Archbishop, using a sensible economy, sometimes preached sermons which had been composed in former years. A dignitary of the diocese—one of the few who was not afraid of him—in whose church he had preached, said after the service: "That was an excellent sermon, your Grace, but I liked it even better when I heard it preached by the Bishop of Gloucester." Thomson looked portentous for a moment, but then had shrewdness enough to perceive the compliment, and smiled benignly.

That accomplished and versatile author, Mr. Baring-Gould, once held a living in the diocese of York, and in 1874—the year in which Tait and Thomson had passed the ill-starred P. W. R. Act—he chanced to be at Bishop-thorpe. In the course of conversation, Thomson said: "Can you explain how it is that in France, which you know pretty well, there exists such a deadly hostility to the Church, whereas here in England there is no such animosity?" "I can explain it," said Baring-Gould. "In France every priest is at a grapple with the devil, fighting for every human soul. Here, the Church plays second fiddle to the World, and is looked on with indifference as a paid musician, to scrape what tunes it calls for." I wish I had been present at this dialogue, if only for the pleasure of seeing the archiepiscopal eyebrows elevated even beyond their wont.

I said above that *Vanity Fair* called Thomson "The Archbishop of Society." The nickname was well chosen. The Sumners and Longleys and Taits neither knew nor cared about society, but Thomson delighted in it, and adorned it. He was an admirable host, whether in town or country, and singularly open-handed in hospitality. He was said to have spent some colossal sum in redecorating Bishopthorpe (reputed to contain a hundred rooms) in honour of a visit paid by the Prince and Princess of Wales, and the dinners at his house in Prince's Gate were renowned.

He was absolutely free from professional narrow-mindedness and abhorred ecclesiastical "shop." An allusion to this trait may be found in the Life of Bishop Wilberforce, who wrote in his diary for the 26th of May, 1873: "Dined Archbishop of York's. A good many bishops, both of England and Ireland, and not one word said which *implied* we were apostles. Eheu! Eheu!"

In one all-important respect Thomson was uniquely equipped for society, whether as host or as guest. In early life he had the singular good fortune to marry one of the most beautiful women in Europe. Mrs. Thomson, born Zoë Skene, was daughter of James Henry Skene, Consul at Aleppo, and granddaughter of James Skene of Rubieslaw, to whom Sir Walter Scott dedicated the fourth canto of *Marmion*. On her mother's side she was of Greek descent, and Greek art, at its highest point, never produced a more graceful form or a more arresting face.

In the fleeting maze of society in London, as I look back upon it across the interspace of thirty years, certain incidents stand out with vivid clearness, not on account of intrinsic importance, but because they were connected with memorable events. In one of them Thomson figures.

In the spring of 1882, Irish disaffection was

at its height. Ireland was in the grip of a treasonable and murderous conspiracy, and our Government of All the Talents, with Gladstone for Prime Minister and Forster for Chief Secretary, had failed, pitifully and ludicrously, in its attempts to protect life and liberty. There were forty agrarian murders undetected, but Gladstone, as always, insisted on believing that things were as he wished them to be, and relied on the power of words to counteract grim facts.

On the evening of May 2, 1882, I was at a party in Eaton Square, where Gladstone and Thomson were among my fellow-guests. As we entered the drawing-room the Archbishop, turning to the Prime Minister with his most impressive air, said: " I want you to tell me about the state of Ireland." Feeling, like most other people who were not wilfully blind, a profound misgiving about the unchecked reign of murderous outrage, I listened intently to the reply. " The state of Ireland," said Gladstone with eager emphasis, " is very greatly improved. Rent is being generally paid." Not a word about human life, which, after all, is a more important thing than rent.

On the following Saturday, May 6th, Lord Frederick Cavendish and Mr. T. H. Burke

were stabbed to death in the Phœnix Park,
and the Irish difficulty entered on the acutest
phase which it has ever known.

ARCHBISHOP MAGEE

WILLIAM CONNOR MAGEE (1821–91) was an Archbishop for only six months; but a six months'
archiepiscopate will serve to complete the
trio. Just after his appointment to York,
he said to a friend: "If it were not for
the incessant 'Your Grace,' 'Your Grace,' of
waiters in clubs and butlers at home, I should
still think myself Bishop of Peterborough.
Truly I am just now the 'well-graced actor,
leaving the stage of Peterborough.'" As Bishop
of Peterborough he played, between 1868 and
1891, a conspicuous part in public life, his
special sphere of activity being that Debatable
Land which Gladstone called "the mixed sphere
of religion and the *sæculum*." He was one
of the greatest speakers in England, and he
had a line of speaking which was peculiarly his
own. In the power of appealing to the emotions
of his hearers he was surpassed by such orators
as Bishop Samuel Wilberforce, and John Bright,

ARCHBISHOP THOMSON.

ARCHBISHOP MAGEE.

To face p. 364.

and the eighth Duke of Argyll; but in the
faculty of closely woven argument he was fully
Gladstone's equal, in terse and effective statement his superior; and in the accessory gifts
of sarcasm and humour he was only matched
by Disraeli.

In private life he resembled a character in one
of Lever's or Miss Edgeworth's novels, unlike
any one else, and quite unforgettable. Like Mr.
Sampson Brass drawing up the description of
Quilp when that worthy was supposed to be
drowned, I might say as I try to describe
Magee, "This is an occupation which seems to
bring him before my eyes like the ghost of
Hamlet's father, in the very clothes that he
wore on workdays. His wit and humour, his
pathos and his umbrella, all come before me like
visions of my youth." And to these characteristics I might add his brogue, his twinkle,
and the mobile curves of his truly oratorical
mouth.

He was even comically deficient in dignity;
overflowing with fun and gaiety; yet easily
irritated, and painfully incapable of suffering fools
or bores gladly. Of his tendency to "levity,"
of which he was fully conscious, he said, half-
ruefully, half-joyfully: "My fate is to be too

good for the bad folk, and not bad enough for the bad ones, and to be abused by both. When I get a *determination of speech to the head*, nothing but speaking will relieve me, and I speak accordingly, good or evil, as the case may be."

On January 22, 1891, just after he had been appointed to the See of York, I chanced to meet him at dinner. He was frankly overjoyed by his promotion, and overflowed with high spirits and rather boyish fun. "Spoonerisms" were then just coming into vogue, and the Archbishop-Designate rolled out specimen after specimen of that form of pleasantry, which he had received from his son, an undergraduate at Oxford. Even now I can seen the amazed and rather pained face of Bishop G. H. Wilkinson (then of Truro), who was constitutionally incapable of a joke, and sate glowering across the table at his frivolous brother, with an expression compounded of pity and distress.

I must now turn back, from Magee's end, to his beginnings.

He was born of clerical parentage and archiepiscopal descent on December 17, 1821. His birthplace was Cork, and he was educated at Kilkenny College and Trinity College, Dublin. In 1844 he was ordained deacon, and became

Curate of St. Thomas's, Dublin, being ordained priest the following year. Some signs of incipient lung-trouble made it desirable for him to seek a better climate, and in 1849 he took a curacy at St. Saviour's, Bath. In 1851 he became minister of the Octagon Chapel in that city, and in the same year he married his cousin, Anne Smith. In 1860 he was appointed minister of Quebec Chapel, London, but left it in 1861 to become Rector of Enniskillen. In 1864 he was made Dean of Cork, and in 1866 Dean of the Chapel Royal, Dublin. A month later, Lord Russell's Government was beaten on his amendment to the Reform Bill, and resigned. There was reason to believe that the See of Meath would soon be vacant, and that it would be conferred upon Magee.

On the 1st of August, 1866, he said :—

"The Bishopric of Meath would, I believe, have been mine had Dr. Singer's death taken place just three weeks sooner than it did. Three weeks of an expiring, and seemingly useless, life lay between me and all that the Bishopric implies. The goal of a life of severe toil and effort was in view; and now it is indefinitely remote, if not absolutely and certainly beyond my reach."

In 1867 he wrote :—

"The Tories will not promote me; the Whigs will leave no church to be promoted in. So there is an end of it."

Disheartened by his Irish prospects, he wrote in September 1868 to Disraeli, asking for some minor appointment in England; and received the surprising reply that his request could not be granted, because he was already nominated to the See of Peterborough. He was the first Irishman since the Reformation to hold an English See.

Irish Disestablishment had been the haunting dread of Magee's early manhood. He foresaw a day of reckoning for the intolerable mischief of Orange bigotry, of uneducated Evangelicalism, of blind and unreasoning hostility to everything that did not utter the current shibboleths of Puritanism. He saw that the utter negation and abandonment of all distinctively Church ideas was destroying the Church's reason for existence and preparing men's minds for the fatal question, "Why cumbereth it the ground?" Staunch Establishmentarian as he was, he was no Erastian. He believed, like Archbishop Whately, in the separate existence, rights, and duties of the Church as a spiritual society, and he laboured to restore such synodal action as would enable the Church to examine her own affairs, speak her own mind, and set her own house in order. But before these prudent counsels could obtain a hearing, the General Election of 1868 took place, and the Irish Establishment was doomed for ever. The last desperate device of the Establishmentarians had been to hold the English Church Congress at Dublin in the September preceding the Election, and it is believed that Magee's opening sermon on the apt text, "They beckoned unto their partners which were in the other ship that they should come and help them," won him the Bishopric of Peterborough.

Magee fully recognized the conclusive character of the national verdict; that he hoped nothing from prolonged resistance; that he urged his Irish friends to agree with their adversary quickly, and make terms with Gladstone before it was too late. At the same time he hated the Bill with all his heart; and, when his Irish brethren declined all compromise and arrayed themselves for battle, he threw himself with all his energies on to their side, and fought his hardest for a cause which yet, in his reason, he believed to be hopeless.

24

His speech on the Second Reading of the Bill
advanced him at a bound to the first rank of
parliamentary orators. Disraeli, listening to it
from the steps of the throne, observed, "I perceive we have got a 'customer' here." Lord
Ellenborough declared that the speech was
"superior, not in degree, but in kind, to anything he had ever heard in either House, with
the two exceptions of Grattan and Plunket." The
great Lord Derby, then nearing the close of his
fine career, spoke of the speech as having contained "the most cogent and most conclusive
arguments upon the merits of the question,"
adding this extraordinary praise, "Its fervid
eloquence, its impassioned and brilliant language,
have never in my memory been surpassed, and
rarely equalled, during my long parliamentary
experience."

This immense success, added to his innate
capacity for affairs, marked him out at once as
a bishop who would have to take a prominent
part in the parliamentary business of the Church.
He said of himself that he was better suited for
the "*haute politique*" of the Church than for
some other episcopal duties. He was a consummate orator, a born debater, a master of
organization and machinery; and, though he

disliked the House of Lords, and felt that the bishops were in a false position there, he was not the least afraid of his audience. Thus he became, what for good or for evil is increasingly rare, a parliamentary bishop, and as such he was brought into very close relations with Archbishop Tait, who seems to have desired to use him as a fighting lieutenant. But there was only an imperfect sympathy between the two men, and the Bishop of Peterborough had a shrewd insight into the faults and limitations of his chief. The Life of Archbishop Tait gave what may be called the domestic chaplain's view of its hero. As such it was natural and becoming, and, from its own standpoint, true. But let us see how the matter presented itself to a very clever man, trained in the rough-and-tumble of the world, and promoted by the sheer force of his own genius to the front rank :—

" The Archbishop's Scotch caution amounts to a disease, with odd outbreaks, at intervals, of impulsiveness. And he is, besides, so utter an Erastian that any move of his for increased power for the Bench will be of a kind generally distasteful even to moderate Churchmen."

In 1874, with reference to the Public Worship Regulation Act :—

"The Archbishop has turned the Ganges into our garden, and I fear it will sweep away other things than the Ritualistic weeds. . . . Evidently we are entering on a great crisis, and, alas! we do not trust our pilots either of Cantuar or York.

"The Bishops are sore at the way the Archbishop has overridden them in the conduct of the Bill. . . . We sorely need a strong and yet a gentle hand at the helm of the Church, and the Archbishop has neither of these *now*."

In 1876:—

"The Archbishop so entirely believes in Parliaments, and so entirely ignores the clergy, that he is becoming, with all his noble qualities and great practical sagacity, a great peril to the Church. He regards the clergy as a big Sixth Form, and acts accordingly.

"We are drifting, and getting nearer and nearer to our Niagara; Cantuar at the helm, quite satisfied that a good strong Erastian wind from St. Stephen's, is carrying us steadily and safely along.

"It is certainly a misfortune at this moment to have two Primates nearly alike in Church views, and singularly alike in their want of imagination, and therefore of power of sympathy with others, or anticipation of events."

In 1877 :—

" He [Tait] will never be a leader; and his office is not powerful enough to make *him* a ruler, who is not something of a leader too."

In 1879 :—

"The laity are astride of them [the Bishops] and the clergy, and they will hold their place. Cantuar likes this! He said so to me lately. He is infatuated for laity and Parliament, and will one day have a rude awakening."

In 1880 :—

"When will the Archbishop of Canterbury give up driving, and take to leading, the Church? More and more I am convinced that the Episcopate under his government is letting the Church drift on the breakers, when a strong hand on the helm might have saved her."

On the Amendments to the Liberal Burials Bill of 1880 :—

"On these points Cantuar may be trusted. It is just in such lesser points, involving caution and canniness, that he shines."

In 1881 :—

"A. Cantuar managed his little speech for the Queen Anne's Bounty Bill admirably. He muddled it up so judiciously that no one knew exactly what it meant."

On Tait's death :—

"He never could endure opposition well, but on the other hand he never bore malice. He was a good man, and in some respects a great one."

Of course the political affairs with which Magee mainly concerned himself were those which affect the Church. In the general field of secular politics he was a moderate Conservative of the utilitarian type, abhorring democracy, and regarding his own countrymen with that singular mixture of intellectual admiration and practical mistrust which is the characteristic of the educated Irishman. In his whole moral and mental constitution he belonged to his early time, and was completely out of touch with the sentimental ethics and poetical economics which played so large a part in the thought of the Seventies and Eighties.

In 1866, during the debates on Lord Russell's Reform Bill, he wrote :—

"Gladstone's speech was the inauguration of an ultra-democratic career, taken up as much from pique and passion as conviction. He and Russell and Bright are an ominous conjunction."

In 1874 :—

"Gladstone turned Radical, and backed by all

the unbelief and all the High Church Ritualistic Radicalism in the country, is a very awkward element in the future."

In 1879:—

" The British Constitution is very dear at the money. Free institutions are becoming unworkable. The revolutionary party in the House received its leader last night in the person of W. E. Gladstone. . . . What bearing this will have on coming domestic legislation it is not difficult to foresee. Disestablishment comes nearer by a great deal in consequence of it, and moreover, Disestablishment by Gladstone the Radical and not Gladstone the Liberal. Marry! this is miching mallecho, and means mischief."

After the General Election of 1880:—

" The Liberal party will then be Radical pure and simple, and headed by Gladstone. Then comes the last struggle between Church and Democracy, and there is no doubt which will win."

In the same year:—

"This Disturbance Bill will go very near to evicting the Ministry, or would do so were it not that Gladstone has still his trump-card to play—a new Reform Bill and a dictatorship afterwards for the term of his natural life."

When once the fate of the Irish Church was
settled, English Disestablishment became his
favourite bugbear. He regarded Establishment
not only as a blessing to the State, but as a
guarantee of order, sanity, orthodoxy, and com-
prehensive tolerance, in the national religion.
By a rough-and-ready process of reasoning, he
connected it with Socialism, Democracy, and
Revolution generally, and he rather grotesquely
assumed that Gladstone was to be the leader
and champion of these allied abominations.

Reviewing the General Election of 1885, he
said to a clerical friend :—

" This means Irish revolution first, and then
an embittered struggle between the revolutionary
and Conservative forces in England and Scotland, the revolution winning and being merciless
after the bitterness of the fight. I give the
Church of England two Parliaments to live
through—this one now coming, in which she
will be merely worried and humiliated; the next,
in which she will be assailed and disestablished
in the Commons; the third, in which the peers
will give way and the thing is done. . . . Say
ten years for all this. Now, please put this
letter by, and let us read it, if spared, *ten years
hence*, on the Lake of Como, whither we shall

have gone to spend our few remaining disestablished years."

In the domain of theology, Magee belonged
essentially to what R. H. Hutton so well
described as "the Hard Church." He was
never troubled by a single doubt. He saw the
fundamental facts of the Christian revelation
with intense clearness; and he regarded all who
had a wider vision as visionaries, and all who
saw less as wilfully blind. One might, or might
not, concur in his premises; but, those granted,
his deductions from them were of irrefragable
force. "Logic," he said, "is as real a fact as
steam"; and he would have seen nothing but
nonsense in the wisdom of St. Ambrose—*Non in
dialectica complacuit Deo salvum facere populum
Suum.*

Probably the good people who originally
brought him to Bath thought that any Irish
clergyman was necessarily an Evangelical, and
so took him on trust: but the Simeon Trustees
displayed the truer instinct when they declined
to present him to one of their livings. He was
strongly opposed to Romanism and Puseyism,
and in his earlier days, at any rate, held no
High Church doctrine. But, eloquent and forcible
and convincing as he was in the pulpit (and he

avowed that he was much more a preacher than a pastor), he had absolutely none of that " unction " which is the true note of Evangelical preaching; nor, as far as one can see, of that passionate zeal for the salvation of the individual soul which is the Alpha and Omega of all Evangelical ministrations. He was stoutly opposed to Calvinism. He was not the least afraid of Biblical criticism, as he showed by appointing B. F. Westcott to the first Canonry of Peterborough which fell to his gift. He confessed himself quite unable to " howl the Gospel." He had nothing but sneers for the " sweet young clergyman of the Simeonite type." The preaching of an aged Low Churchman reminded him of a " spinnet played by an elderly lady." Truly this is not the language of Evangelicalism. Of his famous sermon before the Church Congress at Dublin, the Evangelical Bishop of Cork declared that " it had not Gospel enough in it to save a tom-tit," and the preacher thought the criticism " delicious."

On the other hand, Magee had an unbounded contempt for Ritualism in all its forms and phases, though after the Ridsdale Judgment he conformed, as a matter of obedience, to the use of the cope in his cathedral. His notion of

liturgical reform was such a reconstruction of
the rubrics as should make ceremonial impossible; but he was shrewd enough to see that
any attempt to meddle with doctrine must rend
the Church in twain.

Probably every Churchman who ever met
Magee in society, or heard him on the platform, or ever "sate under him" in the pulpit,
must have felt that he was the most unecclesiastical of ecclesiastics. There have been prelates,
both in ancient and in recent times, whose hold
on the fundamental truths of the Church's faith
has been infinitely weaker; but men of that
stamp have generally tried—and often successfully—to veil their essential scepticism under
the solemn plausibilities of an official language
and demeanour. Sanctimonious fraud of that
sort stank in Magee's nostrils and elicited his
exclamation, "What an immortal thing is
humbug!" What he was, and what he thought,
and what he felt, that he was willing that all
the world should know; and, confident in the
strength of his own convictions, he paid scant
regard to the flaccid nerves or feeble brain-pro-
cesses of those mild pietists, male and female,
whose idea of a bishop is a kind of mincing
demigod.

"I am conscious" (he said) "of my defects
for my high office—lack of dignity, impulsive
speech, too great fondness for sharp and sarcastic utterances, impatience of dulness and
folly."

He spoke, thought, and acted like a thoroughgoing man of the world, who was also a thoroughgoing Christian, with keen humour, strong
opinions, remorseless logic, and a legal bent of
mind.   It would be absurd, according to worldly
standards, to say that a man who reached the
highest place but one in his profession had mis-
taken his vocation ; but one cannot help feeling
that Magee would have been even more at
home in the House of Commons or on the
Woolsack than in Convocation or on an episcopal throne.

Unfortunately, the world is full of excellent
people who "jock," if at all, "wi' deeficulty,"
and who find it impossible to enjoy or even
tolerate the jokes of other people.   To such as
these, it must be confessed, Magee's humour was
a sore trial.   A joking clergyman was bad
enough, but a joking bishop outraged their moral
sense ; and, at all stages of his career, Magee
joked in season and out of season, without the
slightest regard to convention or susceptibilities.

When he was stationed at Bath, he took an active part in the concerns of the Bath Free Hospital, and soon discovered that the chief medical officer was an ex-army surgeon, grossly incompetent for the work entrusted to him. Magee tried to get him removed; and, at the Annual Meeting of Subscribers, the indignant surgeon turned on Magee the full torrent of his wrath. He was, he said, no stranger to the quarter from which these attacks on him proceeded, and, indicating Magee, he thundered, "If it were not for his cloth, I'd have him out and put a bullet through him." Magee promptly rose, and said that if the gallant gentleman insisted on offering him personal violence, he was restrained by his sacred office from retaliating. "But," he added, "one humble request I will prefer. Should he succeed in hitting me, I pray that he will not attempt to dress the wound." This was an admirable thrust, thoroughly well deserved, and was probably resented by no one except the infuriated surgeon; and when Magee, returning to his native land, plunged into the free fight of religious faction, he wielded his sword-stick with admirable effect. But, when he was transplanted to an English diocese, his sprightly sallies, repeated and distorted, caused

dire offence among solid squires and dignified
incumbents. He was reported to have said that,
if he ever opened his study-window, every jack-
ass in the diocese thought himself at liberty to
thrust in his head and bray. When the faithful proposed to present him with a crozier, he
replied that he valued the kindness, but would
have found an umbrella much more useful.
By a rash and quite unsound antithesis between
"England free and England sober," he infuriated the teetotallers. By outspoken criticism
of demagogues such as Charles Bradlaugh and
Joseph Arch, he enraged alike the artisans
and the agricultural labourers. On one occasion,
when consecrating a cemetery, he was mobbed
and insulted by the rabble; and, when attention
was directed to the occurrence in the House of
Lords, he closed the discussion by airily saying
of the rioters: "I inflicted on them the ignominy
of an episcopal benediction, and dismissed them
from my mind." Here is his vivacious portrait
of Mark Pattison, whom another artist, Miss
Rhoda Broughton, drew as Professor Forth in
Belinda. "Imagine the mummy of an opium-
eater restored to life and dressed in the dinner
dress of the nineteenth century; that is Mr.
Pattison, Rector of Lincoln College, freethinker
and free writer, but certainly not free speaker."

These personal skits, when bandied from mouth to mouth at the Athenæum or the Metaphysical Society, did not tend to endear him; but, if he was exposing foolishness or rebuking impertinence, his sense of humour stood him in good stead. When an impudent firm of speculative publishers pirated a collection of his sermons and advertised it under the title of "Magee Extra—Price Sixpence." He wrote to the *Times* :—

"I think it due to any intending purchaser of this particular 'Magee Extra,' to apprise him that, if he expends upon it the sum of sixpence, he will get for his money a good deal more of the 'extra' than of the 'Magee.'"

It is to be remarked that Magee's jokes, like those of Sydney Smith, were never mere appendages, but always formed part of the texture of the argument, and helped to establish the point for which he was contending. It would, therefore, rob them of their point to tear them from their context—the more so as they are to be found in rich profusion in the "Life and Letters" of this brave, brilliant, and high-minded man.

CHAPTER XXII

BISHOP WILKINSON

GEORGE HOWARD WILKINSON was born in 1833 and died in 1907; but he was essentially a man of the Seventies, for the period during which he did his imperishable work ranged from 1870 to 1880. He became Bishop of Truro at the beginning of 1883, and was eventually Bishop of St. Andrews; but it was when he was Vicar of St. Peter's, Eaton Square, that his name became famous.

The Wilkinsons were an opulent family in the county of Durham; country gentlemen, land-owners, and sportsmen; and the traces of his upbringing hung about George Wilkinson to the end. He was short and, in early life, slight, well-built, and active; and carried himself with that natural dignity which supplies the lack of height. He was, alike by instinct and by habit, a horse-man; rode admirably, and had something in

G. H. WILKINSON.

(Bishop of St. Andrews.)

To face p. 384.

his appearance that suggested the stables. He was clean-shaven except for a fragment of whisker on each side: his hair was thick, intensely black, accurately parted, and so well trimmed that not a particle of it was ever out of place; his white neckcloth was accurately tied; his clothes fitted him like a glove; and from the crown of his hat to the soles of his boots you might have searched in vain for a speck of dust. These were the characteristics of his appearance in early manhood, and, barring a certain enlargement of the figure, they were the same to the end.

Horsemanship entered into his life and his ministry. In the summer evenings he generally had a gallop in Rotten Row, when the gay world had gone home to dinner, and so kept himself fresh and fit. If his spiritual children were morbid or gloomy, he recommended riding as a religious exercise; and I remember one of his most effective illustrations in a sermon when, speaking of permitted enjoyments, he instanced among them the sensation of a good horse straining between one's knees when hounds are breaking cover and you see five miles of grass stretched out between you and the skyline.

Having taken his degree at Oxford, Wilkinson

was ordained to the curacy of St. Mary Abbot's, Kensington. He became Vicar of Seaham in 1859, and in 1867 he accepted the incumbency of St. Peter's, Great Windmill Street, which had been recently built by the great Lord Derby. At that time Gladstone was living in Carlton House Terrace, and he became a worshipper and communicant at St. Peter's. Mrs. Gladstone, always active in good works, associated herself with Mrs. Wilkinson, a young and beautiful woman, in parochial labours; and so began a friendship which deepened as the years went on. In 1869 Wilkinson was transferred (by Dr. Jackson, Bishop of London) from St. Peter's, Windmill Street, to St. Peter's, Eaton Square, and entered on a ministry of which the effects are not even now exhausted.

Spiritually considered, Belgravia was at that time a desert. At St. Paul's, Knightsbridge, and its daughter-church, St. Barnabas, Pimlico, there flourished a stiff Anglicanism which was lapsing out of date. St. Michael's, Chester Square, was in the hands of the Low Church party; and two proprietary chapels, one in Halkin Street and the other in Eaton Terrace, were the abodes of a more ultra Protestantism. St. Peter's, Eaton Square, was a church of commanding size and position, built in 1825 to supply the needs of the residential quarter which Lord Westminster was creating on the site of the "Five Fields," and which had acquired from its principal square the nickname of "Belgravia." It was a plain, oblong barn, with a pillared portico, a threefold gallery, a flat roof, and no chancel. The fabric was as ugly as a Georgian architect could make it; the services corresponded to it; and the preacher, gazing down from his tower-like pulpit, might have said with the Rev. Charles Churchill :—

> While, sacred dulness ever in my view,
> Sleep at my bidding crept from pew to pew.

The congregation and the parish were in all respects worthy of the sanctuary; and into this Dead Sea of formalism and lethargy Wilkinson burst like a gunboat. He very soon amended the fabric, making it look less like a lecture-hall and more like a church; but what he did materially was a very small thing when compared with what he did spiritually. His preaching, and the personality of which it was the utterance, instantly struck home. Earnestness ousted formalism; lethargy woke from its slumbers; even worldliness rushed to hear the voice that rebuked it. Society was told, in the plainest English, of its sins and their reward; of its unfulfilled duties, of its neglected opportunities, of its hypocritical excuses :—

> E'en so, of John acalling and acrying
>   Rang in Bethabara till strength was spent,
> Cared not for counsel, stayed not for replying;
>   John had one message for the world, "Repent."

The message of the Baptist to Judæa, the message of Savonarola to guilty Florence, the message of Wesley and Whitefield to the England of Hogarth and Fielding and Smollett, spoke again in Wilkinson's preaching. The force which compelled men to listen was purely spiritual. There was nothing that could be called, in the usual sense, clever; there was no sign of learning, no attempt at reasoning, no rhetoric, no poetry. There were not even the graces of gesture and voice, for the preacher stood stock-still, except in so far as he vibrated with passion, and his voice alternated between a groan and a howl. But there was the force which no human power can resist, the force which, from St. Paul's days to ours, has been "mighty through God to the pulling-down of strongholds."

Of Wilkinson's practical effect on the men and women who submitted themselves to his guidance I shall speak later; but it may be interesting at this point to record the impressions of a perfectly dispassionate observer.

In the year 1872 the two great missionary societies of the Church of England—the S.P.G. and the C.M.S.—agreed on the desirability of holding a united supplication for an increase of the missionary spirit. With the sanction of the ecclesiastical authorities, St. Andrew's Day, November 30th, was fixed for the observance, which has become a permanent institution. But in 1872 it was a startling novelty, and the *Times* attacked it in an article quite remarkable—not for irreligiousness, for that was to be expected, but for ignorance and fatuity. On the 23rd of December Matthew Arnold wrote thus to his mother:—

"Yesterday morning I went down to Belgravia and heard Wilkinson; he is a very powerful preacher from his being himself so possessed. But it was a very striking sermon —on missions, and the *Times* article upon them. The notion was that we are corrupting here from over-vitality—too much life crowded up in too narrow a room—and that the best remedy

was to return to the old Gospel injunction:
Go and preach the Gospel to every creature.
This was in answer to the common objection:
Begin with your heathen masses at home. He
despaired of home, he said; he had at first
thought it was the right place to begin, but
he now saw the Will of God was not so; and
then came pictures of the life of the poor in
London, and of 'Society' in London, and of
the Church of England, all fermenting and corrupting, he said, from too much vitality being
jammed up in too narrow a space; the only
remedy was to disperse into missions. We
ought all to wish to go, and to bring up our
children to wish to go. His triumph was when
he met the natural question, 'Why don't *you*
go, then?' He had wished to go, he said,
prayed to go; he still hoped to go, but he was
not yet suffered; he thought it was because of
the sins of his youth and that he was not found
worthy; and he compared himself to Moses,
not allowed because of his faults to enter the
Holy Land himself, only permitted to send
Joshua. You see what awful risk he ran here
of being unreal, even absurd; and he came out
triumphant. He was so evidently sincere—more
than sincere, burnt up with sorrow—that he

carried every one with him, and half the church was in tears. I don't much believe in good being done by a man unless he can give *light*, and Wilkinson's fire is very turbid; but his power of heating, penetrating, and agitating is extraordinary."

This is, I think, an absolutely just description; and on people less critical than Matthew Arnold the "power of heating, penetrating, and agitating" produced remarkable effects. By his protests against worldliness Wilkinson was said to have "spoilt the London season"; though, as he incessantly thundered: "Pay your tradesmen's bills," he must have done, even economically, almost as much good as harm. It is probably true that any preacher who cares to do it can become a director of women, but Wilkinson's power over men was unique. In a church filled to overflowing, and in a congregation which hung upon his words, one saw men of every age, class, rank, and profession. Something like half of Lord Beaconsfield's Cabinet (1874–80) were his habitual and attentive hearers. Gladstone (who named him for the See of Truro) esteemed him the typical and representative Anglican, and gave him the highest proof of confidence by begging that he

would attend his death-bed. Ordinary men of
the world, Members of Parliament, and mer-
chants and country gentlemen, submitted themselves gladly and trustfully to his guidance;
and of these "many remain unto this day,
though some have fallen asleep." From this
congregation he could raise all the money he
wanted by merely asking for it; and "I want
a thousand pounds" one Sunday, was supple-
mented by "I've received a thousand pounds"
next Sunday. The alms collected in church
amounted to £4,000 a year, besides all the
cheques for parochial and extra-parochial purposes which found their way, often unasked, to
the vicarage.

The sincere respect in which the laity held
Wilkinson was due, in part, to his excellent sense and tact in dealing with devout
women—a troublesome and perilous crew. He
was not only a saint, but a gentleman; and, in
the things of this world, a man of excellent
common sense. No trace of mawkishness, or
love-making, or spiritual flirtation on either side,
was ever permitted to mar his ministry. He
knew how to keep foolish people in their proper
places, and could be fully as stern as he was
sympathetic. To the girls of his flock he was

in the best sense a father, kind and wise; and
these are now mothers, grandmothers, heads of
families, and mistresses of households in which
the Wilkinsonian tradition still lives and works.

Another of Wilkinson's great merits in the
eyes of the laity was his businesslike habit.
He was—what some clergymen are not—
scrupulously accurate in applying, and account-
ing for, the moneys which he received. In
giving to St. Peter's the layman knew that his
money would be used for the specific purpose
for which it was intended, and for no other.
The whole organization of the parish was
thorough and methodical; and the vicar was
"the very pulse of the machine."

Partly on grounds of health, and partly from
a distaste for worldliness, Wilkinson held aloof
from general society. Following a strict rule
about Friday, he once begged to be excused
from dining at Marlborough House on that day.
He was sometimes to be met at the tables of
intimate friends, where he could speak without
restraint about the things which are of real and
durable importance. He had perfect manners,
at once courteous and dignified. He could talk
pleasantly enough about indifferent subjects, and
I always noticed that his conversation tended

towards the occupations and interests of country
life. He might have truly said with Wordsworth :—

> I am not one who much or oft delight
> To season my fireside with personal talk
> Of friends who live within an easy walk,
> Of neighbours daily, weekly in my sight.

He abhorred gossip, and was, perhaps, more
absolutely devoid of any sense of humour than
any man whom I have ever known.

CHAPTER XXIII

HENRY PARRY LIDDON

IN the spring of 1870 a new and astonishing force first made itself felt in the religious life of London.

The Church of St. James's, Piccadilly, has, ever since the eighteenth century, been famed for its courses of lectures on Sunday afternoons in Lent. In 1869 Dr. Jackson, then Bishop of London, suggested to the Rector of St. James's that he might do well to choose, as the Lent Lecturer for the ensuing year, a preacher who had recently attained renown as Bampton Lecturer at Oxford. This was Henry Parry Liddon, born in 1829, named after Sir Edward Parry, educated at King's College and Christ Church, and sometime Vice-Principal of Cuddesdon.[1]

From the very beginning of his ministry

[1] He died in 1890.

Liddon made his mark as a preacher. His sermons were quite unlike the ordinary products of the English pulpit; elaborately prepared, though preached without book, immensely long, exuberantly rhetorical, and delivered with a fervour which seemed to exhaust all the physical energies of the preacher. As years went on Liddon, who was not a strong man, found these efforts more than he could stand, and took to reading his sermons instead of delivering them by memory. In the difficult art of manipulating a manuscript without being tied to it he had, in my experience, no equal; and the enormous congregations which for twenty years hung on his words under the Dome of St. Paul's testified to his unequalled power of attracting and arresting. Even in the opening Collect his vibrant voice struck like an electric shock. His exquisite, almost over-refined articulation seemed the very note of culture. The restrained passion which thrilled through the disciplined utterance, warned even casual visitors to the cathedral that something quite unlike the ordinary stuff of sermons was coming, and they were seldom disappointed.

Here it should be remarked that Liddon belonged essentially to the Oxford of Aristotle

DR. LIDDON.

To face p. 396.

and Butler, ere yet it had been sophisticated by
Kant and Hegel and T. H. Green. He was
less at home when he was speaking on the
abstract ideas of God and the soul, the origin
of Evil and the possibilities of Prayer, than
when he was deducing lessons of faith and
life from the Gospels and the Epistles. He was
indeed a most vigorous thinker, but did all his
thinking in the terms of time and space. He
did not shrink even from applying temporal
standards of measurement to the life of eternity. To him the things of sense were not
adumbrations from intangible existences elsewhere, but realities as real in their own place
and order as the unseen realities of the
Spiritual Kingdom.

He was a consummate rhetorician. He had in
a singular degree the power of leading a
sympathetic hearer to the conclusion at which
he wished him to arrive. In the skilful combination of fact, illustration, inference, and
appeal he had no rival. Regarded as a practical effort for a definite end, his rhetoric was
perfect; but as a literary performance it was,
at least in his earlier days, more open to
criticism. It was over-elaborate, over-ornate,
and tinctured by Macaulayese, which betrayed

itself in the short sentences, the rolling paragraphs, the sonorous eloquence of the descriptive
paragraphs. It was noteworthy that the more
he wrote, the easier and purer his style became.
He gradually got rid of redundant and glisten-
ing ornamentation; and the sermons which he
preached as Canon of St. Paul's are, from the
artistic point of view, much finer productions
than those which made his fame at Oxford
between 1855 and 1865.

Oxford, where he lived almost continuously
from his matriculation in 1846, had always
known and loved him. His Bampton Lectures
on the Divinity of Our Lord, delivered in 1866,
had established his fame among theologians;
but London knew nothing of him till Lent, 1870.
Then he came and conquered. In previous years
he had occasionally preached in London—at
St. Paul's Cathedral, at All Saints', Margaret
Street, and elsewhere; but now for the first
time the denizens of the West End, Cabinet
Ministers, Members of the Houses of Parliament, great squires, leading lawyers, and all
their contingent of wives and daughters, heard
the greatest of English preachers, and heard
him in the fullness of his physical and mental
vigour. My friend Henry Scott Holland, then an

undergraduate spending a vacation in London, thus describes the impression which the lectures created :—

"Was anything ever seen like the sensation which they produce? Those smart crowds packed tight, Sunday after Sunday, to listen for an hour and forty minutes to a sermon that spoke straight home to their elemental souls. It was amazing! London never again shook with so vehement an emotion. "Society" in its vague, aggravating ignorance, believed itself to have discovered Liddon. How indignant we used to be with the rapturous duchesses who asked whether we had ever heard of this wonderful new preacher! Why, for years before we had stood ranked thick on each other's toes in huddled St. Mary's (at Oxford) to catch every word of the ringing voice. Those belated duchesses indeed! Yet it was something that, however late in the day, they should all feel it necessary for their reputation to be there at St. James's."

I may support this witness of a disciple and a friend, with the quite unprejudiced testimony of a writer in the *Times* :—

"To any fresh or earnest word on the most solemn and mysterious of themes, we listen

with some measure of the eagerness which a
fond imagination ascribes to the Ages of Faith.
Generation after generation feels those questions
start up with the greenness of a recovering
spring. Dynasties come and go. Empires rise
and fall, literatures vanish from the memory of
man, forms of polity wax old and perish, and
the ancient homes of great peoples survive as
the sepulchres of the dead; but the broodings
of the soul on the dim hereafter never fade nor
die. With immortal vigour they renew themselves in each generation and baffle the efforts
of logic or sarcasm to numb them into death.
It is these undying problems that Mr. Liddon
has been passing under review, with the help
of a rare erudition and a vigorous dialectic;
it is these yearnings of the soul that have
found expression in the solemn passion of his
rhetoric; whence, despite his constant recourse
to the profundity of German analysis, a brilliant
and overflowing audience have flocked to hear
his lofty discourse."

So much for Liddon the Preacher; and it is,
I suppose, chiefly as a preacher that he will be,
and even is now, remembered. But I must
say a word about him as the man, the companion, the friend.

First about his personal appearance. What was Liddon like? His facial beauty was striking. The nose was very nearly straight and sharply chiselled, the nostrils curling upwards with a critical and rather fastidious curve. The chin was prominent and strongly moulded, the mouth wide but firmly set, and connected by a deep groove or furrow with the corners of the nostrils. His forehead was broad and covered by a mass of straight hair, which once was jet black, but latterly nearly white, though the definitely marked eyebrows, which overhung his piercing eyes, retained their blackness to the end. His complexion was an olive-brown; and the whole effect of his appearance was somehow foreign. "Liddon is half a Frenchman." Vary the phrase by substituting "an Italian" for "a Frenchman," and you have the simple formula in which bewildered London expressed its feeling about the Lent Lecturer at St. James's, who in the same year became Canon of St. Paul's. Some plausibility was lent to the statement by the vehemence of his rhetorical manner, and by the structure and method of his orations, which had indeed been modelled on French preachers such as Bossuet and Fénelon, Père Felix, and Père Hyacinthe.

But it was pure delusion; and Liddon was as thoroughbred an Englishman as could be found between the Solent and the Bristol Channel.

The physical beauty began and ended with his face. He had neither figure nor carriage. In early life he had been spare and ascetic-looking, but in middle life he became portly, and his height was not proportioned to his width. His bearing, except in the pulpit, was not impressive; and a phrase of Lord Acton, likening him to "a deferential sacristan," hit a certain aspect of his appearance.

When I turn from physical to mental traits, the impression which dominates all others in my remembrance of Liddon is that of his vitality. He was alive all through, vivid, vivacious, sensitive, alert. He seemed to be surcharged with moral electricity, which tingled and flashed and sometimes scorched. One form of his vivacity was his effervescing humour, which was not very sedulously restrained. His sense of the ludicrous knew no bounds except those prescribed by reverence and charity. This was a painful stumbling-block in the way of serious people, dons, pedagogues, and dignitaries. We saw in the case of Magee that to "jock wi' deeficulty" is the hard lot of some very excellent people, and there is a still larger class which finds it difficult to enjoy, or even tolerate, the jokes [of other people. To such as these, it must be confessed, Liddon's humour was a sore trial. He told a story excellently well; his stories were nearly always personal; and his dramatic effectiveness made the people whom he was describing live and move before one's eyes. And, apart from story-telling, his humour was still personal, for, though it might be intended to illustrate some topic on which he felt keenly, it always played around some individual personality. He was personal when he wrote one Christmas from Amen Court that London was then buried under a dense fog, "which is commonly attributed to Dr. Westcott having opened his study window at Westminster." He was personal when he wrote with regard to an ecclesiastical appointment in which Gladstone had greatly disappointed him—"The Prime Minister has given us, instead of an alabaster box of ointment very precious, an ornamental jar of scented pomatum." He was personal when he excused himself for spending several hours of a precious Sunday in writing a letter of advice to a friend who had got into a foolish scrape, on the ground that the act was analogous to that of pulling an ass out of a pit on the Sabbath Day.

In the pulpit personalities can scarcely be indulged; but Liddon's humour defied all conventional restraints and broke out in unexpected places. As he preached, he put in bits and hits which he omitted or modified when the sermon came to be printed. Thus one would search in vain for his warning against the perils of the public-house on the public holiday—"If St. Paul could rise from his grave, and traverse the streets of London in the afternoon of a wet Bank-holiday, he would, I think, be disposed to modify his statement that they that be drunken are drunken *in the night*." A sarcastic reference to rationalizing theories of the fall of Jericho was considerably toned down before the second series of his University Sermons was published, though traces of it may still be discovered in Section ii of the sermon as printed. In another sermon, Jowett's translation of Plato suggested an allusion to teachers whose motto would seem to be "I live, yet henceforth not I, but Plato liveth in me."

Socially Liddon was at his best when dining with a small party of friends whom he knew thoroughly well, and with whom he could trust himself unreservedly, without fear of misconstruction. Having worked hard all day, and from a very early hour, he had an excellent appetite, ate heartily, and enjoyed a glass of wine. But his fun was not in the least dependent on these provocatives, for one of his fellow-Students at Christ Church says that "it used positively to disgrace the mild austerities of a fish-tea on Fridays at which he would join us." On all social occasions, if he was in good trim and felt sure of his company, his presence was a guarantee of wholesome mirth. In truth, his cheerfulness was part of his religion, for he held that " light-heartedness is at once the right and the duty of a Christian whose conscience is in fairly good order."

It was Liddon's fate to be frequently involved in controversy. When a cause in which he believed was imperilled he flung himself into the thick of the fighting with absolute and calculated self-surrender. He did not stand aloof to see which side was going to win. Of course the controversies of his life were mainly theological, but once at least he found himself forced to take sides in political contention. In the Eastern Question of 1875–78, he joined with all his heart in the opposition to Lord Beaconsfield's pro-Turkish policy. Though he could scarcely ever be persuaded to appear on a platform, he spoke on the 8th of December, 1876, at a great conference in St. James's Hall, and spoke with extraordinary fire and eloquence. He declined to treat the issue as a question between Christianity and Mohammedanism, between truth and error. He regarded it simply as a question of right or wrong—justice or injustice.

"I do not ask for a law which shall secure exceptional privileges to the Christians. I only ask for a law which shall be just—a law which shall secure to every subject, Mussalman or Christian, equal rights—secure to the Turks the right to live in peace, the right to enjoy their property, secure to them even their harems, so long as their consciences are not sufficiently instructed to wish for something better—but to take from them that which damages them even more than it harms the Christians—the right to injure the latter by continual persecution."

Partly because of his attitude towards the Eastern Question; partly because of some early sermons in which he endeavoured to trace to a Christian source some of the ideas, such as Freedom and Progress, on which Liberalism subsists; and partly because of his personal attachment to Gladstone, Liddon was sometimes claimed as a Liberal; but the claim was unsubstantiated. He once said to me: " The real interest of politics is to watch the course of events, and, when the time for voting comes, to vote for the party which is supporting what one believes to be the cause of righteousness in the prominent question of the moment." Thus he voted for Gladstone at the critical election of 1865, when Oxford dismissed him. He voted for the Liberals in 1880, when the nation dethroned Lord Beaconsfield. He voted for the Tories in 1885, when the Liberals, under Chamberlain's maladroit guidance, were assailing the Church. " As to Liberalism," he once said, "I admire its foreign policy, but I cannot endure it in the sphere of education. It is by instinct heathenish in that matter." About Home Rule he had "an open mind," but he "found it difficult to see how, if granted, it will not create more difficulties than it relieves."

As regards foreign affairs, Liddon's chief concern was for the persecuted Christians in Eastern Europe, and he looked on Russia as their divinely appointed protectress. But he was scarcely less concerned for the well-being of

France, which he loved with an affection born of religious and intellectual affinity. In August 1870 he wrote to a friend: "Yes! my sympathies are certainly with France. Bismarck is a much nearer reproduction of the *bad side* of Napoleon I than Napoleon III is. He is, as the Germans call him, 'a man of blood and iron.' His dealings with Hanover, Frankfort, and Denmark were injustices of the grossest kind; and, apart from the Spanish Question, France has, I think, *ample* grounds for her quarrel with Prussia in the evasion of the articles of the Treaty of Prague."

In the following year, preaching at St. Paul's Cathedral, he uttered a remarkable prediction: "Peace may be concluded (God grant that it may be!) within a few weeks; but who can seriously suppose that a peace based upon an enforced severance of French citizens from their country will last longer than the exhaustion of conquered France?"

On the economic side of politics Liddon's leanings were perceptibly, though not avowedly, towards what is vaguely called "Christian Socialism." He detested the harshness and hardness of the Poor Law as commonly administered. He had scant respect for the stiff dogmatism of Political Economy. A beggar on the roadside was to him a brother in Christ, with a definite claim on his sympathy and help. I well remember his lively interest in the great Dock Strike in 1889, and the alacrity with which he subscribed to the fund for maintaining the dockers' wives and children. " There, at any rate," he said, " one cannot be doing wrong."

This acute and practical humanitarianism was indeed a part of his religion. His controversial zeal sometimes blinded dull people to the fervent love of his fellow-creatures, which was a governing principle of his nature; and perhaps this was not surprising, for when he felt keenly he spoke strongly; and keen feeling and strong speech are alike bewildering to the flaccid and the indifferent. But those who knew him well—and I had the happiness of knowing him from my first term at Oxford to his death—always realized that in him they had one of the warmest, the kindest, and the most faithful of friends.

That he was one of the truest saints ever produced by the Church of England is indeed a commonplace; but he was also one of the most interesting and agreeable people whom it ever was one's privilege to know. If he was not always the wisest, his errors of judgment were due to qualities which in themselves are attractive — enthusiasm, romance, and an imagination so keen that it saw visions as if they were already realities.

CHAPTER XXIV

ALEXANDER HERIOT MACKONOCHIE

THIS is a name—not, it must be admitted, a very euphonious one—which belonged in almost equal proportions to the Sixties, the Seventies, and the Eighties. One might almost say of Mackonochie what Cowper said of Whitefield—that he

> Stood pilloried on infamy's high stage,
> And bore the pelting scorn of half an age.

This infamy he incurred, as his predecessor had incurred it, by a lifelong effort to bring the Gospel within the reach of the poor and the outcast; and his obstinate persistence in the methods which seemed to him effective for the purpose awoke the scorn of the pliable and the easy-going.

In person Mackonochie, though far from

---

[1] 1825–87.

handsome, was striking and impressive. He
was tall and spare, though not emaciated, and
he bore himself with a singular dignity. I
cannot imagine that any one ever took a liberty
with him; and, though the kindest heart in
the world lay concealed under that stern aspect,
his mere glance would have checked forward-
ness or familiarity. His nose was aquiline, his
chin prominent, and his mouth was drawn down
at the corners in a rather forbidding fashion.
His complexion was clear and bright; his
hair a very dark brown; and, though the greater
part of his face was shaved, it retained on each
side a fragment of hair, which in contradis-
tinction to the clean shave of Romanism, and
the luxuriant whiskers of Protestantism, acquired
the nickname of "The Anglican Inch."

Mackonochie was born in 1825, of purely
Scottish descent, his father having been a
colonel in the Honourable East India Company's
service. He received his early education at
private schools at Bath and Exeter, and after
studying for a short time at the University of
Edinburgh he went up to Wadham College,
Oxford. He obtained a Second Class in the
Final Classical School, and then, in obedience
to a vocation which he had felt from his earliest

years, he dedicated himself to the ministerial
career. He was ordained deacon by Bishop
Denison at Salisbury in 1849, and priest in
1850. His first curacy was at Westbury, Wilt-
shire, and thence he removed to Wantage,
where Dr. Liddon was one of his fellow-curates.
During a visit to London in 1857 he went to
St. George's-in-the-East; and he was so deeply
impressed by the solitary and strenuous work
which Father Lowder was there carrying on, that
in the following year he joined the mission and
came to live at the Mission House in Wellclose
Square. It was at this time that, unknown to
himself, he fell under the watchful eye of a
wealthy and devout layman, J. G. Hubbard,
who discerned in him a man fitted beyond all
others for the difficult and laborious charge of
the church which he was then building in
Baldwin's Gardens, Holborn, afterwards famous
as St. Alban's. Never was a more judicious
selection made, for in many aspects of his
character and constitution Mackonochie was
the ideal priest for a Mission-Church. In early
youth his health had been delicate, but strength
had come with years, and long self-discipline
had rendered him almost insensible to fatigue,
and impervious to common ailments. He could

fast absolutely from the evening of Maundy
Thursday to midday on Easter Sunday, and
then sit down to a hearty meal and feel none
the worse. His head was as hard as his body
—clear, cold, and strong. His habit of mind
was characteristically Scotch in its dry logic
and theoretical consistency. No one would
have thought of describing him as a very clever
man; but his astonishing powers of "grind"
enabled him to attain at the University and,
subsequently, a degree of intellectual success
out of proportion to his purely mental gifts.
Nothing was more characteristic of the man
than the dogged resolution with which he would
address himself to the study of some quite uncongenial branch of knowledge, such as an
unfamiliar school of painting or a freshly discovered science. At these he would "toil
terribly"; and, holding that a religious teacher
should keep abreast of all new knowledge, he
would dutifully endeavour to familiarize himself
with ideas and phenomena which in themselves
had only the faintest interest for him. This
intense habit of conscientious study was only
a form of his invincible will. A more resolute
man never lived. When once he had deliberately adopted a course, he pursued it with grim

tenacity, and his power of resistance to pressure
was at least as strong as his constructive
volition.

Hence arose an unfortunate disagreement
between himself and the founder of St. Alban's,
which caused so much pain to two excellent
men. When Mr. Hubbard offered him the
living, he refused to entertain the offer except
on the condition that he should be absolutely
free, and unfettered by any understandings
except those which bound him as a clergyman
of the Church of England. He frankly stated
that his principles of doctrine and worship were
those which have since come to be called
"Ritualistic"; and, in his own words, he made
it plain that he could not accept the responsibility of a parish "except on the basis that my
duty to God and to the souls of His people,
according to the best judgment that I could
form of it, would have to be paramount over
every other consideration. The point I kept
before myself, and as forcibly as I could im-'
pressed on others, was that when once a priest
was licensed to the parish, and the church
consecrated, the work would be neither his nor
Mr. Hubbard's, but God's. With the priest,
as God's steward, would rest the responsibility,

and, therefore, with him alone, after such
security for sound judgment as he might be
able to take, must rest the decision for which
he alone would answer at the Judgment."

These considerations, strongly urged by
Mackonochie, were duly weighed by Hubbard
and other friends of the new church, with the
result that they implored Mackonochie to raise
no further difficulties, but to accept the charge
on his own terms. This he cheerfully did.
All he asked was a free hand. His was the
responsibility, and his must be the power. He
could not share the one; he dared not share the
other. From the moment when he accepted
the charge of St. Alban's, he sketched out for
himself a line of action which, whether wise or
unwise, was bound to develope into the form
which it ultimately assumed. Strong in his
Scotch love of logical coherence, nothing could
turn him back, or modify his judgment, or stay
his hand. Prosecutions, persecutions, admoni-
tions, abuse, ridicule, calumny—all ran off his
robust constitution like water off a duck's back.
And yet, except in matters where his ecclesiastical conscience and judgment were involved,
he was the humblest and most teachable of
men. He was modestly aware of his intellectual

A. H. MACKONOCHIE.

To face p. 417.

defects, always ready to be taught, and full of touching confidence in the superior wisdom of much younger men. By them in turn he was greatly loved. His absolute honesty, sincerity, directness, and fearlessness commanded their respect. His contempt for wealth, ease, enjoyment, worldly advancement, fascinated their imagination. He had acquired, in the most sacred of all confidences, a deep insight into the inner springs of character and conduct, which was as helpful as it sometimes was startling. His intense and most practical sympathy with poverty, sickness, pain, and trouble, whether material or mental, endeared him to thousands who would have been repelled by his stern fidelity to the letter of an unpopular creed, by his prosaic and unimaginative temperament, and by the dignified austerity of his personal demeanour.

He was a remarkable, though not exactly a fine, preacher. His voice was harsh and monotonous; his gestures were ungraceful, and he had a trick of hanging his hands over the front of the pulpit, which suggested that they had just been washed and were hung out to dry. He had not the slightest eloquence, or even rhetoric; but he had quite sufficient fluency, and a complete command of clear, plain, and forcible English. He was wholly free from "gush"; but his spirtual earnestness, his deep sense of sin, and his strong insistence on practical duty, gave his sermons a pecular cogency. For a long series of Good Fridays I attended the service of the Three Hours which he conducted at St. Alban's; and I have never heard that peculiarly difficult ministry so well performed.

But Mackonochie had not been long at St. Alban's when trouble began. The high ritual practised in the church attracted public notice. The daily papers described it in "graphic" articles. The angry bigotry of a Puritan section wholly unconnected with the parish was aroused; and it was determined to test the legality of the ceremonial used at St. Alban's. The difficulty was to obtain a prosecutor, for the great majority of the parishioners were devoted to their clergy and church. At worst they were indifferent. No one was hostile.

The real prosecuter was the notorious Church Association, described by Bishop Magee as "The Persecution Company, Limited," and it secured the co-operation of a certain Mr. Martin, a resident in St. George's, Bloomsbury, whose sole connexion with St. Alban's was that his name stood on the parish rate-book, for some schools of which he was secretary. At Martin's instance, legal proceedings against Mackonochie were begun on the 28th of March, 1867, when the Bishop of London [1] sent the case by Letters of Request to the Court of Arches.

The charge against Mackonochie was that he used in divine worship certain specified practices which were contrary to, or inconsistent with, the rubrics of the Church of England. The case was tried in the Court of Arches, before Sir Robert Phillimore, who decided against Mackonochie on certain points, but with regard to three—namely, altar-lights, kneeling at the consecration, and elevating the Holy Sacrament—pronounced that they were legal. On these three points Martin forthwith appealed to the Judicial Committee of the Privy Council; and an enquiry touching the niceties of eucharistic ritual was conducted by a tribunal "including a Presbyterian, an ex-representative of the Orange town of Belfast, a partisan Archbishop, a lay Low Churchman, and a theologian,[2] who talked about 'the inferior Persons of the Trinity.'" It is not suprising that, under such judges, a Ritualist

[1] A. C. Tait.   [2] Lord Westbury.

fared badly. The case was given against Mackonochie, and he was condemned in costs. Mackonochie, who in truth cared little for the precise forms of ecclesiastical ceremony, so long as reverence, seemliness, and intelligible teaching were secured, immediately conformed to the letter of the judgment. But his prosecutors were not satisfied with the extent of his compliance, and delated him to the Privy Council for disobedience to their monition. It may not be uninteresting, as illustrating the spirit and methods of this prosecution, to cite a portion of the bill of costs presented by the proctors for the Church Association to Mackonochie, exceeding, before taxation, £400, and relating only to that part of the case heard on December 4, 1869 :—

July 1869.

	£	s.	d.
Attending Mr. Pond, instructing him to attend St. Alban's on Sunday, July 11th	0	6	8
Taking his statement and fair copy	0	18	4
Paid him for his attendance	2	2	0
Attending Mr. Pond, instructing him to attend the early Communion on July 12th (i.e. the next day, Monday) and four following days	0	6	8
Taking his statement and fair copy	0	18	4
Paid him for his attendance (two guineas for Sunday, one each week-day). Three persons were employed	5	5	0

Similar entries occur all through, exceeding in the whole £100. Though judgment was given in Mackonochie's favour on two charges out of three, he was ordered to pay the whole costs. Not satisfied with this partial victory, the prosecutors now proceeded against Mackonochie for sanctioning the performance by others of illegal acts. Hired spies were again sent to make observations at the church; and, although their evidence was contradicted on some main points by the affidavits of clergy, churchwardens, and lay communicants, the Privy Council found Mackonochie guilty of disobedience to their judgment, and suspended him from the performance of his clerical duties for three months. During this period the services were carried on precisely as before. Mackonochie returned to his post when the term of his suspension had expired, and for three years the parish was left in peace. In 1874 the second "London Mission" was held, and, partly in connexion with the mode in which it had been conducted in St. Alban's parish, a fresh prosecution was begun by the indefatigable Martin, and Mackonochie was again suspended.

This second suspension was the signal for some very decisive proceedings. A Committee

of Defence was formed in the parish, and an
emphatic remonstrance against the treatment
of the vicar was presented to the Archbishop
of Canterbury.[1] The Bishop of London [2] refused
to receive a similar deputation. During Mackonochie's suspension, A. H. Stanton, as curate-
in-charge, refused to celebrate the Holy Communion with maimed rites, and the congregation
of St. Alban moved in a body to St. Vedast's,
Foster Lane. When Mackonochie returned to
the parish, some alterations were made in the
accustomed ceremonial, and the enemy seemed
to be for a while appeased. Then came seven
years of quiet and successful work, and ever-
increasing activity in the service of the poor.
But in 1882 the inveterate Church Association
prepared a fresh lawsuit with a view to
Mackonochie's deprivation. At this time Archbishop Tait was on his death-bed, and he resolved,
with creditable freedom from petty pride, to
acknowledge and to repair the unhappy effects
of his own Public Worship Regulation Act.
From his death-bed he arranged that Mackonochie
should exchange livings with the Rev. R. A. J.
Suckling, Vicar of St. Peter's, London Docks ; and

[1] A. C. Tait, translated in 1868 from London.
[2] J. Jackson.

he procured the sanction of the Bishop of London
to this arrangement, which defeated the projected
lawsuits.   To St. Peter's Mackonochie accordingly
went at the beginning of 1883, and there he
continued until the threat of yet another prosecution, promoted by the agency which had done
so much to embitter his life, made it desirable,
in the interests of St. Peter's parish, that its
much-persecuted vicar should resign his charge.

The anxieties and hardships of his life had
told on him more severely than his friends had
guessed.   He resigned St. Peter's, and returned
as curate to his old parish of St. Alban, where
he was welcomed with touching and chivalrous
loyalty by his friend and successor, Mr. Suckling.   Before long a gradual failure of strength
compelled him to withdraw from ministerial
work, and to live mainly with his own family in
the country, though he still dearly enjoyed the
society of intimate friends and the beauties of
nature.   On December 15, 1887, while on a
visit to the Bishop of Argyll at Ballachulish,
he went out for a long walk and, being over-
taken by snowstorm and darkness, lost his way
in the Mamore deer-forest.   He was found there
two days later, lying dead in a snowdrift, his
body guarded by two dogs which had accom-

panied him on his walk. Death came as a
merciful release from increasing infirmity, and
closed a life which, though not free from errors
of judgment, was spent with prodigal self-sacrifice
in the service of his fellow-men. The following
words are from the pen of his friend and colleague, Arthur Stanton :—

"It is ungracious, and beyond just surmise, to
say that the enfeeblement of his manly, strong,
loving life was the necessary result of the repeated prosecutions which the Church Association thought it their duty to maintain ; but
there can be little doubt that underneath the
brave cheerfulness with which he met all the
reverses and submitted to the indignities conse-
quent upon them, there lay a very keen sensitiveness, and that the 'iron entered into his soul.'
For although never admitted by him, it was
observable, so that no one wondered at the
storm-beaten expression on his face and the
broken utterances of his lips which marked
the two declining years of his life.

"The mystery of his stern, hard, self-devoted
life completed itself in the weird circumstances
of his death. He seems to have walked round
and round the hollow in which he had taken
shelter from the mountain storm, trying to keep

life in him as long as he could, then as if he knew his hour had come, deliberately to have uncovered his head to say his last prayers, and then to have laid his head upon his hand and died, sheltered in 'the hollow of the hand' of God whom he had served so faithfully; and at His bidding the wild wind from off the moor wreathed his head with snow."

This dramatic ending to a noble life awoke a general and kindly interest in the history and character of Alexander Heriot Mackonochie. A generation has arisen which never heard of the riots at St. George's-in-the-East, and barely remembers the acrimonious litigation which so long harassed St. Alban's. Modern society has learned the lesson of toleration, or perhaps of indifference, so rapidly and so completely, that it can only recall by an effort the passionate animosities which thirty and twenty years ago made ecclesiastical controversy so furious and so vindictive. In this altered condition of the public mind it may not be uninteresting to recall the kind of life which earned for Mackonochie the guerdon of personal violence, protracted persecution, judicial penalties, pecuniary loss, professional discredit, shattered health, and ruined happiness.

That life may be expressed in three words, *Sacerdotium est sacrificium*; and, in Mack-onochie's case, the sacrifice was not more deliberate than complete. In early manhood and middle age and advancing years; at morning, at noon, at night; in summer and winter; in work-days and holiday-time, in popularity and perse-cution, he gave himself, body and mind and soul, to the work which he had undertaken. Indefatigable in the duties of his sacred office, he laboured far beyond its limits for all that could serve the material and moral interests of his fellow-men. He worked for public health, for higher and wider education, for all innocent and national recreation. Not content with teaching, and preaching, and visiting the sick, and guiding the perplexed, he instructed the ignorant and comforted the sorrowful and fed the hungry and clothed the naked, and helped, without pauper-izing, the industrious poor. Frederic Myers portrayed a life so spent when he made St. Paul exclaim:—

> Never at even, pillowed on a pleasure,
>   Sleep with the wings of aspiration furled;
> Hide the last mite of the forbidden treasure;
>   Keep for my joys a world within the world.

It is not to be conceived that such a life, lived with unflagging purpose for twenty years in one of the poorest and most degraded quarters of a crowded city, could fail of its effect. "There is nothing fruitful but sacrifice," cried Lamennais, when no other conviction was left to cheer him; and the sacrifice of Mackonochie's life bore abundant fruit. He enlarged the boundaries of the Kingdom of God by making the lives of men purer, brighter, and more humane.

CHAPTER XXV

ARTHUR HENRY STANTON

IN the year 1862 A. H. Mackonochie, whom I described in the last chapter, became incumbent of the newly created parish of St. Alban's, Holborn, and he soon acquired a remarkable coadjutor.

Arthur Henry Stanton was born in 1839, the youngest son of a manufacturer at Stroud. He was educated at Rugby under Dr. Goulburn, and at Trinity College, Oxford. After his B.A. degree, he spent two terms at Cuddesdon, and in 1862 he joined himself to Mackonochie as a lay-worker in what were then the slums of Baldwin's Gardens and Gray's Inn Lane. In the following Advent he was ordained deacon by Bishop Tait, and so began a ministry which was pursued in the same place and under the same conditions for fifty years.

The square peg in the round hole is pro-

A. H. STANTON.

To face p. 4:8.

verbially a distressing sight, yet in this ill-
arranged world of ours it is painfully common.
How constantly one hears the cry: "What a
first-rate soldier Brown would have made, only
his father forced him into business!" "Jones
ought to have been a clergyman instead of a
politician, for he is always preaching." "Robinson
is really an artist, but he took that family
living, and now neglects it shamefully." Lord
Beaconsfield aimed one of his most poignant
shafts (pseudonymously) at Theodore Hook:
"Nature had intended him for a scholar and
a wit; necessity made him a scribbler and a
buffoon." Matthew Arnold ought to have been
a poet, but his wish to marry prompted him
to become an Inspector of Schools. In a conversation with Arnold, Lord Beaconsfield affected
to regret that he had abandoned literature for
for politics. Sir William Harcourt once told
the astonished Sunday-school children of Derby
that the happiest hours of his life had been spent
in a country parsonage. Gladstone was believed
by some of his circle to be sorry that he had
not taken Holy Orders.

But now and then one comes across a happy
case where the personal qualities and the require-
ments of the office so exactly fit each other that

one says instinctively: "This man is precisely
what he was intended to be, and by being what
he is, he has attained his predestined perfection."
It was so with Arthur Stanton. I simply cannot conceive of him except as a priest, and a
priest working in a church where all social distinctions were obliterated.

He was a Liberal to the backbone. "Where
the spirit of the Lord is, there is Liberty"
—"Ye shall know the truth, and the truth
shall make you free"—were texts on which
he was never tired of insisting. One Easter
Day, addressing the school-children in St.
Alban's church, he pointed to a representa-
tion of our Lord with a banner in His hand,
and thus explained it: "There you see Him,
rising victorious from the grave. And what does
He carry? A banner. Yes, and what banner?
The Banner of Liberty—the liberty which by
His death He bought for every human soul."
It was natural that a mind built on these lines
should have scant respect for authority; and
Stanton was never better pleased than when
proving, from Scripture and history, that infallibility resides neither at Rome nor at Lambeth,
but in that innermost sanctuary of the conscience,
where alone God's voice is heard.

Some twenty years ago a Roman priest, Father Duggan, of Maidstone (who died last year), got into trouble with his ecclesiastical superiors over some point of discipline. Stanton, discerning a congenial spirit, instantly sought Duggan's acquaintance, and soon paid him a visit. Returning to London, Stanton narrated the conversation which he had held with his host, and the narrative ended in this fashion : " On the morning when I came away, I said, ' Well, I've had a delightful time here. I've found myself able to talk quite freely to you, and now I want you to talk freely to me. Answer me one question. I've been a dead failure as an English priest. Do you think I should have been more successful if I had been ordained in your Church ? ' And what do you think the fellow said ? Well, he said, ' I don't think you would have been a success in any Church in which obedience was required.' And I'm not sure that he was wrong."

The immediate reference was of course to ecclesiastical order ; but in matters social and political Stanton was always, by the very law of his being, "for the under-dog." All his politics were governed by his religion. He said with Lacordaire : " I know no Liberalism, except

that which I sucked in from the breasts of the
Gospel." War, he would say, is an evil; and
one of the greatest of evils; "But there is an
evil which is worse, and that is slavery."

Though he had the carriage and manner of
an English gentleman, with a certain dignity
which was all his own, he abhorred social distinctions, and severances between class and class.
In the Workmen's Clubs and Postmen's Leagues
and Homes of Rest, and other institutions which
he organized, he always laid great stress on the
Sunday tea-party. "When men sit down together to a meal, there is no room for pomposity or pride or the feeling 'I'm better than
you.' The common meal recognizes the equality
of man."

I said just now that, in talking to Father
Duggan, Stanton referred to his ministry as a
failure. This was not a vanity or an affectation,
but almost an obsession. In early days he had
been shamefully mishandled by bishops. He
was inhibited from preaching in diocese after
diocese, and treated as if he were an avowed
heretic or a man of doubtful character. The
iron entered his soul, and he never could shake
off the notion that a ministry which had been
thus reprehended by ecclesiastical authority must

have been a failure. Those who knew that it had been more successful, in the great object of all ministry, than anything that the Church of England had known since the days of Wesley, strove long and earnestly to remove this strange and even morbid misconception. Their efforts culminated in a public gathering held on the 26th of June, 1907, when Stanton received an address, signed by 3,800 men, who stated in the plainest words the imperishable gratitude which they owed him for spiritual assistance; and their undying affection and respect. In the face of that testimony, it was impossible to cherish the delusion of failure, and the clouds were rolled away, never to return.

I spoke at the beginning of Stanton's peculiar fitness for his work in life. That fitness was combined of many elements, and each was striking. To begin with, he had perfect health, abundant strength, and that "joy of living" which accompanies them. Then he had an exceedingly good brain, quick in apprehension and cogent in reasoning; which, though he never was a reader or a student, kept him well abreast of what was going on in life and thought. Then again he was wonderfully handsome—tall, slight, yet strongly built; with a straight nose, a wide but firmly compressed mouth, and a most resolute chin. His dark eyes were full of tenderness and fire ; and, combined with his olive skin and raven-black hair, they gave him something of an Italian or Spanish look.[1] Every movement, every attitude, though unstudied and unposed, was graceful ; and his gestures, which he used in preaching with an un-English freedom, though sometimes exaggerated were always effective.

The power of his preaching was extraordinary. He was master of every mood of oratory. All who between 1863 and 1913 attended, even casually, the High Mass at St. Alban's, will remember his eloquence, his dramatic power, his ringing scorn against injustice and hypocrisy, his noble and contagious enthusiasm for the Religion of the Cross and all that it implies. But probably only those who are themselves accustomed to speak in public could fully appreciate the perfect art which underlay the eloquence, or perceive, through the apparent spontaneousness, the lifelong study which must have gone to produce so absolute a result.

It is difficult to describe Stanton in society, for he went into it very sparingly. He was

[1] The same colouring was noticeable in Dr. Liddon ; but they both were pure-blooded Englishmen.

not in the slightest degree ascetic or austere; but I suspect that his ever-present sense of the poverty and misery in which so large a number of our fellow-creatures always live would have haunted him as it haunted Bishop Westcott, and would have prevented him from feeling at ease in splendour and "pomp and circumstance." But in private life, among people whom he loved and trusted, he was absolutely delightful. His rich though sometimes sarcastic humour, his rapid alternations of cloud and sunshine, his eagerness in friendship, his passionate loyalty to *Auld lang syne*, gave him a singularly powerful hold on human hearts. I could not, if I would, express a tenth part of what Arthur Stanton's friendship was to me and mine.

I spoke before of Stanton's perfect health, but a long life of absolutely incessant labour told heavily on his strength; and, after he turned seventy, he began to suffer from some dyspeptic troubles. Towards the end of 1912 those troubles became more urgent; and, after preaching at Colchester on the 24th of November, he was seized by sudden and dangerous hæmorrhage. He never preached again. On the 7th of March, 1913, he received a letter from the Bishop of London [1] asking him to

---

[1] A. F. Winnington-Ingram.

accept a Prebendal Stall in St. Paul's, in honour of the "fifty years of service" that he had given to St. Alban's and the diocese. The offer was most kindly meant, and by making it the Bishop went some way towards rolling away the reproach often and justly levelled against the Anglican Episcopate, that it snubs its best men and promotes their inferiors.

But the suggested dignity would never have been very suitable to Stanton's character and habits, and now it was also too late. In writing to decline it, he said: "Only one thing I ask of you and those who want to show me any kindness, and that is: Let me, after my fifty years' run, slow down quietly into the terminus, not jerking over the points." Three weeks later he was dead.

CHAPTER XXVI

LADY HOLLAND

WHEN one talks of "Lady Holland" people generally imagine that one means that imperious dame (born Elizabeth Vassall) who figures so largely and so disagreeably in the Life of Macaulay and the Letters of Sydney Smith.

To people of my generation the name conveys a very different personality. The Lady Holland whom we remember was to the full as clever a woman as her more notorious mother-in-law, and ten times more attractive. She was pre-eminently a figure of the Seventies; but, as far as I know, no attempts have ever been made to place her character on permanent record.

Lady Mary Augusta Coventry was the daughter of the eighth Earl of Coventry, by his marriage with Lady Mary Beauclerk, daughter of the sixth Duke of St. Albans. She was born in 1817, and a great part of her early life was spent on the Continent, where she formed many of her closest friendships, and contracted habits of thought, sentiment, and conduct quite unlike those which characterize the general run of home-keeping Englishmen. In 1833 Lady Mary Coventry married Henry Edward Fox, who in 1840 became the fourth and last Lord Holland, and who was Minister Plenipotentiary at the Court of Tuscany.

From the time of her marriage, Lady Mary Fox lived principally in Italy; and though, after her husband's accession to his father's title, they spent some part of each year in England, they still considered Naples their home. There they formed and maintained their most intimate friendships, and there they were continually surrounded by the society which they so peculiarly enjoyed. Their foreign associations were made all the stronger by the fact that they had both joined the Roman Catholic Church.

The last Lord Holland died in 1859, and left his widow full control of all his fortune, including Holland House in Kensington, and

LADY HOLLAND.

To face p. 438.

St. Ann's Hill near Chertsey. Between these two houses, most unlike but each perfect in its way, Lady Holland spent the summer months, returning, as long as she could, to Naples for the winter. In her late years she was not strong enough for the long journey to Italy, and she lived entirely in England, except for an occasional visit to some German watering-place.

For the greater part of the year she lived at St. Ann's Hill, once the home of Charles James Fox, and stored with relics of strenuous Whiggery. She rejoiced to tell the story of the seventh Duke of Bedford, who, visiting the widowed Mrs. Fox at St. Ann's Hill, asked her ancient butler if there were many Tories in the neighbourhood, and received the pathetic reply, "Please, your Grace, we're eat up with them."

St. Ann's Hill was a delightful villa, and was enlivened by a constant succession of visitors from London; but for epithets fit to describe the unique charm of Holland House we must go back to Macaulay, who, in 1841, half-seriously, half-fancifully, foretold the possible fate of the noble mansion, famed all over Europe, where so many happy and instructive hours of his early manhood had been passed, "The wonderful city which, ancient and gigantic as it is, still continues to grow as fast as a young town of logwood by a 'water-privilege' in Michigan, may soon displace those turrets and gardens which are associated with so much that is interesting and noble; with the courtly magnificence of Rich, with the loves of Ormond, with the councils of Cromwell, with the death of Addison. The time is coming when, perhaps, a few old men, the last survivors of our generation, will in vain seek, amidst streets and squares, and railway-stations, for the site of that dwelling which was in their youth the favourite resort of wits and beauties, of painters and poets, of scholars, philosophers, and statesmen. They will then remember, with strange tenderness, many objects once familiar to them in the avenue and the terrace, the busts and the paintings, the carving, the grotesque gilding, and the enigmatical mottoes. With peculiar fondness they will recall that venerable chamber in which all the antique gravity of a college library was so singularly blended with all that female grace and wit could devise to embellish a drawing-room. They will recollect, not unmoved, those shelves loaded with the varied

learning of many lands and many ages, and
those portraits in which were preserved the
features of the best and wisest Englishmen of
two generations. They will recollect how many
men who have guided the politics of Europe,
who have moved great assemblies by reason
and eloquence, who have put life into bronze
and canvas, or who have left to posterity
things so written as it shall not willingly let
them die, were there mixed with all that
was loveliest and gayest in the society of the
most splendid of capitals."

Of this highly-wrought description contemporaries said (what one cannot always say of its
writer's handiwork) that it was neither exaggerated nor inexact. In truth Holland House was,
alike in its structure, its associations, and the
society that assembled under its roof, unique;
and the charms which had made it famous in
the Twenties and Thirties of the nineteenth
century were assuredly not diminished in the
Seventies and Eighties. Here Lady Holland
used to establish herself for two months in the
late summer and early autumn, and here her
hospitalities were amongst the most graceful
and delightful incidents of social life. Her
annual garden-parties combined all the solemn

dignity which clings to one of the most historical of English houses, with the fantastic grace and sprightly merriment of an Italian *Festa*.

The hostess's failing health brought these large parties to an end; but, whenever Lady Holland was known to be in London, even in the desolate months of August and September, her shrine was thronged by devotees. Diplomatists of every nation found a second home at Holland House. To its hospitable doors every distinguished foreigner gravitated as by a natural law. Some of the most accomplished of the older men of London were habitual guests, and conversation not unworthy of Fitzpatrick and Jekyll, Mackintosh and Moore, was to be heard at those delightful dinners, un-English in every detail of their composition and service. Half the dishes were French and half Italian; every European language was spoken in turn; the gentlemen returned to the drawing-room simultaneously with the ladies, and the ladies, then greatly daring, ventured, in secluded corners, on the stimulus of cigarettes.

As years went on and the fatigues of hospitality began to tell increasingly on her strength, Lady Holland lived less and less at Holland

House, and, not long before her death, a speculative builder approached her with what would have been to most people a tempting offer. He proposed to buy the reversion of the house, with its gardens, park and farm, for half a million sterling. Lady Holland's reply was worthy of herself. She said that she belonged to the House of Fox not by birth but only by marriage, and that Holland House should not, by her act, pass out of the family which had made it famous. Of that family Lord Ilchester was the senior representative, and to him she left it. I fear that the exactions of recent Chancellors of the Exchequer have converted the hayfields, which I remember, into building-land; but at the annual Flower Show the world sees the lovely house, still standing amid its gardens and terraces, and joins in the pious aspiration of the lines which Hookham Frere cut with a diamond on the window-pane—

> May neither fire destroy, nor waste impair,
> Nor time consume thee till the twentieth Heir;
> May Taste respect thee and may Fashion spare.[1]

One touch of personal description must close this sketch.

[1] On hearing of this inscription, Samuel Rogers said, "I wonder where Frere got the diamond."

Lady Holland was one of the smallest of womankind, less than five feet high, exceedingly slender, with the most exquisite hands and feet. The oldest tree in the pleasure-grounds of Holland House might have described her in the words of *The Talking Oak*—

> I swear, by leaf, and wind, and rain
> (And hear me with thine ears),
> That, though I circle in the grain
> Five hundred rings of years,
>
> Yet, since I first could cast a shade,
> Did never creature pass
> So slightly, musically made,
> So light upon the grass.

Her features were pronounced and sharply cut. Her rich, dark hair retained its colour to the last. But her most conspicuous trait was the extraordinary brightness of her piercing eyes. They sparkled and flashed like a girl's, and when she smiled they lit up her face with a peculiarly bewitching expression. In later years she never laid aside her customary suit of solemn black, and a cap which, to quote Lord Beaconsfield, "should have been immortalized by Mieris or Gerard Douw."

In mind Lady Holland was singularly vivacious. Her mental gaze was of penetrating power. She saw through unreality, vanity, and pretence at a glance; but she was full of the most genial charity towards mere error, ignorance, or indiscretion. She was extremely quick in repartee, loved a joke, and had a peculiarly keen appreciation of whatever was fine in character, art, or literature. For some years she suffered grievously, but her patience and courage in bearing pain, her anxiety that it should not distress other people, and her bright cheerfulness in forgetting it, were models to all like sufferers. In character she was one of the justest, kindest, and most generous of women; overflowing with tenderness alike to man and beast; and the most affectionate and faithful of friends. There seemed to be something specially appropriate to her nature in the beautiful benediction of the Church in which she lived and died—

Lux perpetua luceat ei.

CHAPTER XXVII

A GROUP OF HOSTESSES

IN thus associating the names of the ladies whom I am going to describe, of course I do not mean that they belonged to the same generation. But they all were hostesses who entertained in London during the period which this book covers. Nor do I mean that they resembled one another, or even had much in common. On the contrary, they were as diverse as any seven people commonly are; each had a marked individuality; but it is true of them all that the mere mention of their names awakes a train of pleasant recollections.

I obey a natural instinct when I place first in my list of hostesses Mrs. William Lowther, whose husband built Lowther Lodge, and who made it from 1876 to 1906 a vigorous centre of social life. Statistics in such cases are impossible; but I should imagine that Lowther Lodge opened

MRS. LOWTHER.

To face p. 447.

its doors oftener than any house in London; for, when it was not occupied by dinners and luncheons and teas and dances and garden-parties, it welcomed all manner of organizations which had for their object the cultivation of Art, the diffusion of knowledge, and the improvement of social conditions. But my reason for placing Mrs. Lowther first in my list is the fact that I had known her all my life. Her home and mine were near each other; and I had been accustomed, from very early years, to regard her as the cleverest woman I ever met. Entrance upon society in London gives a young man the inestimable privilege of acquaintance with charming and accomplished women, and I hope I was not unworthy of that privilege; but nothing that I encountered in London ever altered that early impression.

Mrs. Lowther was a daughter of Lord Wensleydale (previously Baron Parke), a great scholar, a great lawyer, and a great judge; and he was accustomed to say: "If my daughter Alice had been a boy, she would have made the name of Parke illustrious in jurisprudence," to which his friends would reply, "It is that already."

Mrs. Lowther's was what men arrogantly call

a "masculine" mind: clear, penetrating, and exact. It was little affected by emotion, and still less by mere assertion. It went straight to the heart of each point submitted to it, and was never satisfied with an answer which logic did not justify. To the gift of penetration she added what Tennyson called "the power of ministration." Her organizing skill was extraordinary, and everything to which she set her hand she did well. It would be hazardous to affirm of anything that Mrs. Lowther could not do it; but perhaps her most remarkable skill lay in painting, and in the decorative arts allied with it. Her conversation was quite first rate: free, bright, responsive, with a considerable vein of sarcasm. Her opinions were strong, and she uttered them unhesitatingly, yet never so as to irritate the opponent with whom she was debating. "A strong-minded woman" is a term of reproach; but such are the vagaries of language that "a woman of strong intellect" is praise. When with such an intellect are conjoined high principle and strong affections, then we see what Wordsworth meant :—

> The reason firm, the temperate will,
> Endurance, foresight, strength, and skill;
> A perfect Woman, nobly planned,
> To warn, to comfort, and command

" The Duchess of Cleveland " is a title which
conveys to people of my generation two very
different characters. Let me take them in
chronological order.

Caroline Lowther, wife of the third Duke of
Cleveland, was born in 1792 and died in 1883.
Her venerable age, apart from anything else,
would have made her interesting ; but there was
a great deal more than mere antiquity about
her, which made her worth observing and remembering.   She had entered society very
young, being presented at Queen Charlotte's
Drawing-room ; she had danced with the Prince
of Orange, had attended Lady Buckinghamshire's " breakfasts " on the site of what is now
Hobart Place, and had hunted in a scarlet habit
with Lord Darlington's foxhounds.

She was a naturally shrewd woman, and well
educated according to the standards of her day ;
she was keenly interested in politics, being
always on the High Tory side ; and, if she could
have had her own way, she would have lived in
a society where literature and politics played a
part, but were kept in due subordination to
birth and rank.   But an early and ambitious
marriage united her for life, or at least for fifty
years, to a good-natured but quite uneducated

sportsman, who loved the company of trainers
and game-keepers and, though he sate in Parliament for Pocket Boroughs, gave political
society an uncommonly wide berth. If this ill-
assorted couple had been blest with a family,
not only would their home have presumably
been happier, but the Duchess would have been
a more popular woman. If she had been a
mother, she would have been less of a gover-
ness—less fond of laying down the law, less
inclined to set every one right, less apt to snub.
Such exercises of social authority do not endear
people to their contemporaries; in fact, they are
intolerable; but, when there is an immense gap
between the age of the corrector and the age of
the corrected, they are inoffensive and even
amusing. Perhaps it was salutary for forward
youths, when they tried to shake hands with
the Duchess on introduction, to see her hand
placed behind her back, and a half-curtsey substituted for the hand-shake. Perhaps it was
instructive to an incomplete letter-writer who
had begun his letter "My dear Duchess" to be
told "I am not *your* dear Duchess." Perhaps
it was good for a well-born man who had played
a clown's trick at dessert to be told "That is
a very ill-bred action," and certainly it was good

for him, when he replied in indignation, " I think I ought to know as much about good breeding as any one in England," to hear the precise reply, " Perfectly. You ought. But, as you do not, I instruct you." Certainly also it was good that there was some one left to make a stand against such solecisms as "The Row" for Rotten Row and "The Zoo" for the Zoological Gardens; "a square" for a quadrille, and "a round" for a valse.

When I first knew the Duchess of Cleveland I was twenty-three, and she was eighty-three. She had been a widow for twelve years, and as Dowager Duchess lived partly at Osterley Park (which she rented from Lord Jersey), and partly at 69 Brook Street. At both houses she exercised an incessant hospitality, and, being still in full enjoyment of her mental faculties, she kept us all alive. One of the rules—an admirable one—was to sit down to dinner at eight sharp; and, if a guilty couple arrived too late, they were punished by being made to sit next each other. " That," said the Duchess, "will cure their unpunctuality, if nothing else will."

Fortunately for such as are interested in the figures of the past, there is an absolutely perfect picture of the Duchess. It is a cartoon in *Vanity Fair*, and exhibits her exactly as she used to look in her little sitting-room in Brook Street. She was a small woman, short and very spare; but she carried herself erect, and moved with great dignity. Her colouring had always been what is euphemistically called "auburn," and in old age she wore, under a rather elaborate cap, a sandy "front." Looking back upon her hunting days, she used to say: "Men called me the intrepid Caroline"; but her nephew, William Lowther, said that he had always heard of her as "Carroty Car." She was always beautifully dressed, though in a rather youthful fashion, and got all her clothes from Paris. In warm weather she used to wear a white muslin costume, with the petticoat cut very short so as to display her exceedingly small foot. She wore gloves all day long, and insisted that the hands of men who walked about London without gloves were "an offence." She had always been active in her bodily habits, and went out in hail, rain, and snow. "No harm ever came," she used to say, "of turning God's leather to God's weather." In walking over rough ground, or getting in or out of a carriage, she scorned all offers of help.

CAROLINE DUCHESS OF CLEVELAND.

To face p. 452.

" No Lowther ever requires assistance." As she
advanced into extreme age she necessarily
became less active. " I am always tired," she
said, " and always cold"; but still she took the
air. She used to drive to one of the bridges
across the Thames, pulling up in the middle
of it to catch the breeze, and she used to make
her footman scull her on the Serpentine—a
sight for Thackeray and Leech. She was, I
think, the last person who drove about London
in the daytime with two footmen standing
behind the carriage. A " carriage," she always
insisted, meant a coach, or at least a chariot.
I was talking to her one day about the
carriage-colours of different families, and I said,
" I can't remember the colour of Lord Salisbury's carriage." Thereupon she said conclusively : " Lord Salisbury has no carriage. He
goes about London in a brougham."

When the third Duke of Cleveland died, he
was succeeded by his brother, Lord Harry
Vane, who had married, in 1854, Lady Dal-
meny, the widowed mother of the present Lord
Rosebery. So from 1864 to 1901 " the Duchess
of Cleveland " meant the lady whom I am
going to describe.

Lady Catherine Lucy Wilhelmine Stanhope, daughter of Lord Stanhope the historian, had been one of the most beautiful girls in England, conspicuous in the famous group of Queen Victoria's bridesmaids. She was also one of the most accomplished women of her time, a considerable artist, and an admirable writer.

As Duchess of Cleveland she was mistress of one of the two or three English houses which challenge Windsor for grandeur; but its tradition had been sportsmanlike and political rather than social or cultivated. The Duchess changed all that, and, under her management, Raby became, during August, September, and October, the resort of all that was brilliant and distinguished in society. But when the winter has settled down on our northern counties, an Edwardian castle is a chilly abode; and the Duchess welcomed the transition to Battle Abbey, on the balmy South Coast, and thence, when Parliament opened, to Cleveland House, in St. James's Square.[1] There she entertained constantly, but not extensively. Her circle was not narrow, but restricted. She welcomed people who had merit to recommend them,

[1] Demolished after the death of the last Duke of Cleveland in 1891. The site is now occupied by flats and shops.

WILHELMINE DUCHESS OF CLEVELAND.

To face p. 454.

without reference to views or positions; but
kept at arm's length the "gay world"—the
huge miscellaneous throng which was even
then beginning to invade society, and had no
credentials except money, smartness, and push.

Perhaps the Duchess showed her quality to
best advantage in private conversation or at a
small dinner. She spoke with an exquisite precision, both of utterance and of diction; she
hardly uttered a sentence without giving it a
turn which one remembered; and her inclination to sarcasm was not unduly restrained.
She was born in a learned home, and had lived
all her life with clever and educated people.
Her information was wide and varied, and she
took keen interest in all the intellectual movements of her time. Her manner, like her figure,
was exceedingly graceful, and her dignity of
movement remarkable. She retained her bodily
activity to the end of her life; travelled all over
the world, and, even when her failing sight
made it dangerous, took her daily ride on her
pony in Hyde Park. She was happy in trans-
mitting her gifts to two sons and two daughters; and the death of her second son, Colonel
Everard Primrose, was a sorrow from which her
vivacity never recovered.

Frances, Countess Waldegrave (1821–79), was a product and an ornament of the Jewish race, being a daughter of the famous singer, John Braham. She married first John Waldegrave, secondly Lord Waldegrave, thirdly George Harcourt, and fourthly Chichester Fortescue, afterwards Lord Carlingford. Fortescue was made Chief Secretary for Ireland in 1865, and his first public appearance was made with his wife at the Dublin Theatre. Inquisitive glances from the pit and gallery were cast upon the new Chief Secretary, and a wag, observing his companion, cried aloud : " And which of the four did ye like best, my lady ? " This was exactly the sort of opportunity that suited Lady Waldegrave's ready wit; advancing to the front of the box she answered : " Why, the Irishman, of course." Rounds of applause greeted the reply, and her ascendency over Irish hearts was established for ever.

It was a curious freak of fate which made Lady Waldegrave mistress of Strawberry Hill. That Horace Walpole should have ransacked chancels and chantries and banqueting-halls to procure stained glass and carved wood for his mock-Gothic toy, and that the toy should have become the home of John Braham's daughter,

LADY WALDEGRAVE.

From her sitting-room window at Strawberry Hill.

To face p. 456.

was a surprising junction of the ancient and the modern world. Lady Waldegrave made admirable use of her position and possessions. She entertained incessantly, and in a gay and unconventional fashion which suggested the friskiness of a "gala" rather than the formality of a "party." But, while she kept this frolicsome side for the frolic-loving world, she all the time played the serious game of politics with assiduity and skill. Her house in Carlton Gardens was a favourite meeting-place for Whigs, and for those more modern Liberals who, under Gladstone's leadership, were beginning to strike out into new paths. Nothing and no one came amiss to the radiant and genial hostess. Her benevolence was universal; her benignity made every one feel himself at home; and her unflagging spirits could console even a shattered party or a defeated candidate. Her merits could best be measured by the consuming grief of the husband who survived her.

As I reflect upon past days, the fascinating group with which I am dealing seems to increase, and some particular trait of character or person clings to each succeeding form. There was Mary, Lady Derby, born Sackville-West, and

wife successively to the second Marquess of
Salisbury and the fifteenth Earl of Derby.
Cardinal Manning, who in his Anglican days had
been intimately acquainted with the House of
Delawarr, told me that, as a girl, Lady Mary
West had been distinguished by a saintliness
and spirituality of character which in his judgment would have best befitted a cloister. But
fate drew out a very different line of life; and,
when I knew Lady Derby, she was esteemed by
competent judges the one woman in London
whose political conversation was really valuable.

Lady Somers, born Virginia Pattle, was pronounced by so fastidious a judge as Henry
Greville "one of the handsomest women I
ever saw in any country"; and, although I never
set eyes on her till she had been married for
twenty-five years, she still remains clearly visible
to my mental gaze as the most graceful creature
I have ever beheld. Every movement, every
pose, every gesture, was a work of art. She lived
in a society essentially and profoundly artistic—
was it not Watts who first revealed her bewitching beauty to the world?—and her artistic spirit
showed itself, not in the mere accumulation of
pictures and statues, for that can be effected by

LADY SOMERS.

To face p. 458.

vulgar wealth, but in the beauty and appro-
priateness of her surroundings, whether simple
or costly. The truly artistic spirit will never be
content with a hideous or unsuitable setting to
its daily life; and, wherever Lady Somers was,
whether at Easthor Castle, or in Chesterfield
Gardens, or in a continental villa, there was
beauty. One of her contemporaries used to say:
" She was the first woman in London to drape
herself. The rest of us only dressed."

Another queen of the artistic world was Lady
Marian Alford, whom, unless I greatly mistake,
Lord Beaconsfield sketched in *Lothair* as Lady
Beatrice, " herself an artist, and full of æsthe-
tical enthusiasm." Lady Marian was a
daughter of the second Marquess of Northampton, and wife of Lord Alford, eldest son of the
first Earl Brownlow. Lord Alford died in early
manhood; and by his death it fell to Lady
Marian's lot to conduct the highly important
litigation by which the magnificent estate of
Ashridge was secured for her son, who became
Lord Brownlow on his grandfather's death. Her
administrative skill and energy evoked the
admiration of the eminent lawyers who
fought the case; but, though she triumphed in

law, her natural sphere was Art. She was an
exquisite and delicate portraitist, accurate in
drawing and brilliant in colour; and was an
admitted authority on all the allied arts of
decorative design. She was the first to introduce
red brick into the domestic architecture of
modern London, and the house which she built
at the junction of Prince's Gate and Ennismore
Gardens still bears her name and her coronet.
Grace and dignity were equally mingled in her
manner. Her artistry was combined with administrative skill, and few great ladies have
exercised a stronger influence on the circles in
which they lived.

By a rather abrupt transition I turn to a
friend who first was my hostess when I was a
boy at Harrow, and "a spread" at the "King's
Head" a high regalement. This was Mrs.
Cavendish Bentinck, born Prudence Penelope
Leslie, and wife of a well-known politician who
sate for Cockermouth. When I came to London,
I found the genial hostess of my Harrow days
still on hospitable thoughts intent; and to her
goodwill I owed my introduction to many of the
pleasantest houses. Mrs. Bentinck entertained
famously, but in herself was even more remark-

able than in her entertainments. She had
unbounded strength, supernatural vigour, unconquerable spirits. She overflowed with a
genuinely Irish humour, and had a happy knack
of verbal fun. Her last years were clouded by illness and sorrow which contrasted sadly with her
earlier life; but when she died her friends realized
that they had lost in her one of the blithest
and friendliest of human beings.

To describe Lady Dorothy Nevill is the less
necessary, because in several volumes of delightful memoirs she told the story of her own life.
Yet I cannot find it in my heart to pass her
without a word. She was one of the smallest
creatures on earth—as small, I should think,
as Lady Holland—perfectly proportioned, finely
finished-off, in fact an exquisite specimen of
diminutive humanity; only to be likened to a
Dresden shepherdess, or a tiny figure from
Greuze or Watteau.

Lady Dorothy delighted in the society of
distinguished men, whatever their distinction
was. Herself an enthusiastic Tory, and a
confidential correspondent of her beloved Dizzy,
she yet welcomed to her luncheon-table the most
dogged Radical or the extremest Socialist, so

long as he did not bore or prate or treat the
party as if it were a public meeting. Her own
conversation was, like her book, all sparkle and
vivacity. She had the finest observation and the
shrewdest insight. Nothing escaped that bird-
like gaze; and, when circumstances were propi-
tious, she would reproduce a conversation or a
scene with the most laughable fidelity. She
lived to a good old age, and enjoyed life to the
last. " Those whom the gods love die young "
is a sentiment which bears an alternative significance. People who have the nature that the
gods love remain young to the end.

I bring my list to a close with a name which
carries with it some most delightful memories.
Lady Margaret Beaumont was, during the
Seventies and Eighties, one of our chief
hostesses. Her husband's wealth and hospitable
instincts, combined with her own peculiar charm,
made 144 Piccadilly the pleasantest house in
London. I never pass its familiar walls (now
disguised in modern stone) without grateful and
affectionate recollections.

Lady Margaret Beaumont was a daughter of
the first Marquess of Clanricarde by his marriage
with a daughter of George Canning ; and, as her
friends were wont to say, she was "not Canning's

LADY MARGARET BEAUMONT.

To face p. 462.

granddaughter for nothing." Clever indeed she
was, light in hand, amusing and amused; full
of fun, quick in repartee; keenly alive to all
that was going on in society and in politics,
eagerly interested in her friends' affairs. But
cleverness was the least part of her charm.
She was exceptionally warm-hearted, quite unconventional in speech and manner, very easy of
approach, very sympathetic in trouble, very
faithful in friendship. She lived in the centre
of the world, yet she was not the least worldly.
Though she passed her days in Vanity Fair,
the odour of its merchandise never clung to her
garments. She enjoyed all that wealth gave her,
especially the power of pleasing others; but,
in spite of all the unwholesome influences which
assail a mother taking out her daughters in
London, she retained to the end of her life a
singular and almost girl-like simplicity. Her
health broke down in middle life, and she fought
heroically against ever-increasing illness till the
end came in her fifty-seventh year. It is sad
to think that since 1888 a generation has sprung
up to which her very name is unfamiliar; but
of this I am sure—that no one who knew her
will ever forget her; and that every one who
remembers her still mingles the remembrance
with affection and regret.

CHAPTER XXVIII

THE THREE CATHERINES

MY title is, in its origin, a morsel of journalese. In the autumn of 1866 there was a bad outbreak of cholera at the East End of London, the whole district which was supplied by the River Lea being affected. The mortality was severe; and, when the disease abated, there were a great many orphans left destitute. A letter, calling attention to their sad plight and proposing methods of help, appeared in the newspapers, and it was signed by Catherine Gladstone, Catharine Tait, and Catherine Marsh. "Penialinus"[1] gladly pounced upon the coincidence of the Christian names, and "The Three Catherines" became a catchword in philanthropic circles. Each of the three was a remarkable woman, and each de-

---

[1] A nickname for a florid journalist; invented by William Cory.

464

serves a word of commemoration among the celebrities of the Seventies.

MRS. GLADSTONE

CATHERINE GLADSTONE was the elder daughter, and in her issue heir, of Sir Stephen Richard Glynne, eighth baronet, of Hawarden, by Mary Neville, daughter of the second Lord Braybrooke, and was married in 1839 to William Ewart Gladstone. To describe Mrs. Gladstone is an extremely difficult task. One cannot compare her. She was not like any one else. Both in her powers and in her oddities she stood alone. No one whom I have ever known made a more vivid impression on my mind, and yet to convey that impression to another seems almost impossible. The attempt, however, must be made.

To begin with outward characteristics. She was tall and splendidly shaped, with a bearing which was queen-like in its stateliness and girl-like in its ease and elasticity. In this respect she never grew old, but was to the end as active and as graceful as when she became "the answering spirit-bride" of the foremost man of his generation. Never did she look more majestic than when, sitting by her husband's grave in Westminster Abbey, she received the reverent homage of the Heir to Throne, and the band of friends and disciples who had borne the body to its resting-place.

Her beauty was on the grand scale—a noble brow, shaded by magnificent dark and wavy hair, eyes full of light and expression, and a wide though well-formed mouth. She was, not only by blood and training, but by temperament and instinct, emphatically a great lady (I eschew the French equivalent, and "aristocratic" sounds pompous). Her walk and curtsey as she passed the Royal presence at the Drawing Room was long the admiration of those whose official duty obliged them to stand by the Throne or in the "general circle." All her habits, manners, and ways of speech belonged to that old school, which in these matters was certainly the best school. The effectiveness of her appearance owed nothing to art or study. She was by nature careless and untidy, and it was only the unremitting attentions of zealous maids that made her even presentable. Yet effective her appearance certainly was—no one's more so—and, when one thought what any other woman of

MRS. GLADSTONE.

To face p. 466.

her age, who bestowed so little care upon her
dress, would have looked, one's admiration was
intensified.

She had a magnificent constitution, and the
activity and joy in living which spring from that
best endowment. No untoward circumstances
could depress her spirits, and her sense of fun
was like a perpetual fountain bubbling up in
unexpected places. She saw the absurdities of
situations, speech, character, and appearances,
with peculiar keenness, and could scarcely keep
her sense of amusement under control. She
was peculiarly intolerant of bores and prosers,
dealers in solemn commonplace, "sedentary
weavers of long tales"; and her skill in
extricating herself from their meshes without
hurting their self-esteem amounted to genius.
Like many geniuses, she was, in the petty
concerns of life, careless and unmethodical; and
this quality, playing round the social duties of
a Premier's wife, not seldom landed her in
difficulties. But here again her mother-wit
always came to her aid, and Mr. Gladstone
once proudly said to me: "My wife has a
marvellous faculty of getting into scrapes, but
an even more marvellous faculty of getting out
of them." There was, however, one "scrape"

into which Mrs. Gladstone never got, and that was a betrayal of her husband's confidence. She told me that, at the outset of their married life, Mr. Gladstone, forecasting his probable career, gave her the choice of two alternatives —to know nothing, and be free from all responsibility: to know everything, and be bound to secrecy. Who can doubt which alternative was chosen? Forty years later Mr. Gladstone said to me: "My wife has known every political secret I have ever had, and has never once betrayed my confidence."

But it was not only in her power of keeping a secret that Mrs. Gladstone excelled. She had been a devoted daughter and sister; she was to the last an exemplary mother and head of a family; what she was as a wife can best be conveyed in her husband's words, uttered on the occasion of their Golden Wedding: "It would not be possible to unfold in words the value of the gifts which the bounty of Providence has conferred upon me, however unworthy I may be, through her." Certainly no statesman ever had such a wife. From the earliest days of their married life, Mrs. Gladstone made her husband's health, not always so robust as in later years, her special charge; and her skill and watchfulness drew from him this characteristic compliment: "My wife is no inconsiderable physician. An even more valuable contribution to his happiness was the sedulous care with which she warded off whatever might tend to disturb his vulnerable and impetuous temper. Their married life was one long honeymoon; and, though indeed charged with solemn interests and issues, it had also a jocose and genial side which was inexpressibly attractive. No one who ever heard it will forget the quaint enjoyment with which Mr. Gladstone, grasping his wife's hand, used to sing the refrain of his favourite Fiddler's Song":—

A ragamuffin husband and a rantipoling wife,
We'll fiddle it and scrape it through the ups and downs
  of life.

The slightest sketch of Mrs. Gladstone would be glaringly incomplete without some reference to her religious life. She belonged by instinct and training to the historic school of English churchmanship which existed long before the Oxford Movement began, though her abounding geniality and readiness to adapt herself to changed conditions enabled her to assimilate all that was best in Tractarianism and even

in Ritualism. She seemed equally at home in
the unadorned worship of a simple Village-Church
or in an incense-bearing procession of copes and
banners. In truth her religion lay too deep
beneath the surface to be much affected by
externals; but, though its home was in the heart,
it energized and made itself felt in numberless
forms of practical benevolence. Her husband
had, in early manhood, bound himself by an
act of solemn self-dedication, to the rescue of
the fallen; and in all such endeavours she was
ever his wise and zealous helper. To Houses
of Mercy, Orphanages, Hospitals, Convalescent
Homes, and the like, she was a most zealous
and generous friend; and, quite outside the
limits of Institutions, her tender-heartedness,
her strong sense, and her buoyant spirit made
her a minister of untold comfort to individual sufferers. She had pre-eminently that characteristic
mark of high breeding, that her manner was
the same to high and low, to rich and poor,
in courts and in cottages; and, though she knew
how to be angry when confronted by baseness
or impertinence, she was never so truly herself
as when she was binding up a broken heart or
helping to rebuild a shattered life. When she
died, I wrote an obituary notice of her in the

Times, and could find no words more descriptive of her later years than those with which Sir Walter Scott closed the story of Minna Troil:—

"Her thoughts were detached from the world, and only visited it, with an interest like that which Guardian Angels take for their charge, in behalf of those friends with whom she lived in love, or of the poor whom she could serve and comfort. Thus passed her life, enjoying, from all who approached her, an affection enhanced by reverence; insomuch that, when her friends sorrowed for her death, which arrived at a late period of her existence, they were comforted by the fond reflection, that the humanity which she then laid down was the only circumstance which had placed her, in the words of Scripture, 'a little lower than the angels.'"

MRS. TAIT

CATHARINE TAIT (1819–78) was born Catharine Spooner. The Spooners were bankers in Birmingham, and were connected by marriage with the O'Briens, the Calthorpes, the Noels, and the Wilberforces. One brother was Squire of Elmdon, some seven miles from Birmingham; one was

Rector, and one was Member for the county.
Catharine was the Rector's daughter, and she
was educated in the profound seclusion of a
Warwickshire village, when railways were only
just beginning, and people still regarded a
journey as a serious undertaking, not to be
lightly enterprised. The Spooners were High
Tories, fervent Evangelicals, and even fanatically
opposed to Popery, Jesuitism, and all allied
evils. In this environment Catharine Spooner
was educated; the best part of it—the Evan-
gelicanism—remained with her to the end, but
before she had grown up other influences had
begun to mould her life. The teaching of the
Oxford school reached her through her cousin,
Edward B. K. Fortescue, a devout and brilliant
man, sometime Provost of St. Ninian's Cathedral,
Perth. Under his guidance she became what,
for want of a better word, may be called a
Tractarian—an adherent of the moderately High
Church party; staunchly loyal to the Church
of England, profoundly devout, and unwearied
in good works.

The other influence which helped to enlarge
her outlook in Church and State was that of
Archibald Campbell Tait, a mild Whig and a
still milder Latitudinarian, who became Head

MRS. TAIT.

To face p. 472.

Master of Rugby in 1842. Dunchurch is near
Rugby; the Spooners had friends at Dunchurch,
and, when she was staying with these friends in
the winter of 1842, Catharine Spooner became
engaged to the new Head Master. I have said
in another part of this book that Tait's Head-
mastership was not the most successful portion
of his career; but it would have been a good
deal less successful than it was if he had not
been aided by the prettiness, the social gifts,
and the genial kindness of his wife. She was a
second mother to the boys (whom Tait was
incapable of understanding). She was friendly
and accessible to parents and assistant masters;
and she soon became a popular member of
society in the surrounding county. In later
life she used to say that the years which she
spent at Rugby formed the happiest part of
her life.

In 1849 Tait became Dean of Carlisle, and
there an event occurred which set a permanent
mark on Mrs. Tait, and gave her a peculiar
place among the women of England. It has
been truly said that there is " an instinct,
wholesome and touching, which ennobles a
woman whom God has made desolate—whom
bereavement, like the lightning of Heaven, has

smitten and made sacred." But for the event which, in Mrs. Tait's case, evoked this instinct, she would probably have lived and died unknown to the world at large. She might have spent her life at the Deanery of Carlisle, or perhaps in the modest " Palace " of some remote see; exemplary as wife and mother, diligent in good works; an "example to godly matrons "; but scarcely more conspicuous than when, in her bright girlhood, she plied her daily task amid the scattered cottages and elm-lined meadows of her village home. The event which thus determined the complexion and order of her life was narrated by herself, immediately after its occurrence, in language singularly natural and restrained, but irresistibly pathetic. It is a pardonable exaggeration in her son-in-law, now (1916) Archbishop of Canterbury, to affirm that this narrative "will live in English literature," though it may well be "known and remembered in every land." Some may even doubt whether a story so intimate, of hope and fear and agony and resignation, ought ever to have been given to the world; but, when the hand that wrote it was still in death, the bereaved husband discovered a paper which distinctly authorized its publication and he allowed it to appear in a

Memorial of his wife and of his only son, which was published in 1879.

What Mrs. Tait wrote in the hour of her bitter sorrow must here be condensed into the fewest and driest words. In March and April 1856 scarlet fever in its most virulent form invaded the Deanery of Carlisle, and five of the Taits' little children died.

Very likely, tragedies as grievous as this have occurred at other times and places, and have passed without public notice. Indeed Archbishop Tait noted the fact that he once found in a churchyard a tombstone recording a loss almost exactly similar to his own. But, probably because this tragedy occurred in an official residence and in the family of a well-known man, the tidings of it flew far and wide, and everywhere excited the liveliest sympathy with the parents who had undergone so singular an affliction. Among the people most keenly touched by it was Queen Victoria, whose motherly heart always responded to the cry of sorrow and bereavement, whether it came from a castle or from a cottage.

Dean Tait's work on the Universities Commission had brought him into close contact with the Whig politicians. He was known to desire a bishopric and was believed to be fit for it. Lord Shaftesbury, who at that moment was "Bishop-maker" to Lord Palmerston, thought that the Broad Churchmen must have their turn, and regarded Tait as the most innocuous member of that party. Palmerston who, though a heathen, was thoroughly good-natured, thought that a man who had suffered such a misfortune as Tait's had been, deserved some consolation; and so, by a curious combination of events and circumstances, Tait, a Presbyterian in all his sympathies, with no episcopal and very little ecclesiastical experience, found himself at forty-five placed at the head of the most important see in Christendom.

Of course this unexpected elevation had its bearing on the life and work of Mrs. Tait. She now entered, perforce, that great world of which hitherto she had known nothing. Under her control London House and Fulham Palace became the centres of a constant and generous hospitality. The Bishop of London was a prime favourite with the Queen, whose heart always warmed towards a Scotsman, and Mrs. Tait shared the sunshine of Royal favour. All the great houses, at least of the serious sort, opened their doors to the Bishop and his wife;

and even worldly people looked with respectful
interest on a couple whose domestic life had
been so cruelly darkened. But the world and
its witcheries held no spell for a woman who
had passed through that hot fire of tribulation.
Mrs. Tait filled her appointed place in London
with dutiful care and unostentatious dignity;
but her heart was always in her home and in
the innumerable works of mercy, some public
and some concealed from view, in which she
had always delighted, and for which her new
position gave her fuller scope. Her own
sorrows had given her a passport to every
darkened home; but she never suffered pathetic
memories to interfere with present duties, nor
even to mar the outward cheerfulness which
even stricken people owe to the society in
which they move.

Bishop Tait's translation to the See of
Canterbury brought no change to Mrs. Tait,
except extended opportunities of usefulness and
an increasing burthen of domestic responsibility.
As one looked at her in quiet moments one
could see the "divine hieroglyphics of sorrow"
written legibly on her expressive face; but her
activity, her interest in life, her vivid and
practical religiousness, showed that she had

learnt to live her life "as sorrowful yet alway rejoicing." I saw her for the last time in the private chapel at Addington on the 18th of March, 1877.

When the tragedy at Carlisle came to an end, the Taits had been left with one boy of seven years old and an infant daughter. Two more girls were born, and at Fulham and Lambeth these four children made as bright a family as any home in England could show. The son grew up to be an exemplary and well-loved clergyman, and a life of happy usefulness seemed to be opening before him ; but in 1878 the most melancholy of texts was illustrated again in the case of this much-tried family, and "the clouds returned, after the rain." In 1878 Craufurd Tait died in his twenty-ninth year, and from this final blow his mother never rallied. Her strength, which through all toils and trials had been the astonishment of her friends, began to fail, and before the end of the year she passed into that higher life for which she had been so graciously yet so severely trained.

MISS MARSH

CATHERINE MARSH was born in 1818 and died in 1912. Her father, Dr. William Marsh (1775–1864), was a leading spirit among the Evangelical clergy of his time. He preached so insistently on the Millennium—a topic which religionists of all schools now seem to avoid—that he became known as "Millennial Marsh," and, when he was appointed to a benefice in Birmingham he was enthusiastically received by the local Chartists, who fondly believed that "Marsh's Millennium" was identical with the Golden Age of social betterment which they had been led to expect.

Catherine Marsh was from first to last an enthusiastic adherent of the religious school in which she had been reared; but she was marked out from the main body of her co-religionists by certain qualities which were specially her own.

(1) Though of course she gave the concerns of the Eternal World the first place in her heart and in her life, she had a keen sympathy with temporal misfortune and a strong sense of social duty. In her philanthropic zeal and energy she far outran the rather jog-trot pace

which in her young days was thought binding on young women. "You thought, miss!" cried Mrs. Malaprop, "I don't know any business you have to think at all—thought does not become a young woman"; but Catherine Marsh persisted in thinking, and expressed her thoughts with unflinching courage both in word and in act. She began her work in quite early days among the citizens of Birmingham. Later, when the Crystal Palace was building, Dr. Marsh was living at Beckenham, and the neighbourhood was overrun by navvies, of whom some three thousand lived in the parish of Beckenham alone. They were in those days a rough and untended set, and Miss Marsh felt herself constrained to do something for them. Her practical good-sense, always one of her most marked characteristics, suggested the way, and she opened a Savings Bank for them. This led to friendly relations with their wives and children, and tea-drinkings on the Vicarage lawn. These good offices created a friendly footing, and on Sunday evenings she used to gather the men for what would now be called a "Mission Service" in a barn, where she presided and spoke, sitting at a small table at the top of the room. In those distant days there were

MISS MARSH.

To face p. 481.

many who thought it indecorous for a woman
to speak in public, even though her motives
were the highest; but even those who accepted Dr. Johnson's surly judgment on women's
preaching could not say that, in Miss Marsh's
case, it was not well done. She had an
immense fluency, a rich choice of words, a
singularly soft yet penetrating voice, and an
earnestness which carried conviction almost
before she opened her lips. She was in great
request all over the country as a speaker on
public platforms, and any one who heard her
once wished to hear her again. Her effectiveness as a speaker was enhanced by her personal
appearance, which has been well described by
two friends well qualified to judge. Lady Victoria
Buxton writes: "She was very tall and stately,
one of Nature's noblewomen, and was always
tastefully though simply dressed." Lady Frances
Balfour says: "One associates her with all gentle
movement; her tall, ample figure was always
robed in soft colours and rich materials, for
she said that those who dwelt much with the
poor should dress in a manner which showed
as much respect for them as for the rich"—
an eminently characteristic touch. The mixture
of stateliness and benignity in her bearing and

countenance always reminded me of George Richmond's famous picture of Elizabeth Fry.

When the navvies were drafted from Sydenham to the Crimea, to dig the trenches at Sebastopol, Miss Marsh followed them with her interest, her sympathy, and her letters, and in 1853 she became the Foundress of the "Navvy Mission," which subsists unto this day.

In 1866 a plague of cholera swept through England, and specially devastated the East End of London. Mrs. Gladstone, Mrs. Tait, and Miss Sellon, Foundress-Mother of the Sisters of Mercy at Devonport, were among the most energetic workers in Whitechapel and Bethnal Green, and they were soon reinforced by Catherine Marsh, who had learnt a good deal about cholera through her friendship with Florence Nightingale. She spent her days in the London Hospital, ministering with undaunted courage to the sufferers in the plague-stricken wards; and, when the pestilence abated, she applied her characteristic good-sense to the work of creating Convalescent Homes, which, to a great extent through her powerful support, became permanent institutions of benevolence.

(2) Miss Marsh was an inexhaustible and admirable writer. More than forty works, of various

sorts and sizes, are attached to her name in the catalogue of the British Museum. Her style was copious, correct, harmonious to the ear, and often really eloquent. It is true that she was rather over-abundant in quotation; but quotations, if good in themselves and aptly introduced, are immensely attractive to the class of readers which she aimed at influencing. T. suppose her best-known book is *Memorials of Captain Hedley Vicars*, a gallant and devout young soldier who was engaged to her niece and was killed in the Crimea. Her Life of her father, though a little polemical, is excellent reading. *English Hearts and English Hands* is a book about, and for, navvies; and *Light for the Line* was similarly devoted to railway-servants. To enumerate her books would be a superfluous task, but it is worth noting that to the end of her long life she used to send every New Year's Day to each of her friends a little booklet of cheerful and holy greeting, which generally touched national as well as personal troubles, and always with the uplifting sense of a vivid and unconquerable faith.

I reckon Miss Marsh among the really important woman-writers of her time; worthy, as regards the influence which she exercised, to rank with Mrs. Browning and Miss Yonge.

(3) A third characteristic of Miss Marsh I
notice separately; because it is very rare in Low
Church people, and not common in women of
whatever belief. I mean the sense of humour.
No one could imagine her flippant, or foolish,
or given to inconvenient jesting; but there was
deep down in her nature, as in that of so many
saints, a true fountain of fun, which leapt up
and sparkled at unexpected moments, and was
unmistakably refreshing where an undue or
affected lachrymosity prevailed. She appre-
ciated a good story, and loved a joke, and—
rarer grace still—enjoyed it even when it was
turned against herself. Let one instance suffice.
I believe that the beloved lady was in politics
a Conservative, and I know that she had inherited from her father a vehement, and what
in most people would have been a fanatical,
horror of the Church of Rome, and therefore of
Home Rule. One New Year's Day, when the
Irish Question was at its hottest, she circulated
among her friends a prayer which, among other
petitions for national favour, implored that the
evil counsels of misguided men might be brought
to naught, and that the hands of the rulers of
Ireland might be strengthened. (Those are not
the exact words, but they convey the sense.)

As I happened to be a supporter of the Liberal policy for Ireland, I could not forbear to write back to my kind old friend, suggesting that she should issue an alternative form for the use of Home Rulers. Most " Unionists " would have been furiously angry, and most Low Church people would have replied with a sermon on the errors of Popery; but dear Miss Marsh only responded with a laugh—if one can laugh with a pen—and thanked me for a bit of fun, of which, as she said with a rather arbitrary exclusiveness, "no one less than six feet high would have been capable."